"*Open Deeply* is BRILLIANT! As much as it is for anyone who wants to explore consensual non-monogamy, this book is also for any relationship that could use a tune-up or tune-in. Plus, *Open Deeply* should be on every mental health professional's must-read list. Full of insights and examples that will help you feel empowered to navigate any form of relationship model with compassion and understanding, *Open Deeply* is the non-monogamy book we all need to read right now."
—**Jamye Waxman**, LMFT, Author, Sex Educator

"*Open Deeply* honors all relationships as meaningful and legitimate, while addressing benefits and challenges of both monogamy and open relationships. Always brilliant, and always with compassion, Loree reminds us that true love is about freedom, and with that freedom comes a much deeper love."
—**Chris Donaghue**, PhD, LCSW, CST,
author of *Sex Outside the Lines* and *Rebel Love*

"I am excited that never again will I have to refer non-monogamous clients to a relationship guidance book with the caveat, "this book is helpful, but it's very monogamous…". This is more than a guide; it is not just about how to DO non-monogamy, but how to BE a more connected human."
—**Nicoletta Heidegger**, MA, Med, LMFT,
Sexologist and host of *Sluts and Scholars*

"Whether you are monogamous and looking to explore consensual non-monogamy, or have already embarked on that journey, this book is an essential read. Using real-life examples, Kate's conversational yet informative writing style invites readers to learn effective ways of communicating by tapping into the wisdom of our nervous system. Blending knowledge of both attachment theory and somatic modalities, she offers practical therapeutic tips to help foster and deepen secure attachment which allows relationships to blossom and thrive."

—**Jennifer Burton Flier,** MFT, CDWF, Trauma/Resiliency
Specialist; Senior Faculty, Trauma Resource Institute

"Kate Loree, LMFT, has written a practical and thoughtful book on ethical, nontraditional relationships, which will stimulate curious people wishing to discover a new version of themselves, offer new perspectives and a road map for people already journeying down this new path, and provide a teaching tool for clinicians seeking a solid introduction to non-monogamy. As a therapist, I appreciate how Kate weaves trauma informed phrasing, somatic awareness, body cues, and clear communication skills throughout her book, making it a wise and refreshing resource to offer my diverse clients."

—**Andrea Mikonowicz,** LMFT, Sex-positive,
Trauma Informed, Somatic Psychotherapist

OPEN
DEEPLY

OPEN
DEEPLY

A Guide to
Building
Conscious,
Compassionate
Open
Relationships

KATE LOREE, LMFT

SHE WRITES PRESS

Published 2022

Printed in the United States of America

Print ISBN: 978-1-64742-335-3
E-ISBN: 978-1-64742-336-0
Library of Congress Control Number: 2021919102

For information, address:

She Writes Press
1569 Solano Ave #546
Berkeley, CA 94707

She Writes Press is a division of SparkPoint Studio, LLC.

This book is dedicated to all those who resonate with a love language that is beyond Chapman's famous five—a love language that includes freedom, carefree fun, and adventure.

CONTENTS

INTRODUCTION

In my sex-positive private practice—a practice that serves the non-monogamous, kink, porn, and LGBTQ communities—I have noticed a pattern. Even before the first session, my client couples have often read the classics (*The Ethical Slut* or *Opening Up*) and therefore have the basic concepts and principles of ethical non-monogamy down. However, I quickly find myself referring them to other books, ones that speak through a monogamous lens. Now, why on earth would I do that?

Because there hasn't been a non-monogamous book I can find that truly addresses what comes up every day in my private practice. Couples want and need to go deeper. They read the basic principles and issues, but the books available don't go deep enough. Harville Hendrix's *Getting the Love You Want* beautifully addresses attachment theory and the intricacies of communication, but through a monogamous and often heavily traditional lens. It can inadvertently help some non-monogamous people, but it's lacking in that it doesn't speak to their experience.

This book attempts to fill this void for a more nontraditional and explorative audience. However, it might help more traditional, monogamous couples as well. *Open Deeply* provides a guide to successfully restructuring your relationship model while also addressing the deeper aspects of love, compassion, communication, and attachment. Interwoven is my personal story of being non-monogamous since 2003, along with helpful anecdotes inspired by what I have witnessed in my practice or experienced for myself. My hope is that this compassionate, attachment-focused template for non-monogamy will allow you to avoid pitfalls and find adventure even as you build healthy relationships.

The focus of this book is mainly on the dyad. You might question this focus, since triads, quads, etc. are plentiful within non-monogamy. But I've found that regardless of how many other partners actually exist back at home, and whether the individuals I see practice a hierarchical relationship model with primary, secondary, and even tertiary partners or a nonhierarchical structure with many partners all on equal footing, almost always only an individual or a couple chooses to see me. For this reason, and also for reasons of clarity and simplicity, I focus on connecting and communicating with one other partner in the chapters ahead. Many of these strategies and philosophies could be generalized to your triad or quad family weekly discussion. They could also be utilized with another partner who is not a primary or nesting partner. But in order to convey a clear message, my focus will remain on communication and connection between two non-monogamous people.

This focus does not mean that I condone "couple privilege"—the (often unconscious) belief that committed, emotionally and sexually intimate relationships are fundamentally more important than other types of intimate relationships—which so often leads to additional partners being disrespected. In polyamorous relationships, couple privilege manifests from the common presumption that the couple's relationship, or any primary-style relationship, should be protected at all costs. This stance often leads to other partners being left out of the communication loop or—at worst—unkindly discarded if the couple hits rocky waters.

I have also chosen not to focus on either polygamy or infidelities within a monogamous relationship, despite both being forms of non-monogamy. Polygamy is beyond the scope of my professional expertise—I have never met or had a client who identified as polygamous—and has not been a part of my personal experiences of non-monogamy. And as for broken relationship agreements or infidelities, those will only be discussed through a non-monogamous lens as an issue to contend with, not as a separate form of non-monogamy.

You will notice the pronoun "they" used throughout this book as a preference over "he" or "she." This is a conscious choice. When it comes to sexual orientation, relationship models, and certainly gender, the future is fluid.

Finally, you might read parts of this book and experience misattunements. You might think, *But this isn't MY experience of non-monogamy.* Keep in mind that this book reflects only what I have seen in my practice and what I have experienced off the clock in different non-monogamous communities. In all matters in life, each of us is like the proverbial blind men touching one part of the elephant and trying to describe the animal from our lens. This is mine.

SECTION I

GETTING
YOUR FEET WET

"You must love in such a way
that the person you love feels free."
—*Thich Nhat Hanh*

Chapter One

EMOTIONAL READINESS
TO OPEN DEEPLY

Your big, thumping heart. It's been injured a few times, hasn't it? The more you've been hurt, the harder emotional risk is. Merely opening up to a dear friend about a shame-based secret can be brutally hard. That vulnerability takes courage and an emotional fortitude that only comes from self-work.

Let's therefore consider what it takes to open up your relationship. It takes an even greater cultivated sense of trust than sharing a deeply held secret. You are risking being hurt, betrayed, or misunderstood. Making this shift is deciding to potentially share your love, your greatest treasure, with another.

For those of you who have been emotionally injured by past family or partners, non-monogamy might be harder for you. If loved ones have hurt you, you may struggle with trust issues, jealousy, and fear of abandonment more than others. These attachment injuries do not have to prevent you from being successfully non-monogamous, but they are issues to work through and not around.

This book is about what blocks and builds intimacy between partners when they are opening up. It's designed to help couples restructure their relationship model and navigate non-monogamy successfully, but the information here can help any couple, even those who identify as monogamous, because it looks at attachment theory as the key to successfully negotiating non-monogamy. Consistently, I will be looking through this lens.

My Journey into Non-Monogamy

The concept of non-monogamy opened up before me in September of 2003. I was in my second year of my master's program in marriage and family therapy. I was also working two jobs—as a graduate assistant and as a behavioral therapist working with children with autism—and completing an internship working with mentally ill adults. Life was intense for me, to say the least.

One night, I came home tired after seeing many clients and going to class. Entering the small bungalow in Los Angeles that my artist boyfriend and I shared, I anticipated my precious hour of cuddle time with him before beginning the homework that would absorb the rest of my night.

Upon walking in, I found Richard seated in front of the computer. When he turned to look at me, he had a gleam in his eye. His intensity was a large reason that I'd fallen in love (and in lust) with him, but that day, his intensity made me nervous.

Behind him on the screen was a woman—provocatively posed, her pussy proudly displayed. As I took the image in, Richard explained that he had an idea, a big one. I looked from him to her and back again. Her eyes seemed to join in his mischievous glee. I became more nervous.

Even though we were only about three months into our relationship, I had already learned to take even Richard's most outlandish, seemingly impossible dreams seriously. This was a man who knew how to manifest dreams. And what he was about to propose was going to be a lot for a girl from the Deep South.

But let's take a few steps back. My first (three-hour-long) phone call with Richard, and the subsequent voluminous emails we sent one another, were filled with passion and ideas. We both agreed that we had been cheaters and that we wanted to have a relationship that would allow us to break past patterns. We wanted to find a better way. We joked about a once-a-year hall pass of hot sex with the person of our choosing. But I hadn't really taken any of this talk seriously. It was all just fun and games, right?

In hindsight, I can see how it was all ramping up to that fateful day from the beginning.

Richard launched in. He had been talking to his friend Sadie Allison, a sex educator. He had been telling her the quandary he was in. He was falling in love and didn't want to treat me as he had past women he'd dated. She had suggested swinging!

Immediately, a vision of an orange van with pea-green shag carpet popped into my mind's eye. A lascivious man with an open polyester shirt and a thick gold chain motioned me inside with his creepy but emotionally beaten down wife behind him.

I shook the image from my mind, breaking the pregnant pause, and launched into a series of reasons why this idea was clear insanity. *Only creepy people swing. If I swing, my peers will find out. My mom will find out. My career will be ruined.*

I look back to that version of myself and wish I could whisper in her ear—tell her that everything would be okay. More than okay. I'd tell her that a life of growth, passion, and possibility were before her. And yes, pain would be part of the process too, but it would all be worth it.

That fall all those years ago, I became non-monogamous, and I've been providing therapy since that time as well. Today, I no longer identify as non-monogamous but rather as fluid. You might run into other definitions of fluid, but here is mine: a relationship or person that may shift from monogamy to non-monogamy depending on what suits all partners involved and their changing life circumstances. A fluid relationship is not trapped within the confines of non-mo-nogamy. Instead, a fluid relationship inherently has the full range of freedom to shift across the continuum, from extreme monogamy on one end to extreme non-monogamy on the other end, as life changes. Such relationships have the greatest ability to adapt to emotions and needs, and thus the highest ability to survive over time.

I think many couples that define themselves as non-monogamous, polyamorous, or swingers are actually often in fluid relationships. The term "non-monogamy" was born as a result of a pendulum swing away from monogamy. I believe we have grown past such reactionary, binary terms. When we dig our heels in and proclaim to be rigidly monogamous or non-monogamous out of fear of the challenges that a more flexible stance might bring, we are in danger of misattuning with what is truly ideal for us in any given moment.

Non-Monogamy: Outline for Success

When Richard, who would become my partner for the next thirteen years, initially proposed non-monogamy, it took me some time to move through my initial shock. My knee-jerk, hard "no" quickly melted into a "maybe" as we discussed the possibilities. He was the excited one. I was the wary one. He patiently addressed all my fears. He assured me that we could take baby steps and stop at any time. He told me that I would always be more important than being non-monogamous. He was compassionate and patient during those initial discussions. This kindness allowed me to eventually let down my guard and take the first steps with the assurance that he had my back.

Perhaps you are seeking some security as well, some guarantee that non-monogamy will work for you. One thing to know is that **neither monogamy nor non-monogamy is the golden chalice**. Both paths are hard. Both have their challenges and their benefits. And one may be more appropriate than the other at a given point in your life.

With monogamy, a couple may struggle with monotony, but at

its best there will be a deep sense of feeling special. You may feel like your partner's sun, moon, and stars.

With non-monogamy, you might struggle with feeling less than special; your attachment might feel threatened. You may feel jealous, or empathetically feel your partner's pain when they feel ignored or slighted. However, any long-term non-monogamist will tell you that these issues can be sorted out, and that the benefits to being open outweigh the struggles if you choose your partners wisely and come from a place of compassion for yourself and others. If anything, the heightened intensity of non-monogamy can push the types of issues that might lie dormant like a cancer in a monogamous relationship into the light, forcing partners to deal with uncomfortable feelings. I believe this is one reason that couples who already have compassionate communication in their toolbox often report feeling more in love and closer than ever when they first become non-monogamous.

That said, non-monogamy is a more complicated, and therefore more challenging, relationship model. To set yourself up for success within non-monogamy, you need to cultivate your emotional connection to: 1) your community or support system, 2) yourself, and 3) your partner(s). When we feel emotionally connected and in tune in these three areas, our relationships are most likely to be successful.

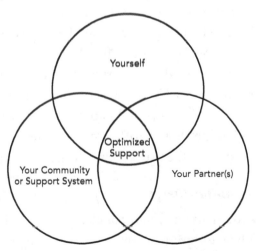

Connection to community

Community can give you an outside perspective and support that can reduce stress and enhance clarity. It is often a cornerstone of emotional stability when non-monogamy gets hard—even if "community" is just one good non-monogamous friend who you can say anything to. Anything is better than having no one within the non-monogamous community to talk to beyond your partner(s) about your relationship(s).

Monogamous ethics are different than non-monogamous ethics. A monogamous friend might say, "If your partner really loved you, they would only want to be with you." This is monogamous thinking and, frankly, often completely untrue and even damaging. So please find at least one non-monogamous friend, if not a wider community (online or in person), that you can confide in.

Connection to self

Connection to self includes tracking your thoughts, feelings, and body sensations as you traverse new adventures in your open relationship. These three components form your compass. Then you take responsibility for your own self-care, which may include joining a non-monogamous support group, starting a practice of mindfulness or meditation, or seeing a sex-positive psychotherapist or sex educator. Self-work leads to knowing yourself and being able to articulate your needs, desires, and boundaries. If you avoid this work, your partner might be happy in the short run, since it will likely mean they'll get their way most of the time. But when your resentments, negative emotions, and thoughts build up, they will become a toxin within your relationship. Better to be deeply honest with yourself and your partner(s) when the issues are small and more manageable.

Connection to your partner(s)

Connection to your partner(s) and couples work includes teaching your partner(s) how to love you well and attempting to love them well in return. Upon opening up, you will need to revisit what makes you feel loved well. This is a new ball game with new dynamics. Cultivating being loved well includes asking your partner for what you need/desire and asserting yourself when your partners' behaviors or verbalizations make you uncomfortable. They should be doing the same. (The communications skills needed for couple's work will be addressed in Chapter 13.)

Back in 2003, when I began my non-monogamous journey, I wasn't aware of any resources to help me process my feelings or what I needed for my relationship with my partner. I was close to two years into it before we began to connect to community. Don't let that be you; you don't have to go it alone. This book is here to help you connect to community, yourself, and to your partner(s). In the chapters to come, you will learn how attachment theory impacts your non-monogamy, which will support you to be way ahead of the game. And as we cover how to blend cutting-edge, neurobiology-informed grounding skills with effective communication skills, challenging conversations regarding non-monogamy will become manageable. Non-monogamy is a wild and woolly ride—but I'm here to help you make it a great one.

Chapter Two

THE BASICS

O ften, when I speak before groups about non-monogamy from
my perspective as a psychotherapist, I invite audiences to envi-
sion their current or potential open relationship as custom-made. If
you and your partners can dream it up, you can manifest it. But for
the anxious and newly learning audience member, this indeterminate
analogy can inspire a desperate need for the concrete. A hand will
shoot up and an anxious voice will ask, "But what does a non-monogamous relationship *look* like?"

To that I say, "It depends. What would you like *your* custom-made relationship to look like?"

This response is usually met with an unsatisfied, scrunched-up,
distressed face—a face I have *all* the sympathy in the world for,
because I've been there.

This book is designed to help you ask yourself the right questions as you consider whether and how to practice non-monogamy.
When we are new to something that feels scary, we want a template
to follow, a clear path. But non-monogamy is an ongoing discovery
process unveiled by experience. There is no template. But there is a
lot of solid information that can help you make crucial decisions in
a healthy way.

Before we can dive deep, I want to make sure you have some key
concepts under your belt. The vocabulary words I'm about to share

are ones most commonly used throughout this text that you might not already be familiar with.

First off, I want to drive the point home that **despite what you have heard, monogamy is not the only relationship model.** Your custom-made relationship model will fall on a continuum—somewhere between the most traditional monogamous relationship and the most full-tilt non-monogamous relationship—and it will almost certainly shift along that continuum over time. There is vast room in between these two poles.

An **ethically non-monogamous** relationship can be defined as one in which partners consciously choose to allow space for intimacy between more than two people. Partners may identify in many different ways: open, swingers, or polyamorous, for example. And the partners involved may vary in sexual orientation: asexual, pansexual, straight, queer, gay, etc. This opens up a universe of possibilities. However, one through line is always there: transparency and consent. No one is being lied to or deceived.

Ethically non-monogamous agreements are a great way to ensure transparency and clarity. Such agreements delineate needs and boundaries; however, they need not be cast in stone. They should not be weaponized as a means to crush your partner if mistakes are made either. Mistakes will be made. We are human. Your collective relationship agreements are merely a harm-reduction model. (Suggestion: If you and your partner often have wildly different versions of reality regarding past events, then write down your relationship agreements. You might ask questions such as: "Will we see outside lovers separately, or will we always play together?"; "Is it okay to have sexual texts without my partner included, or will it always be a group text?"; "At a play party, will we always play in the same room, or might we play in separate rooms?"; and "How often will we check in with each other? And will we sometimes just stay together the whole time?")

These are the kinds of thoughts and questions that lead to the formulation of a relationship agreement. If there are any memory challenges in your partnership, having a hard copy will save a lot of grief. A lot of potential arguments and pain will be dodged.

To more deeply explain, ethically non-monogamous relationships may run the gamut from swinging, which can be defined as emotional/romantic monogamy with sexual non-monogamy, to polyamory, which is romantic/emotional non-monogamy with or without sexual/erotic non-monogamy. And a million hybrids exist beyond these two definitions. For instance, a couple might play together during group sex (swingerish behavior) but may also have two separate lovers, as many polyamorists do. Such a couple may identify as swingers or as a "lifestyle couple," but when they find themselves emotionally attached to lovers that started out as merely sources of great sex, they may shift their identity to polyamorous. It happens all the time. What was once fixed becomes fluid.

In addition, be forewarned that some labels can be misleading. It's always best not to over-rely on labels, such as polyamorous or swinger, when getting to know other non-monogamous people. As in the example above, a couple who participates in threesomes and group sex together but also play separately with other lovers may still identify as swingers. You might assume they are polyamorous upon hearing about their other lovers and be left scratching your head when they call themselves swingers. But a smart newbie will ask for more detail. For instance, they may still regard themselves as swingers because they are part of the swing/lifestyle community, keep heavy emotional boundaries between themselves and other lovers, and make concerted efforts not to become too emotionally connected. You can't find out this information unless you ask.

Incorrect assumptions can lead to a grander social faux pas, like attempting to be romantic with someone who is romantically monogamous and only sexually open. Such a boo-boo may simply be an awkward moment but can also lead to a pissed-off partner glaring you down.

So what's a newbie to do? Ask questions about people's practices.

You can get a more accurate read on their current relationship model by asking questions like, "What are your boundaries around romance and love?" or "What are your sexual and erotic boundaries?" instead of simply asking, "Are you a 'swinger'?" or "Are you 'poly'?" (In Chapter 3, we'll explore the practices and community of polyamory and swinging as a means to provide markers or anchor points that might reduce confusion as you explore the vast land of non-monogamy.)

Now, let's talk about you. Many people who come to my practice question whether they are truly non-monogamous or simply a monogamous person who can't get their shit together. The fear in their eyes says, *Perhaps I'm truly an inherently bad, selfish, and immature person because if I were good, I wouldn't keep failing at monogamy, right?*

This line of thinking breaks my heart. You're not bad. Instead of swimming in shame, let's spend some time trying to find the most authentic *you* and what relationship model suits you as of now. If you already know your truth, please feel free to skip the next chapter and go straight to Chapter 3, where we'll discuss the two major communities: polyamorists and swingers.

So You Suspect You're Non-Monogamous

At this point, you may be considering your orientation and asking yourself if you identify more strongly as monogamous or non-monogamous. The answer may not be as black and white as you think. For instance, there was a time that people asked themselves, *Am I gay or straight?* but now some have realized that their sexual orientation has shifted over time. In other words, their sexuality is fluid. Your relationship model may be fluid as well.

Even if you come to know that non-monogamy is an orientation for you, you will still have fluidity within your non-monogamous relationship agreement. The binary of monogamy versus non-monogamy doesn't serve us. Breaking down rigidity and realizing that there will be a flow to your relationship is a good starting point.

For instance, a non-monogamous couple may choose to be monogamous in practice during and directly after a pregnancy and return to non-monogamy when the time feels right. Another couple may be poly for a while but decide to swing for a bit and keep things light after a bad breakup with another couple. Then, after some healing, they may slowly shift back to poly.

Embracing fluidity is a key component of adaptability and thus success for your relationship. So what is best for you right now? Consider the following questions.

- Have you ever had more than one romantic crush at a time?
- Have you ever been sexually attracted to more than one person at a time?
- While taking a walk on the beach with your love, have you been able to simultaneously enjoy being with them and notice the hotties on the beach?
- Have you ever cheated and thought to yourself, *I wouldn't lie and deceive if I could be in an open relationship.*

If you answered yes to any of these questions, you might be non-monogamous.

On the other side, consider these statements.

- When I go to the beach, I only notice my partner.
- When I have a sexual fantasy, I only fantasize about my partner.
- I have no real need to be with anyone sexually or romantically beyond one person.

If you answered yes to any of these questions, then you might be monogamous.

There are also those who *choose* monogamy, like a person might choose to be vegetarian. As Dr. Christopher Ryan says, "They may choose to be vegetarian. That doesn't mean the bacon doesn't still smell good." If you fall into this category, I encourage you to ask yourself why. Is this truly what is best for you, or is it what you have been influenced or even pressured to do by a partner, your community, or your culture?

Some people consciously choose monogamy, not out of fear or conditioning but because they feel deep intimacy is more easily attained without the stress that non-monogamy can inherently put on a relationship. This is fair. Non-monogamy pokes at any unresolved attachment injuries. A major focus of this book is coping strategies for moving through these stressors.

But first, please consider one last series of statements:

- I notice other sexy people, but the thought of sharing my love is terrifying to me.
- I get crushes on people, but non-monogamy isn't a consideration because I refuse to risk losing my love.
- I've cheated on every partner I've had, but when I think about non-monogamy, I feel like I'm about to have a panic attack.

If you identify with any of these statements, even a little bit, then this book will help. It will help clear the fog of your confusion and support you to make a decision about your relationship model from a place of psychological understanding and insight versus a place of fear.

A final consideration is integrity. One question I like to ask all my clients, regardless of whether they identify as monogamous or non-monogamous, is, "Are you good at it?" You may believe strongly that you are either monogamous or non-monogamous, but let's go deeper. If you identify as monogamous, are you good at monogamy? Or, when you look back in your history, do you have to admit that you have cheated many times on each of your partners? And if you identify as non-monogamous currently, are you good at non-monogamy? Or do you have a history of leaving lovers feeling mistreated, ignored, and slighted?

If you aren't good at either model, it's time to pause and work on yourself for the sake of your and your loved ones' well-being. (See Chapter 16 about infidelities within non-monogamy for those whose issues run deeper than any non-monogamous model can solve.)

Are You an Out-of-Control Sex Addict?

So often when we begin to explore our sexuality, we open one door only to discover multiple new doors behind it. Through non-monogamy, you may discover that you are also kinky and perhaps pansexual. Or maybe you'll realize that you are gender-fluid rather than cisgender. This evolution is part of the discovery process.

A common question my clients ask is, "If I think I might be non-monogamous and/or kinky, does that mean that I'm out of control? Am I a sex addict?" No. If you believe this to be true, you have swallowed cultural toxicity, my friend. Please cough that nasty hair ball up; it need not choke or poison you anymore.

In my practice, I am only concerned about a client's sexual behaviors if the behaviors are 1) truly dangerous to themselves or others, 2) potentially putting them, their job, or their loved ones in jeopardy, or 3) a compulsion rather than a conscious, controlled choice.

Sexually compulsive behaviors that are damaging to the self or others are symptoms, not the root issue. A person may be bipolar and in a manic episode, for instance. But I usually find that such behaviors stem from a history of attachment injuries. Such a person likely had a childhood during which they felt desperately alone. They likely have a sea of accumulative memories, such as being forgotten on birthdays or crying alone, with no one there to attend to them, when they fell and scraped their knee. As a result, they came to distrust others who said they cared about them. And then one day, they had sex. Within that experience, so many unmet needs were finally fulfilled. They were told they were beautiful or handsome. They got cuddled. And, of course, they had great sex. Sex became their safe place within a lonely, cruel world. And thus the seeds were planted for sexually compulsive behaviors to grow.

We are quick to pathologize our healthy sexual curiosity and vitality. If someone started out reading a basic gardening book and that led them to an interest in making bonsai trees and then building garden ponds, we wouldn't worry that such a person was out of control. In fact, we might say, "Isn't that lovely that your initial interest is blossoming into so many other areas!" We would be encouraging and impressed.

And yet when a person begins to explore their erotic life, so often they and/or their loved ones fear that they are becoming a monster or a sex addict. This shame, this horrible self-hatred, comes from toxic cultural programming. (I will talk more about this in Chapter 9.)

Just as most monogamous people are not sexual compulsives, most non-monogamous and kinky people are not either. Being non-monogamous or kinky is not an indicator of a mental health issue. It is, however, an indicator of an outside-the-box thinker—and I don't know about you, but I find such people charming.

Stuck at the Starting Gate: Blocks and Questions That Stall Non-monogamous Momentum

Non-monogamy. Just the thought of it can create a whirling dervish of excitement and anxiety that can overwhelm the mind. But overwhelm need not stall your progress. Instead, let's break down the common blocks and answer a few key questions, one at a time.

Threat of personal loss

Regardless of whether you are 100 percent sure that you're non-monogamous, you may have the very real fear that if you disclose this self-knowledge to your partner, you'll run the risk of losing them, breaking their heart, or creating an irreparable chasm between the two of you. This fear may be valid, and only you can decide if broaching the subject is worth the risk. However, I believe that authenticity is one of the primary keys to happiness. Living an inauthentic life often causes not just the individual but also their loved ones to suffer. Don't you owe your partner the very basic gift of revealing your true self? They have consented to love you and be with you. And it's not a true consent if they don't fully know the real you.

Fear that coworkers, friends, or family will find out

In my first year of non-monogamy, I was terrified of my peers finding out. Clearly, that fear is in the past for me, but coming out was a slow process that took me years. If you have anxiety related to being outed or running into work associates at a sex party, that's a normal and a typical initial concern.

This fear of being discovered usually passes. And if you have good boundaries and don't leave your laptop open or leave your computer history available for your tech-savvy mom or brother to find while visiting, they probably will never know unless you tell them. Unexpected family discoveries happen, but in my experience, both personal and professional, it's rare.

Should I come out as non-monogamous or keep it a secret?

If you can delay coming out until you are emotionally comfortable with non-monogamy, that is highly advisable. The first year of non-monogamy is often filled with second-guessing yourself. The last thing you need is for your God-fearing uncle George to lay down his own layer of fears and anxiety on top of whatever you are personally sorting out for yourself. Slowly, you will hone your non-monogamous identity. It will grow strong and clarify over time. Your relationship model may shift and change over time, but your sense of confidence in your ethical code and life choices will solidify.

Once you do decide to come out, keep in mind that doing so

can take place on a continuum; you decide how much you want to disclose and how many people you tell. You might decide to keep your non-monogamy a complete secret at first. Then, after a while, you might decide to tell your best friend. And then, over time, you may tell more and more people—when you are ready.

Of course, you may not have the luxury of waiting to come out until you are emotionally ready. Maybe you want to take both of your partners to Thanksgiving dinner. Maybe someone has outed you. Perhaps a lover has asked you to come out to a loved one, and, despite being terrified, you have decided to oblige them. There are a million reasons that a person might come out before being entirely ready. And really, are we ever truly ready? (We'll get into this more in Chapter 20, where we'll explore how to come out most effectively, as well as coping skills to help with that process.)

Cultural and religious norms

Despite how enticing a proposition of non-monogamy may be, for many, culturally imposed guilt and shame stand in the way of what might be a more fulfilling existence. (We'll discuss this more fully in Chapter 9.)

Is it worth it to consider a relationship model that goes against pretty much everything you were taught? Becoming non-monogamous may feel like a butterfly's metamorphosis. You have to break down everything within the cocoon and turn into mush first, but then you can rebuild and eventually break free from your binding, revealing yourself as a beautiful butterfly.

Except maybe you don't have faith that you will become a lovely butterfly. Maybe you fear that you will break down into an ugly creature driven by ego, ravenous lust, and harmful behaviors. I mean, isn't that what conservative religion and culture teach us? That we can't control ourselves, so we need religion to keep us from becoming deviants?

Please consider the alternative. If monogamy isn't your truth, culturally imposed sexual and emotional repression can lead to deception, unhealthy sexuality, guilt, poor self-esteem, and anger. When we are silenced, shamed, or shut down, our sexuality is most at risk of becoming an unhealthy, distorted version of our actual truth.

Fear of failure

You may fear that non-monogamy is a pipe dream with little hope for success. Well, first let's redefine success. It's not the seventeenth century anymore. Back then, people married, had babies, and died, on average, before age forty. These days, most of us will have many loves across a lifetime. So let's define success not by relationship longevity but relationship quality instead. And that quality could be determined by the degree of emotional, intellectual, and sexual connection. Although I know plenty of non-monogamous couples who have been together for decades, length of time is not always an indicator of emotional health. Instead, I'd say a successful couple is lit up and energized by their mental, emotional, and sexual connection. They are each other's muses, helping each other find their optimal and authentic self.

Non-monogamy is often a catalyst for such growth and discovery. That may sound strange to you, but countless times, both within and outside of my practice, I have witnessed this process. As an individual begins the emotional and often sexual journey that non-monogamy provides, they begin to grow in unexpected and unrelated ways. Perhaps they take that art class that they had been putting off, or begin to build new friendships. And all of this individual growth, in turn, often feeds back into the relationship—revitalizing it, creating increased happiness, and renewing love.

Fear of growing apart

Couples who are drawn to non-monogamy tend to be growth-oriented adventurers. This exploratory ideal is often why they fell in love in the first place. However, when two mutable individuals fall in love, they may grow together but may also grow apart. So yes, there is that risk that non-monogamy may expedite growth that is not in tandem. However, do you really want to make choices based on fear? Rather than have this awareness stop you in your tracks, why not use this insight to be mindful of your mind, body, and emotional connection to your love? Keep those three areas strong, and you will be able to weather much greater hurdles than non-monogamy.

Common Questions That Come Up in My Practice

Is non-monogamy superior to monogamy?

Non-monogamy is not the golden solution to all the woes of monogamy. Both relationship models are challenging and both have their wonderful benefits. And the question cannot be answered in consensus for all mankind. You must figure out what is best for you.

If you're still on the fence, then experiential knowledge is your next step. If you are brave and willing, take baby steps. Go to some non-monogamous socials. Just hang out and talk. Or go to a non-monogamous lecture and stay afterward to talk with the audience around you. Non-monogamous folk tend to be warm, inviting, and receptive. If you try to engage them in friendly banter, I think you will be happily surprised by how easy it is. Patience and mindfulness win in the end. With this mindset, you will unveil the path that is superior for you now, at this point in your journey.

Can you open up your relationship after an affair?

Every sex educator under the sun will tell you adamantly that no, you shouldn't open up your relationship after an affair. In reality, people do it all the time; it's incredibly common. But just because it's a common phenomenon doesn't mean it's a good idea.

You may be in this very situation right now. So let's be clear: what I'm saying is that this is a painful time to open up a relationship. So often, people attempt to bring in the affair lover as their new non-monogamous partner—a form of opening up that is usually devastating to the partner who has weathered the affair. They are still reeling from broken trust and a broken heart. If there is any hope of mending things with your primary, I suggest ending things with the affair partner and starting your non-monogamous relationship with a clean slate regarding partners. This choice shows an act of good faith and an intention to make things work with your partner. Once this decision is made, it will take some time to earn your partner's trust back. Yes, you may feel that you had reasons for the affair. You may feel that your partner holds some responsibility for why your relationship is in this current state. Regardless, trust has to be earned back.

If you decide to attempt to earn trust back concurrently with opening up, please find a psychotherapist who is not only non-monogamous friendly but has also personally walked the walk and knows what it's like to be non-monogamous. This opinion is controversial. But so often, clients come to me feeling shamed by their last therapist—a therapist who seemed kind and open-minded initially, but whose reactions and statements regarding non-monogamy were bigoted due to ignorance, which can be traumatizing. This can be avoided by asking for referrals within the non-monogamous community or asking potential therapists some direct questions regarding their education and stance on non-monogamy before proceeding with treatment.

Is non-monogamy a practice or a culture?

It's your choice. As you try to define your relationship model, you may choose to keep your non-monogamous relationship model a practice that you keep private, just between partners, or you may choose to join a non-monogamous community.

Some don't feel the need to connect to community. However, connecting to community has many benefits, such as emotional support and social activities. For instance, the swinger community is very organized. In large cities, hotel takeovers and parties are plentiful. The poly community, as well, has parties, Meetup groups, websites, and conventions. And these days, there are sex-positive communities that embrace a wide range of members who may vary in sexual orientation (asexual, pansexual, kinky, LGBTQ, etc.), sexual proclivities (kinks and fetishes), and relationship models.

What are some basic forms of non-monogamous relationships?

I would invite you to create a unique non-monogamous model that fits the emotional, intellectual, and erotic needs of you and your partners as perfectly as possible. Doing so will set you and your partners up for success. That said, there are some basic relationship models and configurations you can use as a starting point.

First, let's discuss the difference between hierarchical versus nonhierarchical non-monogamy. Within a hierarchical non-monogamous relationship, certain sexual/romantic relationships, like a spouse or long-term partner, are prioritized and usually referred to as "primaries." Primaries often live, share resources, and make financial and life-planning decisions together. In addition, they most likely spend more time together compared to their relationships with other partners, who may be referred to as "secondaries." A secondary partner often gets less time and resources and has less say in their relationship than the primary. However, they may have their own primary or may be dating other people. They may have also been very clear about the relationship boundaries and limitations going in.

This dynamic can become ugly when "couple privilege" rears its ugly head—when the couple puts the wants, needs, and feelings of their unit above all other partners. (This concept will be discussed more in Chapter 14.)

Meanwhile, nonhierarchical non-monogamous relationships don't impose hierarchies. A spouse or long-term partner may be referred to as a "nesting partner" rather than a "primary" to avoid hierarchical lingo, and no partner is prioritized over another partner, regardless of marital status or relationship length.

I tend to think of nonhierarchical versus hierarchical non-monogamy not as a black-or-white binary but rather as a changeable continuum. Personally, I don't have a bias toward either one. I only have a bias toward kindness and respect.

Basic Relationship Models and Configurations

Monogamish

This cheeky term was coined by Dan Savage. "Monogamish" refers to couples who are mostly monogamous but will give some wiggle room for the occasional adventure—for example, having a spontaneous threesome while on vacation in Vegas or giving one's partner a sexual hall pass because it's their birthday.

Swing lifestyle

These are generally committed couples who are romantically monogamous but sexually non-monogamous. They usually play together. Such couples may participate in group sex, threesomes, or foursomes, but their intention is to restrict their emotional connection with their other partners to great friends at most.

I should note that the terms "swingers" and "the lifestyle" are often used interchangeably. The latter term was adopted in an effort to avoid the negativity associated with the term "swinger," but both refer to the same practices and/or community. You can safely use either.

Polyamorous relationship

Allows for being in love or romantically involved with more than one person at the same time. Here are some common polyamorous formations:

The Triad: Three-way relationships that may be nonhierarchical, with all three pairs being fairly equally involved. Another common triad consists of a primary couple in a committed relationship with a third-party individual. For example, a married couple, Bridgette and Kyle, are both in a relationship with Denise.

The V: This formation usually consists of an individual with two other partners who are not involved with each other. For instance, Athena is married to Joel and also has a boyfriend, Johnny. Johnny and Joel are not sexually or romantically involved with each other (although they might spend time together as friends).

The W: The center peak of the W represents a person who is linked to two partners (the W's two bottom points), who in turn have their own outside partners (the W's outside top peaks). For example, Grant is married to Juliette but also has a girlfriend, Amber. Juliette and Amber are not involved romantically, but each has their own relationships apart from Grant.

Quad: Two couples or four people who are in a relationship together. For instance, Jack and Daisy are married. Becky and John have been living together for seven years. The four of them date each other. The foursome may be exclusive or open. It's not unheard of for two couples to (spiritually) marry each other.

Solo Polyamory: People who generally do not have or seek intimate relationships that involve a primary-style merging, such as moving in together or sharing finances, as traditional cultural norms encourage. In addition, solo polyamorous people generally don't identify very strongly as part of a unit, such as a couple or triad; rather, they operate and present as individuals. This doesn't mean that they only want casual relationships; they may be deeply in love. They simply value autonomy as a core value. (Note: Solo polyamory is not to be confused with a polyamorous single, who is unattached and dating and may be looking for a partner or partners to build a conjoined life with.)

The Polyfidelity Group: This version involves a group of people who consider all members as exclusive partners. All members are in relationship with one another and do not date outside of the group.

Mono/Poly Relationship: One partner remains monogamous while their partner has other romantic relationships. In my practice, I have found this relationship model to be incredibly challenging and painful for the monogamous partner who is sharing their love. It's not a relationship model I recommend, but it works for some couples.

Relationship anarchy (RA)

A term coined by Andie Nordgren, "RA" refers to the practice of forming relationships of all types (sexual, romantic, platonic, familial) devoid of the influence of societal norms or rules. There need not be a formal distinction between sexual, romantic, or platonic relationships. Furthermore, one type of relationship is not regarded as more important than another. For instance, Sean's romantic relationship with Albert is not regarded as more important than his friendship with Alexandra. In this way, relationship anarchy goes a step beyond nonhierarchical non-monogamy, which only addresses sexual/romantic relationships.

Open relationship

"Open" is an umbrella term for a consensually non-monogamous relationship. Swinging, monogamish, polyamorous/polyfidelitous, and anarchistic relationships can all be considered "open." Such a relationship is based on a committed couple who are "open" to romantic or sexual involvements with other people. Generally rooted in specific rules, expectations, and communication between those involved, open relationships may take a variety of forms and may evolve over time as necessary to meet the needs of the persons involved.

Chapter Three

COMMUNITY

Years ago, a social anthropologist buddy of mine, upon hearing that I intended to write a book, strongly advised me to avoid discussing non-monogamous communities and stick to discussing practices only. Her valid belief was that in talking about community, one runs the risk of inaccurate stereotyping. Also, communities are subject to change over time. What may be a decent generalization at the moment may be horribly untrue five years from now.

I get that. But I feel compelled to discuss community here because it's so important in so many ways. It can be a critical anchor, reality check, and support system for anyone who is non-monogamous. This is especially true when one is new to non-monogamy and needs guidance. Community can be a compass if you get lost in a toxic relationship—to help you find your true north again. Plus, there is a lot of heart in community. For many non-monogamous people, talking to their bio family or conventional friends is not an option. Community can be a surrogate family that will love and support you as you navigate this journey.

For the sake of this book, let's discuss the two traditionally largest cultural groups within the non-monogamous world, polyamorists and swingers, and the fluidity inherent in both. What makes them different? Mainly, polyamorists are willing to love or deeply connect with more than one person, while swingers create social rules and boundaries that limit emotional connection. They are sexually non-monogamous but romantically monogamous. They may have other friends who they plan vacations with and have had sex with for decades, but they have a code that demands that they stop short of love.

Intro to Polyamorists

From a sociological level, polyamory challenges many of our cultural norms and beliefs: the nuclear family, monogamy, romantic love, child-rearing, and religion.

Even those who identify as swingers often get nervous when they consider the concept of polyamory. I remember when my former husband and I began to "break it" to our swinger friends that we each had our own girlfriend and boyfriend. It was as if we'd announced that one of us had cancer; more often than not, a look of sincere concern came over our friends' faces. Another common reaction was one of confusion and judgment. (These reactions were partially due to the rarity of "playing separately" within the swing community at that time, around 2007.)

This initial awkward moment was usually followed by questions, such as, "Aren't you afraid that your partner will fall in love with the other person?" If we asked one thousand polyamorists that very question, I'd bet money that most would say that love and real connection are the whole point. Polyamorists feel it's completely possible to have many loves and that it doesn't need to be a threat to other partners. In fact, most would say those feelings of love can benefit all involved.

But back to you. If your internal dialogue is still plagued by critical thoughts such as, *I still wonder if I'm misguided, creepy, or selfish for liking the idea of having more than one love*, I invite you to have compassion for yourself. You are one of countless thousands who have begun the journey through your culturally imposed shame to find your truth on the other side. You might have experienced a con-demnation of the concept of abundance, especially related to love and sex, all your life.

And while we are discussing ethical and consensual non-monogamy (CNM), let's not forget the countless monogamous-identified people who are engaging in non-consensual infidelities. When we add all these groups together, it becomes clear that non-monogamy is common. So I reiterate, *no*, you are not creepy, crazy, or selfish for being curious about consensual non-monogamy. Actually, it's quite natural.

What's the difference between polygamy and polyamory?

Polygamy, technically and legally, means "many marriages," while *polyamory* means "many loves." Some researchers believe that polyg-amy was born from economic necessity. With more children, a family had more workers to help one survive and build wealth. In popular Western culture, polygamy has been correlated with misogyny, even though this is not always the case worldwide. Regardless, polyamory advocates have put a lot of work into delineating the differences between the two concepts for our court systems and media sources, mainly so that polyamory is not confused with the subjugation of women and/or illegal practices here in the States.

It's common for people to get polygamy and polyamory con-fused, since both involve multiple relationships. But polyamory has an egalitarian cornerstone that may not be found in the prevalent form of polygamy, called polygyny. (The rarer form of polygamy, polyandry—one woman married to multiple men—is so rare that it is never confused with polyamory.)

Who Are Polyamorists?

In Meg Barker and Darren Langdridge's 2010 book, *Understanding Non-Monogamies*, Elisabeth Sheff, PhD, relays her research findings from a longitudinal study (1996–2003) of polyamorous families in two regions of the United States confirming the popular belief that mainstream polyamorous communities are overwhelmingly white, college educated, and middle- or upper-middle-class, with professional jobs. However, in the 2019 article "Demographic Comparison of American Individuals in Polyamorous and Monogamous Relationships," published in *The Journal of Sex Research*, Dr. Rhonda Balzarini reveals a different picture entirely. In her study, polyamorous people more often reported a lower income bracket than the monogamous cohort. She found no major differences in groups when it came to ethnicity, except that polyamorous respondents were more likely to identify as multiethnic. An unexpected finding was that polyamorous folk were much more likely to choose "other" if given the option, eschewing labels related to anything from sexual identity to political affiliation. When reporting their sexual identity, polyamorists were more likely to state that they were pansexual or bisexual.

This might lead you to believe that the times they are a changin', but in reality, it's more likely that researchers have simply improved their ability to capture the diversity that has always existed. In the article "Why Do We Think Polyamory Is Only for the Rich, White and Privileged?" Isabelle Kohn points out that historically people with a low socioeconomic status and people of color have not fully been captured in research studies due to where the studies are done, such as on college campuses or at polyamorous conventions, which require a higher income to attend. And as sex therapist Jamila Dawson explains, polyamory is "not necessarily called the same thing as it is in white, higher SES communities" by different communities, and therefore groups practicing polyamory but using different language to describe it may go unrecognized by researchers.

Diversity is also evidenced in television shows like *Insecure* and *She's Gotta Have It*, which both take on non-monogamous themes within Black communities. As consensual non-monogamy becomes more and more mainstream, I believe its demographic diversity will be increasingly depicted.

Are Polyamorists Commitment Phobic?

Before answering, let's look at the idea of loyalty and commitment through the lens of polyamory. Ask yourself, *Can a person be committed and loyal to one love if that person is also committed and loyal to another?* If your gut reaction is no, then think of a parent's love for more than one child. The parent is expected to be committed and loyal to all of their children. Polyamorists simply apply this same principle to their romantic relationships. If anything, it could be argued that polyamorists are more "in love" with commitment than monogamous people are, at least in the sense that they are committed to many partners. Polyamory is about abundance and the belief that we shouldn't deprive ourselves in this life but rather revel in love and affection from all directions!

Polyamory for the Newbie

If you are considering exploring polyamory, or even just playing separately, then there are a few concepts and dynamics to be aware of. First off, let's discuss "New Relationship Energy" (NRE), or limerance. Remember the first time you fell hard for someone? Your first big crush? Perhaps you stared out the window for long hours, dreaming of kissing them. That, my friend, is NRE.

NRE is a natural drug high produced by your body. It's wonderful and blissful. We all adore this feeling.

I must insert a word of caution here, however: having a new, passionate love relationship come on board can be destructive and devastating to an already existing primary or nesting partner relationship. When you are newly attracted to someone, chemicals like adrenaline, dopamine, and serotonin flood your body like a tsunami, hijacking your thoughts—and actions, if allowed. Supercharged with these neurotransmitters, people often feel like they want to have sex every waking moment with their new partner, and then (thanks to serotonin) think about them constantly when they're apart. It's amazing. What's not to love?

At this point, the unaware polyamory newbie might be caught up and think, "My God, this is the person for me! The passion! The perfection! I've been wasting all these years with my spouse! This is what love is supposed to feel like!" If this poor, misguided soul takes action based on these drug-induced feelings, emotional damage to their primary or nesting relationship is sure to follow. And the truth, plain and simple, is that NRE fades. With familiarity, the release of these neurotransmitters diminishes, and the new partner ceases to seem as perfect as they did in those first few months. We all have flaws, and as NRE fades those quirks become less "cute." So, enjoy the bliss of your NRE. It's one of the best feelings under the sun. Just please, be realistic and don't forget to have gratitude for your long-term partner. Remember the biology of human connection, and always remember to honor the love who has trusted you with their heart.

Which leads us to another polyamory heavy hitter: compersion. Compersion can be described as the opposite of jealousy. It takes a developed trust and confidence in your love to feel joy when they speak fondly of their other amorous relationships. And it's okay if you never experience compersion. Just getting to the point where all parties involved feel good about the relationship model is a great goal and sufficient. If you don't experience compersion, that does not imply that you're less evolved.

And if you experience jealousy, there is no shame in that. Jealousy is natural, and it's designed to inform us when something does not feel right. But just because you experience jealousy doesn't mean you can't experience compersion as well. Look for it. You might have experienced it already and not even recognized it. With awareness comes cultivation.

I find that compersion is most easily felt when a person feels solid and secure—emotionally, sexually, and intellectually—with their love. If, for instance, you've injured your back and can't have the rough, intense sex you're both used to, and then your lover finds a partner who is kinky and loves it rough, you might feel loss and grief for a connection that once was, making compersion hard.

If you're wondering, *How can I get to the point of feeling compersion when jealousy, sadness, or grief still rules my heart?*—yes, jealousy and other associated difficult feelings are a *huge* topic within non-monogamy. So much so that we will continue to discuss it through much of Section II of this book. So, hold your horses for a bit (or, if you're feeling impatient, skip to Section II).

Pros of Polyamory

Authenticity

There are many positives to polyamory. First and foremost, if you have a primary or nesting partner, additional relationships can take away some of your perceived responsibilities to your partner. No longer are you expected to be *all* things for one person. If you don't like your lover's fascination with zombie flicks, then guess what? That's okay! You can send them off to be with someone who does. You get to be your authentic self. You don't have to pretend to love baseball or feel pressure to watch a rom-com movie marathon just because your mate wants to. Someone else can fill those needs for them, leaving the two of you to share the things you both truly love to experience together—something that always deepens the bond between a couple.

Expansiveness

Other loves will help you discover things about yourself you never knew existed, which will allow you greater opportunity to become a more fulfilled person. You might say to yourself, *But can't my friends do that?* Sure, they can, but romantic relationships tend to run deeper and richer. Some of the best lessons about life are learned while holding someone's hand.

Extended family

If you develop several loves, they may become an extended family—one that can provide a broadened support network for both emotional and financial challenges. This also applies to children in the household. Ongoing research by sociologist Elisabeth Sheff, PhD, indicates that children often benefit from polyamorous households due to a higher household income and increased emotional support. Sheff writes, "Many parents say their children's lives, experiences, and self-concepts are richer for the multiple loving adults in their families. This abundance of support frequently leads to children with higher self-esteem and psychological well-being. That is not to say that polyamorous families do not have challenges as well, especially from the outside community, but the strengths are powerful and vast."

Cons to Polyamory

Not being the "one and only"

Many people desire to be at the center of somebody's universe. Ideally, polyamorists attempt to make *all* their loves feel special and honored. But sometimes an individual is left feeling like a sidekick, disposable, or a victim of "couple privilege." If you find yourself having such thoughts, it's time to own your feelings and have a voice. If you can't come to some resolution after considerable effort, seek a different relationship—one that leaves you feeling peaceful and content.

Complications

Being committed to one person is hard enough. Being committed to many loves compounds the difficulties and potential stressors. If you are considering this path, please don't go into it with blinders on. You have to cultivate amazing skills at setting boundaries and be ready to *really* communicate. The need to negotiate sleep and date schedules is a given. Spontaneity often becomes impractical and/or impossible.

Successful non-monogamy takes a responsible soul who is ready and willing to hear all their lovers' feelings and attend to them.

Legal difficulties

Polyamorous families can face *many* legal difficulties. Currently, we can only marry one person legally, regardless of how many people we might be in a loving relationship with. This barrier leads to other legal constraints, such as not being able to add multiple people to health insurance policies. If a girlfriend or boyfriend is in the hospital, you may be denied visitation due to not being immediate family. Other legal matters, such as wills, custody agreements, powers of attorney, joint property, and medical powers of attorney are all impacted. However, there are websites (such as www.polyfamilies. com) and books (such as *Opening Up*, by Tristan Taormino) that offer guidance and suggestions to circumvent these roadblocks.

Perhaps one day we will let go of our negative associations with the concept of having more than one spouse. If such a cultural zeitgeist shift occurred, legislation might change as well and thus dissipate painful legal issues that polyamorists contend with. The reality is that some polyamorists would like to marry more than one loved one and want the legal privileges that come with that status.

Connecting to the Polyamory Community

Let's discuss how to connect to the polyamory community.

Online communities

Websites like Meetup.org have a plethora of polyamorous meet-up groups, such as "poly cocktails." Just put in the key word "polyamory" and you will find events and groups in your area. Also, Facebook has many polyamory and non-monogamy support groups that can get you connected and give support. Once connected online, you can pick the live support groups and polyamory socials that work for you.

Internet dating apps

OkCupid has gained a reputation as being friendly to alternate sexual lifestyles and, unlike some mainstream dating apps, allows users to identify as pansexual, bisexual, queer, sapiosexual, and a whole range of other options. You can also answer questions about non-monogamy that can up your chances of finding your match. Searching by the interest topic "polyamory" is a great way to cut to the chase!

Feeld is another app that caters to non-monogamous individuals and couples. It's presently set up more for hookups than love and deep connections, but it's still a great resource when hunting for your next partner. Once you have done your research and begun to make personal connections through the Web, you can take the final and most exciting step by actually meeting others like you.

Conferences

The longest-running non-monogamy-related conference in the United States is the Poly Living Conference, which is put on by the nonprofit group Loving More. This is a strong conference with a host of nationally recognized speakers and amazing events. Conferences are a Google search away and happen worldwide.

The bottom line here is that there are many paths to fulfillment in life and love. Polyamory is an adventurous path that deviates from the direction many have been conditioned to believe is right and proper. Emotional expansion begins with respecting and honoring your own intuition. A heightened ability to love can only branch out from the self-love and awareness we allow for ourselves.

In Deborah Anapol's 1997 book, *Polyamory: The New Love without Limits,* she described polyamory as a "lovestyle" that arises from the understanding that love cannot be forced to grow, or not grow, in any particular direction. Polyamory emphasizes consciously choosing how many partners you wish to engage with rather than accepting social norms that dictate loving only one person at a time.

Intro to Swingers

For some, swinging is a less stressful way to enter into the world of non-monogamy. That may or may not be true for you. I guess that all depends on what you find stressful. With the swing lifestyle, you're solely adapting to sexual non-monogamy. It's more boundaried, which is good for someone who is new. Although I could argue for Anapol's view that love cannot be truly controlled, boundaries do have an impact. I know swingers who have had sexual adventures for decades without falling in love with their other sexual partners. How? Again, boundaries. We will talk more about this soon enough.

Many people struggle with the idea that if they want to have other sexual partners, that means they don't truly love the person they're with—but that's simply not true. One experience does not negate the other.

The fear of being out of control may also enter your mind again here. A good way to prove this fear wrong is to stay away from the booze when you are in new situations like a play party or a chemistry check date. This policy will help you make clear decisions that you don't regret. Also, allow yourself to emotionally process one event before booking the next. So often, people get excited and go to a ton of events back-to-back and ignore or are in denial about mounting emotional injuries and unhealed wounds within their primary relationship. Based on my experience in private practice, during this phase, folks are often too excited to listen to sound advice. Or they don't think such caution is necessary. But once their excitement abates a bit, they almost always come around and see the value in it.

Meanwhile, the lifestyle provides a community of sexual adventurers who more often than not will happily support you as you experience the highs and the lows of swinging. As long as you 1) aren't judging or disrespecting them and 2) fit in and adapt to swinger cultural norms, they will not judge you for your curiosity in their world.

In fact, they will most likely champion and guide you as you navigate your way through their community.

You get to choose how far you go with swinging, from just being a voyeur to becoming a full-on participant. You have complete control over your actions and can always say no to the things that make you feel uncomfortable. Do only what feels good and right for you and your partner!

A note on swinger norms: every community has their norms and limits, which can feel judgmental if you do not fit within them. Previously, the non-judgmental atmosphere of the lifestyle compared to our larger society was stressed. However, there are some glaring exceptions. Within the lifestyle, a variety of sexual orientations exist—but historically, the norm has been the bisexual female–straight male couple, and lifestyle gay, bisexual, or pansexual men, whether they are identified as a single male or within a couple, have frequently been discriminated against. However, according to a 2019 study in *Culture, Health & Sexuality* entitled "Changes in the Swing Lifestyle: A US National and Historical Comparison," between 1982 and 2016 a shift toward greater diversity and an increased connection to the Democratic Party occurred. Such shifts are evidence of increasing inclusivity.

Cooper Beckett, a self-identified swinger and author, has made a valiant effort to expand the concept of what a swinger can be by hosting international swinger events that welcome all walks of life. Another group, Sex Positive World, puts on events and holds group meetings in many major cities that meet the needs of swingers, polyamorists, and everyone in between.

If you want community but don't feel you have found your tribe, keep looking. You will find it. And if you discover that you are viewed as fringe within the swing community and therefore do not feel accepted, explore the secret groups on swinger websites or perhaps explore polyamory, kink, or other communities that are known to be more embracing regardless of gender or sexual orientation.

Ultimately, the lifestyle provides a safe arena to embrace yourself as a sexually adventurous person who has the courage to embrace sex as good and healthy despite all the social pressures to conform. No matter what word(s) you choose to identify with sexually, exploring your sexuality is healthy! It can lead to personal growth, insight, and connection if you explore from an emotionally honest place. Being curious about sex just means that you are truly alive. So, that being said, let's explore.

Getting Started in the Lifestyle

If you have any reservations about the swing lifestyle or looking for group sex, then by all means, go slow and cautiously. Jumping in too fast is the primary mistake new couples or singles often make. There are many ways to slow the process down; let's discuss some.

Utilize community
You can find a date at a bar or a sex website, but without the context of community, it will be harder to vet who you pick. If you choose a lover on a swing website, you can see that person's or couple's reviews and thus have an idea of what other people think of them.

Flirt, text, or email
Before your first date, spend some time getting to know your prospective play partner or couple by communicating with them. Sexy communication can build sexual tension and excitement while reducing anxiety and reservations. If you email within a lifestyle website, you can also postpone revealing your identity until you are ready. This approach gives you time to weed out anyone who doesn't seem quite right.

Go on a "chemistry check" date
There is no need to "seal the deal" on your first date. A great way to increase your surety and decrease your anxiety is to have a no-pressure

chemistry check date. A chemistry check allows you to meet the couple or single and get to know them over drinks or dinner, so you can see if you click without any expectation of sex. If there is chemistry, then such a meeting also allows everyone to communicate expectations, limits, and desires before everyone is naked and articulate conversations become more challenging.

Find your sexual comfort zone

In the beginning, some people are only into flirting and sexy emails, while others are ready to move forward and experience same-room partner play. If you're past the point of just being curious but are wary of jumping into the deep end, consider "soft swapping"—swapping partners with another couple, but only for kissing and making out, and at the very most having oral sex. With soft swapping, no penetration is permissible unless it's with your own partner. Later on, when you feel more comfortable, you might choose to ramp up to "full swap," in which full penetration is permissible (but not required, of course).

Some players in the lifestyle remain at soft swap. In fact, some people in the lifestyle community don't ever have sex with other couples or singles; they just love being part of a sexually free world. These people enjoy the lifestyle parties simply because they love the people; ultimately, they choose to only have sex with their partner—and that's okay. Remember, this is your adventure and you make the rules.

Our culture puts a lot of "shoulds" on us regarding what is right and moral. It's hard to escape culture-induced shame. But, in the end, each of us has the freedom to decide what's right for us personally. Some naysayers regard swinging as sanctioned cheating. Ideally, swinging is not about cheating at all; rather, it's about honesty and loyalty while exploring sexual diversity with your partner.

Singles, too, can profit from an atmosphere bereft of shame. In a world full of responsibilities and pressures, the lifestyle can be an amazing stress reliever. Even beyond that, it can be surprisingly healing in its open acceptance of sexiness and normalization of desiring many sexual partners.

The Kink Community

It's hard to discuss non-monogamy without mentioning kink, which includes fetish and BDSM practices. A fetish is a sexual desire to an unusual degree for a particular object or body part—anything ranging from shoes to sweaters to balloons. BDSM, meanwhile, actually stands for six practices: bondage, discipline, dominance, submission, sadism, and masochism. The kink community is huge, especially in major cities—and many of its members are non-monogamous. However, despite having a practice of consensual non-monogamy (CNM), many kinksters identify more with the kink community than with the swing or polyamory community, so one is more likely to find them at kink events, munches (non-play kink socials), and dungeons (BDSM play spaces). If you are non-monogamous and kinky, this might be your preferred community as well.

Bigotry between polyamorous, swing, and kink communities

Can't we all just get along? You might be surprised by this, but a fair amount of bigotry exists between alternative sexual communities. We can't always assume that alternative sexual communities will be supportive of one another just because all their members are alternative.

People in alternative sexual communities, in my experience, do have much more tolerance for sexual variation than within the general public—but some are still guilty of being judgmental of sexual or gender norms that fall outside of their own social boundaries. I've often heard swingers say that poly folk are on a speed train toward divorce and that kinksters are just weird. Meanwhile, I've heard poly and kinky folks pigeonhole swingers as being superficial.

Perhaps the most bigoted individuals, though, are those who

project their own sexual shame. If someone feels the need to slut-shame another person, it seems to me that it's time to look hard in the mirror.

Personally, I have seen firsthand what each of these communities has to offer, and I still cherish the time I spent connected to the swinger (lifestyle) community. When I was working in mental health clinics, which are incredibly rewarding but stressful environments, the swing community's no-drama, all-fun policy was just what I needed. I still have friends from those days who I'm connected with well over a decade later.

And fun is not the only reward; community support, which can show up in various ways—classes, emotional support groups, and even community outreach—is another benefit. We aren't surprised when a religious or social justice group goes out of their way to help someone in need. But would you be surprised to hear that people in swing, poly, or kink communities will do a similar outreach for members of their community? It's a common occurrence.

So the moral of the story is that if you choose to explore the various alternative sexual communities out there, they can be a great support to you as you explore the exciting but often difficult experience of being non-monogamous. They can help you find your truth. In the process, maybe you'll even find your tribe. And within any of these groups, you may find a gem that might end up being an amazing friend. Community is not a necessity, but it sure is an asset.

I believe the future is fluid. This concept applies to community as well. Many CNM folks have read *Sex at Dawn* and are aware how the agricultural revolution and colonialization broke down tribal communities, nomadic living, and extended families, greatly reducing CNM in the process. The monogamous, nuclear family became the norm. But there is still much to learn from leaders who speak on the decolonization of sex, especially with regard to CNM, such as Dr. Kim TallBear. As we do so, we will almost certainly find that intimacy, deep connection, and support can be found not only between two people but also, as indigenous tribes have always known, in our connection to the whole—community, nature, and our world. But embracing a communal non-monogamous relationship model will not be successful if it's driven by the narcissism colonialism fueled. My hope is that one day all relationships will become more conscious, connected, and compassionate so that all relationships, especially our relationship with nature, can reach their full potential while given dignity and respect.

SKILLS & STEPS FOR SUCCESSFULLY SWIMMING TOWARD THE DEEP END

"To open deeply, as genuine spiritual life requires,
we need tremendous courage and strength,
a kind of warrior spirit."
—*Jack Kornfield*

Chapter Four

BUILDING TRUST, EXPANSIVENESS, AND PASSION

The crux of my professional passion is helping people cultivate a conscious, connected, and deeply intimate love within non-monogamy and fluid relationships. At its best, non-monogamy is a catalyst that fuels deeper intimacy. Before you can navigate this terrain successfully, you need to lay some groundwork.

Specifically, non-monogamy requires an extensive and cultivated emotional intelligence toolbox. Sound daunting? That's okay. The road map is here. From this point forward, we will be cultivating the skills needed to demonstrate emotional intelligence in your relationships. With this foundation, you will be able to successfully build powerful and positive ethically non-monogamous connections.

I believe the key to success in non-monogamy is understanding our attachment styles and their roots. Non-monogamy pokes at our attachment injuries *way* more than monogamy does, and yet I rarely hear attachment theory mentioned in the non-monogamous literature I see. In both monogamous and non-monogamous relationships, it's our unresolved attachment injuries and our associated fear of intimacy that create destructive blocks between couples. Once we heal those injuries, conscious, connected, and deeply intimate love is possible.

Open relationships shine a light on our wounds, revealing what needs to heal within us. This is the immense gift and the terrifying reality of non-monogamy. These wounds can remain dormant in monogamous relationships for decades, but once you open your relationship up, there is no hiding them.

So what is an attachment injury, anyway? Attachment injuries can come in many forms. Abuse or neglect from a parent or a past loved one are powerful attachment injuries that may stay with us for decades. Other attachment injuries can come from isolated incidents. Imagine being left alone in a hospital and fearing for your life. If your partner chooses a business meeting over being by your side in your hour of need, guess what? You have experienced a massive attachment injury. Your partner chose business over loving you well.

These past memories impact us at a cellular level and get projected onto our current intimate relationships. (If you want to read more on this topic, I recommend *The Body Keeps the Score*, by Bessel van der Kolk.) Furthermore, these injuries are often at the root of non-monogamy issues such as jealousy. How can one trust another person with their loved one if their life experience has been a series of betrayals, disrespect, and lies?

It's possible—but before it can happen, we have to do the work to heal and build a strong safety net of trust with all partners involved. Chapters 5 through 7 will unpack how to have compassion for our very tender underbellies as we navigate non-monogamy. Going forward, everything in this book is designed to help you build trust. And please note that this security might land very differently within your non-monogamous relationship than it did, perhaps, in your previous monogamous relationships. Trusting your partner to take the kids to karate practice is very different than trusting your partner with another lover.

The Crucial Role of Trust and Learning to Love Well

When I was younger, I often fell in love fast and hard. At age twenty-two, when I first saw Derek, the man who I would spend over a decade with, his GQ model looks, swoon-worthy rocker hair, and brilliant mind had me hooked.

Today, that starry-eyed girl is long gone. Now I know that the first onion layer of a person may be pristine, but it's simply that: the first layer. And it takes time to find out what is underneath. Love is built gently, with patience and over time. You are best served by looking for a partner who not only eventually says, "I love you," but who knows *how* to love well. Non-monogamy provides tests that will reveal how well you love others and yourself. Sometimes you won't pass the test. But when you wake up with your lovers after a kick-ass, sexy threesome in which all involved felt attended to and cared for, you may feel like you can shoot for the moon or take on anything. CNM is its own kind of hero's journey.

A conscious, connected, intimate love within CNM does not happen organically. It comes from the work of two invested people who are dedicated to learning and using hard-earned skills to love deeply.

Let's unfold what I mean by that. For a moment, let's consider the difference between the two ideas above. In a monogamous relationship, too much security can lead to a companionate relationship that includes stellar cuddling but is completely devoid of heat in the bedroom. Within non-monogamous relationships, in contrast, trust is the springboard to adventure.

This type of trust may be brand new to you. It's great that you trust your partner to take care of you when you are sick, pay the bills on time, and listen to you when you're mad at your boss. However, trust within non-monogamy is completely new terrain. You will have to learn to trust your partner's judgment in whole new ways. Do you trust their ability to choose another partner who will be kind and respectful to you? Do you trust them to check in on you at the play party? There are endless moments that will build or break down the trust you have for one another.

Trust is built from a consistent pattern of benevolent words, actions, and deeds played out within non-monogamous situations. It is also tested and impacted during discussions regarding your open relationship. It will increase or decrease depending on how well you and your partner comply with relationship agreements, how completely you have each other's back, and how attuned you both are to each other's needs. All of our actions and words have an impact on trust. And while it is impossible to bring up every situation that may affect trust, I can front-load you with some important things to think about.

The following are some key ideas to consider when attempting to build security within your open relationship.

Patience Wins Out in the Long Run

If you are the one who wants to leap, skip, spring down the path of non-monogamy, your enthusiasm is a lovely thing. But every admirable trait has its downside, and in this case, it may be that you tend to push too fast and hard. Just remember, it pays to be patient and gentle. If, in your excitement, you become blind and deaf to your love's needs, you might very well shoot yourself in the foot. All your forward momentum could come to a screeching halt if you push and pressure too much and your partner breaks down in overwhelm, lashes out in anger, is overcome with sadness, or completely shuts down.

Being compassionate not only makes your partner feel seen and heard, it also sets you both up for success in the long run. So I invite you to try to find a happy medium between your needs and your partner's needs. Look to the long view. Having the patience of a busload of nuns in the first year may very well yield a lifetime of increased sexual authenticity and freedom in the years to come.

Also, be mindful that your words and deeds match the agreements you have made. For example, if you consent to a break from non-monogamy, give your partner a true break. So often, I see the opposite play out in couples therapy. One partner will ask for a break from an activity within their non-monogamous agreement—asking to be monogamous in practice for a while, or to only play together until some issues are worked through. And the new relationship practice is agreed upon, but then, during every session going forward, the consenting partner sounds like that little kid in the back seat of the car saying, "Are we there yet? Are we there yet?"

This is not a true break.

Take Ashley and Denise. They had been together for five years and non-monogamous for nine months. But Ashley found herself grieving the loss of the white picket fence ideal of monogamy she'd dreamed of as a young woman. Consequently, she asked for a break from non-monogamy to work on the lack of connection she was feeling to Denise. Neither of them had any deep attachments to other partners, so taking a break was ethically and logistically easy.

Denise, who was all in for non-monogamy and excited to have new lovers and new experiences, was disappointed that Ashley felt they needed to stop their non-monogamous adventures to work on their partnership. She reluctantly consented to the break, though it bothered her that there was no stated end point. (Ashley had simply stated that she needed time.)

The fact that Ashley's pain was compounding was also difficult for Denise to understand. She was mainly experiencing joy and wanted Ashley to feel the same. Her lack of understanding, coupled with her impatience to move forward, made compassion difficult for her.

In our sessions, instead of solely focusing on unpacking what would make her and Ashley feel connected, loved, happy, and respected within the relationship, Denise fixated on the lack of an end date for the break. Her frustration and confusion was palpable. The result was that Ashley didn't feel that she was getting the break she'd asked for. She needed an *emotional* break from non-monogamy, not simply an activity or time break. And Denise's failure to honor the break left Ashley feeling that she and their relationship were not being honored. The result was a heartbreak that she never really recovered from and that continued to mar their relationship years later.

The moral of this story is to be patient, honor your love, and look to the long view. Giving your partner what they need now will almost certainly pay off later. Patience is a core way to build trust and security.

If you are the more fired-up one, you might be saying, "But what about my needs? Don't they matter?" Yes—and throughout this book, I will discuss communication strategies that will make hard conversations about fears and concerns more successful. When you use compassion during those conversations, your partner is more likely to begin to feel at ease. And with a sense of safety and security comes a willingness to step out of the familiar, move forward, and take risks from an authentic and happy place.

Never Shame Your Partner

Now, you might be thinking to yourself, *I'd NEVER shame my partner!*—but it can happen more easily than you might imagine. Usually the shamer doesn't even realize they're being hurtful, and their intent is rarely malicious.

These kinds of topics take a great deal of finessing. If poorly delivered, the result could be a partner plummeting down a shame spiral or shouting in righteous indignation. How can you kindly express that your partner stepped over your boundaries without shaming them? That's a tough one. I'll give you an example.

Josh and Veronica had been non-monogamous for about a year and had been going on dates with other couples most of that time. However, they were new to play parties.

At their third play party, they knew a lot of people. The crowd and the music were amazing. They quickly got caught up in the energy. After chatting and flirting for hours, they headed for the bedroom. Upon entering, they discovered a passionately engaged foursome in full swing on the bed. One of the couples, who they knew, waved them over. It was a huge bed, and there was plenty of room for two more. Another couple was using a sex swing next to the bed that was attached to an eye bolt in the ceiling.

Josh and Veronica had discussed their play party rules and boundaries and had even gone over associated feelings in therapy. Regardless, that night, Josh got hit with some new, unexpected feelings when Veronica, for the first time, really let go. While Josh was going down on their friend Monique, Veronica was getting lifted into the sex swing. Soon, she was getting fucked hard by Kent, a strapping, six-foot-two gentleman. Her moans grew to a crescendo, and everyone on the bed giggled a bit without breaking their focus—everyone except for Josh, who was devastated. He had never heard her be that loud before, or look quite that blissful.

For the next thirty minutes, he tried to hide his feelings, but eventually he whispered to her, "Let's go"—and the fight that ensued in the car was heated and painful for both of them.

"I just never knew how insatiable you could be!" Josh said at one point. "You were so loud. Everyone was looking. I felt so embarrassed."

Now Josh is simply expressing his unfiltered hurt, which is probably more about his fear of losing her or not being good enough than a fear that Veronica will become an out-of-control sex banshee. However, all Veronica hears is that she was a shameful embarrassment to him at this party—so, as you might expect, she lashes out in anger and defensiveness.

How could Josh have expressed his hurt more effectively? First, to avoid shaming our partner we need to cool our jets and ground ourselves before speaking. Even a few deep, slow breaths can calm the body a bit. (I know this can be super hard when you are pissed. Don't worry. We will continue to talk about how to pull this off throughout this book.)

Once you have taken some deep breaths, take a moment to imagine how your words will be felt on the receiving end. Let's imagine that Josh is able to put his ego in his back pocket and say, "Look, I'm happy you were having fun. I know you've wanted to try out a sex swing for years. But when you got so loud, I got sad that I wasn't the one experiencing your first time in a swing. And I was also fearful that I've been failing you somehow, if Kent can elicit that kind of reaction from you."

With this approach, instead of jumping to guardedness and rage, Veronica might have softened with compassion. "Oh, sweetie," she might say, "I'm so sorry. I should have grabbed you for that first experience in a swing. You'll always be my favorite lover. But I think that swing is my new kink! It just really hit the spot."

Upon hearing Veronica's reply, Josh might not have been ready to wink and make a cheeky joke like, "I guess we will be swinging by the sex shop tomorrow," but he probably would have felt a bit more validated.

Yes, I know this is easier said than done, but these self-calming and communication skills are there for the taking, and if you can utilize them in tense moments, you will be able to navigate the hardest part of non-monogamy. When you're able to engage in self-care and make your partner feel cared for all at once, you are off to a very good start. And when respect and validation are mutually felt, a predominantly happy non-monogamous journey is within reach.

Always Have Your Partner's Back

So often in couples therapy, when someone expresses why they are falling out of love, they will say to their partner, "I just don't think you have my back." In non-monogamy, providing that "I've got you" feeling means everything to your partner—it's a key security that most people want.

In the case of polyamory, this gets more complicated. If two people you love are pissed at each other, how do you have *both* of their backs? This request also becomes challenging if you have a partner who has distorted thinking and projects the worst onto others. Still, where possible, it's best to choose your partner over the chance at a new sexual experience. So often I have borne witness, both in and out of my practice, to that non-monogamous person who is like a kid let loose in a candy store, frenzied and gluttonous, forgetting their love who's crying in the doorway. But it doesn't have to go down that way.

I'll give you an example from my personal life. Within my thirteen-year non-monogamous relationship with my former husband, he had many girlfriends. And during all that time, I only once asserted "veto power," asking him not to see a potential girlfriend.

One day, I came home from work and this new potential girlfriend was sitting on our sofa. I had been given a heads-up; her presence was not a surprise. I sat down to chat with her. Very soon, she began bragging that the married non-monogamous men she had dated previously had always told her that they could be honest with her in a way they could not with their wives. I could see her Mount Everest–size ego. Her competitiveness was transparent. This gal was not intending to be my ally.

After she left, I reached out to a few members of the lifestyle community about her and quickly found out that she had been banned by two of the major lifestyle party promoters due to belligerent behavior. When I told my partner that I did not want him to see her, without skipping a beat, he agreed. And just like that, she was gone. That meant the world to me, and I breathed a big sigh of relief. I trusted him more for it. (Side note: I don't believe veto power should be used willy-nilly. And veto power does not work within every relationship. It can be too dictatorial. But within some relationships, in which both parties trust each other not to use it except in extreme cases, it can lend to that sense that your partner has got you.)

Megan and Tom had been married for four years and had a two-year-old daughter when they decided to open up their relationship. Megan found lovers relatively easily, while Tom had a harder time.

Eventually, Tom expressed desire to take on his coworker Anya as his lover. They'd had a flirtation for years. Megan knew her and liked her. To him, Anya made perfect sense. He'd already begun to talk to her about the arrangement and she was willing to try it, though this would be her first time dating a non-monogamous man. By the time he brought it up to Megan, both he and Anya were completely invested in the idea and assumed Megan would be on board.

To his dismay, Megan's reaction was not what he'd anticipated. "Anya doesn't have the first clue about non-monogamy," she told him. "She could cause a lot of devastation to our marriage just out of ignorance. What if your boss finds out? You could be fired. We need your paycheck. I'm not ready to go back to work yet. And what if your coworkers find out? They don't know we're non-monogamous. They'll think you're cheating on me. Imagine what your company picnic will be like for me, with all the stares. And what if I ask for certain boundaries? How will I even be able to ask for boundaries if you are seeing her every day at work? Oh, and you both go to the same gym on the weekends!"

Tom immediately lashed out in anger. "Oh, you're just being jealous. You don't want me to have anything for myself. You know that Anya is a nice person, my coworkers and boss are open-minded, and everything will be fine. You've always been selfish."

Megan collapsed. Suddenly, non-monogamy felt like something that was creating a wedge between her and Tom rather than increasing their closeness and passion. She wondered if opening up was just one big mistake that she couldn't take back. Both partners were left feeling that the other didn't have their back.

How could this have gone down differently? Tom could have talked to Megan first about taking on Anya as a lover. At that point, Megan could have asked him not to take on lovers he worked with. In reply, he might have expressed his dismay that finding lovers had been much harder for him. Maybe he could have shared that he was envious that lovers just dropped in Megan's lap. Imagine if she had said, "Hey, honey, I want to help you out. Let's go to a few Poly Cocktails meetings or some parties. I think it would be fun to be your wingwoman and help you find a lady. Maybe we'll even end up having a threesome in the process, who knows? I get that finding a lover has been harder for you. I just don't feel comfortable with either of us finding lovers at work. It's too risky."

If your partner feels like you have their back, they will be more likely to open up like a flower, unfolding their authentic sexual truth and in turn giving you more freedom. However, if you pressure or manipulate them, or prioritize an isolated conquest over the health and longevity of a cultivated relationship, then they will most likely remain tight in the bud—making your experience within non-monogamy one of pain rather than joy and connection.

Respect Your Partner's Vulnerability

Too often, we are not conscious of the impact of our words. We are simply fighting to be heard and get our needs met. But when we are reactive rather than thoughtful, our partner learns that it's not safe to be vulnerable with us. A type of trust is damaged.

Consider Chelsea and Marcus, who have been together for five years.

Chelsea says to Marcus, "I hear that you're struggling with my relationship with Jack. I know that when I'm with him on Fridays, you feel anxious. What do you need?"

Marcus replies, "Well, if you know that, then don't go."

In this example, it took courage for Chelsea to validate Marcus's feelings and ask what he needed, knowing that what she might hear may not be advantageous to her own needs and desires. In this case, Marcus is probably unaware that he's taking advantage of her generosity and vulnerability. He is simply trying to hurt less.

What if their interchange goes down like this instead:

Chelsea says to Marcus, "I hear that you are struggling with my relationship with Jack. I know that when I'm with him on Fridays, you feel anxious. What do you need?"

Marcus replies, "Thank you for caring enough to talk to me about this. I'm uneasy because it's new. I don't trust Jack yet. I'd like to talk to him over Skype."

"Sure," Chelsea says. "I'll let him know that you plan to reach out to set up a time to talk."

In the first example, Chelsea validates Marcus's pain regarding Jack, and in response he attempts to yank her whole relationship with Jack away from her—a heavy-handed move. Now, in some cases (for instance, if Jack has toxic behaviors), such a response might be warranted. But in this situation, it clearly wasn't.

In the second response, Marcus honors Chelsea's vulnerable outreach, thanks her, and replies with a reasonable request. Such a response inspires trust in Marcus, which means that Chelsea will be more likely to confidently check in with Marcus, making sure his needs and emotions are being considered, in the future.

Have a Good Attitude

Having a good attitude inspires trust in our partner. They trust us to always attempt to bring our best self, our higher self, to the relationship. This type of trust is calming and happiness-inducing.

When I think of applying a good attitude to non-monogamy, I think of Dan Savage, who coined the term "GGG" to represent the qualities that make for a good sexual partner. The *GGG* stands for "good," "giving," and "game." "Good" refers to being good in bed. "Giving" refers to giving equal time and equal pleasure during sex. "Game" refers to being game for anything sexually, within reason.

I believe in GGG non-monogamous relationships. Let's look at each of these ideas a little more closely.

Good

"Good" might translate to learning to love your partner well (how they want and need to be loved) within non-monogamy. For instance, your partner may ask you to send them a text that says, "Good night, sweet dreams," when you are away seeing a lover in another city. With this request, you have a choice: you can view the request as an opportunity to love your partner better, or you can choose to view it as a burden and perhaps passive-aggressively forget to do it.

Our partners are always trying to teach us how to love them well. Listen and take action, and you will build a rich, connected relationship.

Giving

"Giving" might refer to hearing your partner's non-monogamous needs and attempting to make sure both you and your partner feel there's a balance in needs being met. It implies an intention of mutual generosity within your non-monogamy. But this intention need not yield a matchy-matchy relationship model. Your partner might want a variety of lovers or threesomes. You might simply want two deep relationships. The two of you may have wildly different needs. This is okay. What matters is that there is a sense of balance combined with mutual and consensual generosity.

Game

"Game" might refer to a willingness to try new things within non-monogamy. This doesn't mean overextending your boundaries to the point of psychologically damaging yourself. Within both sexuality and non-monogamy, any yes should be a true yes. However, let's imagine, for example, that you're a bit nervous about a chemistry check date with another couple. Your partner has been hoping for a future foursome. With only a few threesomes under your belt, the couple dynamic seems daunting to you. But part of being game is working through some manageable anxiety to at least meet the couple. You can ponder later whether you are ready to take the next step; by at least meeting the couple, you have shown your partner that you are game to consider the adventure they have fantasized over.

Have Humility

If we show humility within this challenging, non-monogamous journey rather than charging in like a bull in a china shop, our partner will trust us to have good judgment and make sound choices for the relationship. I often have long-term couples come limping into my office because non-monogamy has given them a humility lesson they did not expect. Before the brutal reality check, they often say to themselves, "We've been great parents, business partners, and lovers for all these years. We will be good at non-monogamy too. It will be fine!"

The problem, of course, is that they aren't aware of what their non-monogamous journey will reveal about them. Non-monogamy brings out all our unresolved psychological stuff. That's the beauty and the curse of it: it can provide corrective, healing experiences, enhancing trust, intimacy, and growth while concurrently being erotic and fun, if you have a patient, compassionate partner—but this growth can be painful, even if it's worth it. Non-monogamy is challenging for *everyone*. It's a much more difficult relationship model than monogamy.

Another mistake folks make is to assume they will know how they or their partner will react before they have actually experienced something new firsthand. They are overly confident about how they will respond to their first sex party, or with their first partner beyond their spouse. How confident were you about how you would respond to sex back when you were still a virgin? It's really not that different. I find that people don't know how they'll feel until they literally have experience under their belt. And yet people commonly make assumptions about how they'll react to non-monogamy. They are sure their partner will be the jealous one and that they will be the cool cucumber, only to find out, as reality unkindly smacks them in the face, that they are the jealous one and their partner is as comfy as a kitten with catnip.

Having humility is a large stepping-stone toward navigating this journey with grace. Non-monogamy is a catalyst. It can strengthen the connection and love of a strong couple and just as quickly derail a fragile one. A surfer becomes great by having humility regarding their relationship with the powerful wave. A surfer would never surf with a broken leg, and so a relationship should not be opened if there's an existing rupture. You would be attempting to take on a powerful force without being strong enough to attune to it properly.

Although being open can be a wonderful addition to your life, it also complicates things. These are all reasons to cool your jets and remain thoughtfully humble—and with this humility comes the realization that you can't do this on your own. Learn from others. You need not always find out the hard way.

Educate Yourself

Practicing non-monogamy is a multifaceted and involved way to live. Therefore, beginning your journey fortified with knowledge and community support is highly advisable. If you are the reader in your relationship, please push your partner to self-educate as well. I often see couples having difficulties because only one partner has done the work of self-education. This ignorance and lack of effort can create serious damage in a relationship.

With non-monogamy, intuition is not enough, especially when you're new to it. A great first step is reading this book, and I hope this will be just one of many that you read over the course of your continued journey.

Avoid Lying, Even by Omission

Those who lie or mislead within non-monogamy tend to be harmony addicts (this is not an actual diagnosis). They cannot tolerate discomfort within the relationship.

This lack of tolerance for discomfort can be due to many reasons: 1) hating to see their partner in pain, 2) fearing rage or criticism, 3) fearing a sense of being controlled, or 4) fearing abandonment. But their partners often sense their deception. And once your partner discovers one lie, they will most likely feel as though they're standing on quicksand. Trust disintegrates, and they fear that behind this deception are many more.

At this point, if you're the one who's been lying and you had hopes for having a partner who feels compersion for your other love relationships, you can kiss that dream goodbye for the foreseeable future. You have just paired non-monogamy with pain, my friend.

A bit of Psych 101 for you: There's a classic behavioral study about mice who discover cheese, only to be shocked upon trying to eat it. Imagine your partner is the mouse and non-monogamy is the cheese. It seems so good, something your partner wants. But then they pick it up and get shocked. Your lying by omission is the shock. The mice eventually stopped trying to eat the cheese altogether, even though the shocks were administered only half of the time. Humans learn the same way. If you keep shocking someone, they will eventually lose faith altogether.

The eight keys to building trust within non-monogamy that we've just reviewed will create a strong foundation to build upon. Mistakes will be made, but deeper intimacy is often found within the repair. Trust and security are everything in non-monogamy. And compassion for yourself and your partner during the hard times will be easier if a strong safety net of trust is in place.

Chapter Five

SELF-COMPASSION

The longer I'm a psychotherapist, the more I realize how rare self-compassion is. Many of us beat ourselves up with a critical inner dialogue that we picked up in childhood. Many of my clients will confess, "I'm bad at poly. I'm a selfish person. Why is it so easy for everyone else? Why am I so weak? I'm so petty and jealous."

That critical voice or internalized bully insists, "You must be good at poly or else you are failing everyone." And when that voice wins out over intuition and self-care, that's the beginning of saying "yes" when really your answer is "maybe," "not yet," "I'm scared," or "I need comfort." When our "yes" isn't a true yes, we allow things to happen that aren't good for us—and the result can be traumatizing, leading to PTSD symptoms, such as insomnia, hypervigilance, or panic attacks. Sound extreme? I've had plenty of clients who've had panic attacks related to non-monogamy. That's why your yes should always be a true yes. A true yes is a big part of self-compassion and self-care.

If you're confused—wait! Give yourself some time and ground yourself. Bring your body back to the parasympathetic nervous system, a place of calm, with some deep breathing. *Then* check in with your mind, body, and emotional compass. These three components, in tandem, will steer you true.

Practicing Compassionate Self-Talk

Compassionate self-talk is the most important first step toward self-compassion; it clears a path to a more peaceful you. For those with a strong inner critic, this suggestion is easier said than done. Self-flagellation can be brutal and endless. You may even beat yourself up for beating yourself up. This tendency comes from the bullies in our past—a parent, a teacher, a coach, or a peer—who told us, through words or actions, that we were bad. Eventually, their messages become the messages in our own head.

Guilt says, "I did something bad," but shame tells us, "I am inherently, at my core, bad." Guilt can inspire. It can invite us to change a bad pattern and develop a better version of ourselves. But shame breaks us down. It can even send us into a debilitating emotional spiral that leaves us incapable of being there for ourselves or others.

Instead of beating yourself up, begin to talk compassionately to yourself. Notice the critical voice that, like an abusive parent, says things like, "You're petty, jealous, and weak." Let those thoughts drift by like a cloud and bring on board the good parent. Perhaps they would say, "Non-monogamy is really hard. You're having a difficult time right now, but you'll work through this if you're kind to yourself. Be patient with yourself. Be kind. You deserve self-care."

Many in the non-monogamous community over-rely on cognitive strategies as the be-all, end-all solution to coping with problems like jealousy. This often compounds the damage. Cognitive strategies alone often heighten shame. For example, I've frequently heard a well-intentioned partner advise their emotionally distraught, self-flagellating partner to "just be logical." Rather than providing any sort of empathy, they say, "Logically, you know that Alex isn't out to hurt you or our relationship. They have always been good to both of us. You're just being jealous and emotional"—an approach that leaves the distraught partner feeling dismissed and misunderstood, beaten up by themselves *and* their partner. Such an unbalanced philosophy frequently becomes a toxic force rather than a helpful one. (We'll discuss a better, more balanced approach to this in Chapter 13.)

Cultivate compassionate self-talk and remind your reality-checking partner that these feelings often run deeper than what simple logic can fix. Our emotions are one-third of our internal compass; just like our body sensations and thoughts, they should not be disregarded.

Building Positive Affect Tolerance and Its Impact on Intimacy

One of the primary blocks to self-compassion is poor positive affect tolerance. Positive affect tolerance is the degree to which one can take in, believe, and enjoy the best parts of life. It's also our ability to tolerate positive emotions.

Those with poor positive affect tolerance are easy to spot. Have you ever said to a friend, "Oh, you look beautiful in that dress!" only to have them reply, "Thanks, but I feel ugly and gross today." In my private practice, I might say, "Tell me about a memory, belief, person, place, or thing that makes you feel happy inside." Someone with poor positive affect tolerance might reply, "I loved my cat, but my cat's dead." Now, how long were they able to stay with the positive thought? Not even a few seconds.

What does this have to do with non-monogamy? A lot. Because this same person is the one who says, "I'm horrible at poly." If a person only notices the bad moments within non-monogamy, their perception of non-monogamy will quickly become negatively skewed; they will only notice their mistakes and ignore all their wins.

So how does one retrain the brain, the neural connections that have been built over a lifetime? Begin with a practice of gratitude. Neuropsychologist Dr. Donald Hebb says that at a neurobiological level, neurons that fire together wire together to form pathways in the brain. For instance, if we experience daily road rage, that rage may become our default mode of operation. Similarly, if we begin a practice of gratitude within non-monogamy by simply interrupting the critical mind to notice times that we handled things well—had fun, or felt charming, confident, and sexy—then neural circuitry will form that improves our positive affect tolerance and, in turn, our capacity for self-compassion. This gratitude practice will take tenacity and commitment at first, but over time it will become your default way of thinking.

We can build our positive affect tolerance like we build our muscles at the gym. Don't pick up the hundred-pound weights first. Start light. Next time you receive a compliment, simply say thank you rather than discounting the compliment. The next time someone gives you a wanted hug, notice what part of your body connects with the good feeling and focus there. In this way, you will slowly build your ability to tolerate self-love and the love of others without pushing them away or sabotaging their attempts. And when you have a strong ability to both receive and give love ideally in equal measure, your core relationship will be better able to successfully negotiate non-monogamy with strength, security, and confidence.

Healing Attachment Injuries

Past attachment injuries have a deep impact on how difficult non-monogamy may or may not be for you. Jealousy is not petty. It's a manifestation of how your past attachments have impacted you. If, as a child, you found out that one of your parents was unfaithful and this traumatized you, this is an attachment injury. If your first sweetheart lied to you, betrayed you, or cheated on you, these are also attachment injuries. Such injuries inform us. They tell us how safe the world is and how safe we are. If life has taught you that those closest to you will leave you, lie to you, and/or betray you, why would you ever consider non-monogamy? Why would you trust?

This is not to say that those with attachment injuries should not be non-monogamous. If you have chosen a loving, compassionate partner who communicates well and is willing to negotiate with you, corrective experiences—experiences that support you to heal because they mirror those damaging experiences from your past but have different, more positive outcomes—are possible.

For instance, imagine Bekah witnessed her father cheating on her mother and then Dad said, "Don't tell your mother. It will be our little secret." Then, in adulthood, Bekah marries Rob. They have a discussion about cheating and decide to try non-monogamy. During that discussion, Rob says to her, "I will never cheat on you. I want us to find a way to be partners in crime instead." Non-monogamy may feel scary to Bekah, but the fact that Rob is clearly attempting to be honest with her is a corrective experience from how she witnessed her father operating.

The more you face the pain from your backstory, the more manageable your feelings of jealousy will become. But facing those messages must be done gently, with self-compassion and proper timing. Forcing yourself to face what triggers you too quickly or harshly can retraumatize you. Psychotherapy trauma modalities, like EMDR (eye movement desensitization and reprocessing), can help heal what cannot be cleared on your own or via couples therapy. It is not something to simply rationalize through. If you use only intellect to power through your feelings, or if you try to box up your feelings, no true progress will be made.

As I mentioned at the beginning of this chapter, I often hear clients say, "Why am I so jealous? Why am I so scared? I'm having panic attacks at night. Why is non-monogamy so easy for my partner?" When this happens, instead of giving them a pre-packaged answer, I'll ask questions that lead me to their personal truth. Such an inquiry will go something like this: "Tell me about your backstory. In general, has your childhood and your life informed you that the world is safe—that people have your back and are honest? Or has it been your experience that you cannot trust loved ones, whether they are parents or partners?" Through this line of questioning, I find, people begin to see that they aren't weak. They are simply affected by the pain from their past.

If you puncture a tire with a large knife, you don't blame the tire's integrity when it goes flat. And yet we expect people with a lot of pain in their backstory to be unaffected by that past trauma. Now, that's delusional thinking, but it's how our culture shapes us to think. This lack of self-compassion comes from an internalized message from our culture that says, "You should just get over it!" when in fact, it's not that easy. When I have a person in my practice with a lot of attachment injuries, I tell them, "I know non-monogamy is way harder for you. That's okay. It just means that you need to take it slower. You need to tell your partner when you're scared, and not say yes to anything unless it's a true yes."

Healing Our Ego States: The Warrior, the Child, and the Nurturer

There are at least three ego states within the human psyche that are always at play along the non-monogamous journey. All three have a massive impact on the success of our non-monogamous relationships, and they can sometimes be at odds with one another.

What is an ego state? Well, the theory behind ego state therapy is that the human psyche is actually a family of selves and each is an adaptation to life circumstances with different roles. Think of that friend who becomes the angry girl or the horny guy when they're liquored up. Rather than assume that this is their true nature that's been repressed, it's more likely that this is a facet of that person, an ego state.

An ego state can come forward for various reasons. Ego states vary in quantity and intensity and can differ from person to person. Traditional ego state therapy discusses the parent, the adult, and the child. However, the most common three ego states I see in my practice I refer to as the warrior, the child, and the nurturer.

The warrior is the ego state that gets things done and achieves dreams. The warrior is generally pretty badass but is not very forgiving, patient, or understanding. The warrior powers through situations that are hard despite emotional or physical pain and is stellar at blocking out discomfort. My clients with strong inner warriors tend to over-rely on cognitive therapy coping skills, value the mind over feelings, and have contempt for the wounded parts of themselves, including the parts that struggle with non-monogamy.

The child is often the part of us that holds the pain; you might have heard the term "the wounded inner child." However, in moments of feeling safe or healed, the child can be our carefree, lighthearted, joyful self, as is typical of a happy child. Oftentimes I have witnessed this at non-monogamous events where everyone feels safe and happy: there is a carefree glee filling the room that runs tandem with the sexiness. Thinking of sex party participants as having an almost childlike, carefree glee may be hard to fathom. But such parties, at their best, strip away the deep sexual shame that permeates American culture, and what is left is a rediscovered lightness of being that most of us leave behind as we get older.

However, in moments when we are triggered, the wounded inner child is the first to feel it. For instance, if we feel ignored by our partner as they attend to another partner, we may feel hurt—and if we're not careful, the child will come forward and run the show, throwing a tantrum or bursting into tears.

As you can imagine, the warrior tends to *hate* the child—its volatility, its sensitivity—and wishes it could just get rid of it.

Of course, it's not that simple.

The warrior and the child will never work things out alone. They need a third-party negotiator. This is where our inner nurturer comes in. The nurturer can negotiate between the warrior and the child using kindness, emotional intelligence, and empathy. Its role is to make sure the wounded inner child is protected, cared for, and allowed to feel feelings. The nurturer advocates for self-care, self-love, and compassionate self-talk, and in doing so creates a bridge between the warrior and the child. The nurturer knows that the only way to get the warrior to where it wants to go is to attend to the vulnerable child.

This internal triad has a major impact on self-compassion. The warrior, if given a voice, might say, "Dear GOD! If I could just get rid of this kid, I could do anything. This freakin' kid is always holding me back." If the warrior is ruling the internal system without any balance from the nurturer, the inner child, metaphorically, will be in a locked and chained hall closet in the psyche's basement with the light turned off—sometimes for years! And people do go for years, and sometimes decades, without attending to their internal injured child. Meanwhile, the warrior may be saying yes to non-monogamous adventures when their yes is not a true yes. And because the vulnerability of the child is suppressed, there may not be full awareness that the individual is pushing themself to do things that parts of their psyche aren't ready for.

To get in touch with your inner nurturer, warrior, or child, try an experiment: First, write what the warrior thinks about your current non-monogamous situation. Second, write down what the child is feeling. These expressions are likely to be very different. Finally, imagine that your inner nurturer can sit down and say to the warrior, "Look, we are only going as fast as the most vulnerable part of us can handle. If we start to show compassion to the child, you will be able to achieve all your hopes and dreams. You will be able to handle more challenges. And you will be able to negotiate life's stressors with more composure." Eventually, the warrior will come around.

Now, let's focus on your inner child. If you have a wounded inner child that you have been neglecting, just know that it might get worse before it gets better. Imagine we take the chains off the basement door, unlock it, and pull the child out of the dark closet and into the light after years of being locked away. For a while, it may tantrum—but what happens if you show consistent love to an upset child? The child eventually gets better and starts to trust. So ask your inner child: *What are you scared of? What do you need? What are you afraid to ask for?*

The next time you're upset regarding anything to do with non-monogamy, ask yourself, *How old do I feel right now?* Almost always, when I have asked this question of my clients when they are upset, the response is age six, eight, or ten. And why is that? Because that's often the age the person actually was when they experienced an attachment injury that emotionally or somatically mirrored what they're experiencing in the present.

Let's take a look at Jessie and Elise's story. They had been non-monogamous for many years and had explored many forms of non-monogamy. Jessie had never been a jealous person and had given her partners a lot of freedom. Recently, however, Elise had wanted more time away to see two other partners, and suddenly Jessie was panicking. Recently, she'd even had a full-blown panic attack.

In therapy, Jessie had learned to check in with herself. While Elise was on a date and Jessie lay alone in bed, she noticed that she felt about six years old. In her mind, she thought back to age six and realized that was how old she was when her dad left her mother and her without leaving so much as a note. As a teenager and young woman, Jessie had a history of being drawn to unavailable partners. And right now, all she wanted was to hear the key turn in the door.

Elise loves you, she told herself as she lay there. *Talk to her. Tell her what you need. She's not like all the others. She will listen.*

At that moment, she heard the key turn in the door. It was 2:00 a.m., and Elise came straight to the bedroom, crawled into bed, cuddled up to Jessie, kissed the back of her shoulder, and whispered, "My sweet girl, I love you so much." She knew Jessie's tender underbelly.

"You're gone too much lately," Jessie whispered. "I miss you."

Elise kissed her. "Let's work it out in the morning. I don't want you to hurt. I'm not going anywhere. I'm right here."

Reassured, Jessie cuddled up to her and fell asleep, knowing that she had finally found someone she could always be honest with and who would be there for her.

So what happened in this example? Jessie, through therapy, had cultivated her benevolent nurturer, her internalized good parent, and that part of her was able to soothe her inner child. She was able to ask for what she needed, and because she chose a compassionate partner, chances were they would create an agreement that worked for both of them.

In healing our inner child, it's possible to transform that child from the one who holds our unresolved pain, shame, and fear to the one who meets life with joy, vulnerable openness, and creative brilliance. That happy child that was "socialized" or "traumatized" into a recessive part of ourselves can be found again. This healing process is an integral part of the journey toward opening and loving deeply.

Chapter Six

COPING WITH JEALOUSY AND OTHER UNCOMFORTABLE FEELINGS

Jealousy—it's the terrifying beastie that lurks in dark corners, threatening your ability to achieve non-monogamous bliss. If you could just beat it down, all would be well. Right?

Have you ever been with a child who was overwhelmed by putting on and tying their shoes? Behavioral therapists who work with children advise breaking down the overwhelming task into small steps. You might say to the child, "Just put your foot in the shoe. Great! Now tighten the laces. Wonderful! Now tie a knot." And so on.

Just as shoelaces overwhelm that small child, the term "jealousy" overwhelms many adults. It's a complex emotion with many emotions packed inside of it—we often think we are jealous when really we are feeling disrespected—and therefore it needs to be broken down in order for us to understand it. Jealousy is a confusing experience.

Many things can bring out the green-eyed monster. Your partner flirting with a hottie in front of you, paying more attention to another partner than they're paying to you, or taking on a new lover—all of these things may bring up jealous and uncomfortable feelings and shake up your life. If there is anything that makes humans fearful, it's the unknown. That's what jealousy is tied to—an uncontrollable, unpredictable, or unknown threat. Wanting to batten down the hatches is a human response. Rigidity might take hold in your psyche. However, flexibility and willingness to open yourself up to change and growth is crucial. I know that's a lot to ask, but it's necessary.

What Is Jealousy in the Context of Non-Monogamy?

Jealousy in the context of non-monogamy is usually defined as the emotional reaction to a threat to one's relationship from a real or imagined romantic rival. Traditional evolutionary psychology suggests that jealousy is an inherited survival response. This means that, at least in the case of extreme jealousy responses, your primitive brain literally kicks into survival mode. If you've ever felt like you were having a panic attack due to issues within non-monogamy, this hypothesis may partially explain why.

Evolutionary psychology goes further by separating gender responses. Have you ever heard that men are more jealous of sexual affairs and women are more jealous of emotional affairs? This primitive response from men, coinciding with territorial behaviors, may have increased surety that the male was the biological father of the children he provided for, thus guaranteeing that his DNA would be passed on. For our female ancestors, *emotional* security in a relationship may have increased the likelihood of maintaining a provider for themselves and their children, thus increasing the likelihood of survival. This theory purports that survival instincts gave rise not only to our tendencies to be jealous but also to the *ways* in which we exhibit jealousy.

An additional factor in the mix is cultural. Some of us buy into the cultural indoctrination that says our partner is our sexual and emotional property, and consequently we may subconsciously feel robbed and violated by non-monogamous practices, thus explaining the rage some people experience.

To define jealousy as simply a fear response to the threat of losing one's partner to another person is limiting. Within this swirling brew of emotion, fear is only one ingredient. Jealousy often encompasses other emotions, such as sadness, disgust, and rage. And our *internal* emotions and triggers often comingle with *external* forces, such as cultural influences and relationship dynamics.

Beyond a fear of losing one's partner might be an unconscious or conscious resentment at being put in this horrible, tortured state in the first place. These feelings may be directed at a primary, their romantic/sexual interest, or both.

Everyone experiences jealousy. It's a normal human emotion. And just because you feel a lot of jealousy doesn't mean non-monogamy is wrong for you; it just means non-monogamy will be more difficult for you.

On the bright side, jealousy can actually be a catalyst for deeper intimacy. Vulnerability usually is. If we can learn to listen to what our jealous responses are trying to tell us and be gentle with ourselves, we can build trust and security within our non-monogamous relationships. Our partners need to consciously listen without being reactive, feeling controlled, or fearing their lovers and connections will be yanked from them. Such mutual compassion can lead to opening deeply rather than having angry fights that devolve into throwing spaghetti plates at each other's head like Frisbees.

How to Tackle Jealousy and Other Uncomfortable Feelings

I have a three-step approach for tackling jealousy and other uncomfortable feelings in a relationship. These three steps are: 1) read your body, 2) define the antecedent, and 3) get to the root of your jealousy or other uncomfortable feelings.

The first step, read your body, is heavily influenced by my education in and professional use of somatic psychotherapy via the Trauma Resource Institute (TRI). Don't let the word "trauma" scare you. It sounds daunting, but jealousy often bridges back to either big traumas, such as a parent abandoning a child, or smaller traumas, like a high school sweetheart leaving us.

The second step, define the antecedent, is influenced by my training in and professional use of behavioral therapy. My training in this area originated from my early work with children with autism, but it's helpful for us all for making the unmanageable manageable.

Finally, the third step, get to the root of your jealousy, stems from the work I've done since 2003 with trauma and my education in EMDR.

Together, this trifecta, which harnesses some of the most powerful tools psychotherapy has to offer, can truly empower you, making your jealousy something you can successfully work through.

Let's look at the ways we can better listen to jealousy when it shows up:

Step One: Read your body

If we only utilize intellect to navigate jealousy, unattended negative emotions build up, which often leaves us mired in generalized anxiety or anger. When we shove down our uncomfortable feelings, negate our jealousy, and pack it all away in boxes, there is a long-range price to pay. For some, ignored emotions can lead to health issues, like IBS or fibromyalgia. For others, generalized anxiety or anger may lead to emotional numbness if neglected for too long. Finally, over-intellectualization hurts our relationships. It sabotages opening deeply. It's symptomatic of a deep intolerance of vulnerability, and in time it results in festering, unhealed emotional wounds. A lack of vulnerability and unresolved trauma are two major blocks to building a deep, connected, and conscious love with another person in any relationship model, including non-monogamy.

To track your body, I invite you to notice your heart rate, depth of breath, and where and to what degree you feel tension, along with any other sensations, such as: tingling, pain, warmth, arousal, itchiness, etc. If you notice an uncomfortable feeling but are having trouble labeling it, ask yourself, *What part of my body knows about this feeling?* Upon checking in, perhaps you'll realize your heart is racing, your breathing is shallow and rapid, and there is a tightness in your throat and chest. With this extra information, it becomes apparent to you that you are afraid—very afraid, in fact. With your body honored as a powerful part of your compass, you will be much more able to be honest with yourself and your partner, take care of yourself, and ask your partner for what you need before uncomfortable feelings escalate.

Consider Daniel and his wife, Lilly. Daniel says to Lilly, "I'd like Heather to be my new lover and sleep with her this Friday. What do you think about that?"

I've known Heather for ten years, Lilly reasons with herself. *She's always been good to us and respectful to our marriage.* So she replies, "Sure! Have a great time."

Daniel spends the night with Heather and comes back Saturday at noon. Lilly is furious, but she doesn't know why. Daniel senses her anger and lashes out, saying, "You're just jealous. You told me I could go, and now you're punishing me for doing what we agreed to. You're not being fair."

Lilly is miserable. She questions whether Daniel's right and whether she can do this non-monogamy thing at all.

Now let's do a redo. This time Lilly will check in with her thoughts, emotions, and body sensations before responding to Daniel's proposal:

When Lilly checks in with her body, despite having all the same thoughts mentioned above, she notices a sensation that feels like a little knife dropping through her gut when she thinks about Daniel spending the night with Heather. This time she's able to say to

Daniel, "I need to have some time to sit with your request. I'll get back to you in [two hours, a day, fill in the blank]."

After a couple of hours, Lilly notices the sadness attached to the pain in her gut and gains some insight. She is able to come back to Daniel and express her true needs. Perhaps she says one of the following:

1) "Our anniversary is two days away. Can you wait a couple of weeks after that before you see her?"
2) "I'm not ready for you to spend the night. Can you come back by two a.m.?"
3) "I'm not ready for you to play separately. Can we have a threesome instead?"

Or perhaps she simply says, "I'm not ready." Regardless, she's expressing a more truthful answer here—which will allow her, when Daniel does have an experience with Heather, a greater probability of experiencing compersion, or at least feeling calmer, instead of descending into a jealous rage.

Step Two: Define the antecedent to your somatic reaction as internal or external

Sometimes it's tricky to figure out why you're jealous. Take your time to think about it. The truth will be unveiled in due time.

To start, consider keeping a journal of feelings and sensations and their associated antecedents (what precedes the feeling or sensation). These antecedents might be external, such as something your partner or their partner said or did, or they might be internal, such as a thought you've had. Write down any other feelings/sensations besides jealousy that you notice as well. Keeping such a journal of feelings and associated antecedents can help reveal triggers and patterns.

Let's imagine we can peek into Claudia's journal. She has listed steps one and two in an inverted order for ease of reading later.

Antecedent: Josh laughed at every joke Sally said at the party, touched her more, flirted with her more, and made more eye contact with her than with me.
Feelings/Sensations: Loneliness. Sadness. Rejection. Jealousy. Tightness. Sinking feeling in gut.

Antecedent: Thought: "Sally is more fun than me."
Feelings/Sensations: Jealousy. Insecurity. Anxiety. Rejection. Tension in core. Tearful eyes.

Antecedent: Josh went on and on about how much fun he had with Sally at the party.
Feelings/Sensations: Fear. Competitiveness. Hot face. Tense body.

After accumulating a list of antecedents and their associated feelings and sensations, a further step could be to mark these feelings/sensations as "E," "I," or "B"—"E" for externally created antecedents, "I" for internally created antecedents, and "B" for both.

By marking them in this way, you begin to subjectively suss out with whom the responsibility might lie for this particular issue—you or with your partner. The purpose of this exercise is not to cast blame but rather to assign responsibility. And no, that's not the same thing. Assigning responsibility does not include the shaming inherent in blaming someone. It simply helps you to either avoid taking on emotional work that does not belong to you (if the antecedent is external) or realize that you need to work on yourself (if the antecedent is internal).

Let's take the first antecedent on the list by way of example:

Josh laughed at every joke Sally said at the party, touched her more, flirted with her more, and made more eye contact with her than with me.

This antecedent may belong in both categories—your responsibility and your partner's. Perhaps Claudia blew up in her mind the discrepancy between the attention Josh paid to Sally and her (internal), or perhaps Josh needs to take ownership that he could have done a better job of balancing his attention between the two women (external). If both Claudia and Josh take ownership where appropriate, Claudia will likely feel more at ease when they attend their next party, and consequently the relationship will be stronger as a whole.

Step Three: Get to the root of your jealousy

Once the antecedent to our emotional and somatic reactions is pinpointed, we can find the root of our struggle. Let's go back to Claudia to explain how.

If Claudia were to look at her journal entries, she would easily see a trigger: the fear that Sally is more fun than she is. Once she pinpoints the trigger, gets in touch with the associated emotional pain, and senses the tension in her body, she can then bridge back to her past to locate where this fear is coming from.

Oh! A memory so easily pops up. Claudia remembers her sister. She was the class clown and received all the positive attention from her parents. She remembers a trip to Disneyland when she was left at a gas station for an hour because her parents were laughing so hard at her sister's jokes that they didn't even notice Claudia running after the car as they pulled away.

Boom! Okay. Now she doesn't feel as crazy. This trigger is more understandable now. She felt she played second fiddle to her sister her whole childhood. Now she feels second to Sally. This is how we work as humans; we are biocomputers. When we have an emotional reaction that we later realize was not commensurate with the situation at hand, there is a good chance we reacted that way because of an earlier experience that created a neurobiological road map in our body.

After Claudia goes through the three-step process delineated above, she realizes that she has some self-work to do to manage this trigger, but she also realizes that Josh can help too. If she trusts him enough to share her feelings, he will be let in on the fact that she struggles with feeling rejected. Does compassion for her trigger mean that he needs to walk on eggshells and pretend to laugh at all of Claudia's jokes? No. Not at all. He merely needs to make an effort to gain insight and put his resulting compassion into action—make a point of attending to Claudia and connecting with her as evenly as possible when they're at a party Sally is attending as well. Claudia will feel less rejected and more relaxed, and they'll both be able to have a good time.

Other Emotional Reactions Linked to Jealousy

Emotional reactions, such as feeling disrespected, are frequently mislabeled as jealousy. The truth is, jealousy is a large umbrella feeling (otherwise called a "complex emotion") that often contains other emotions as well.

Let's shine a spotlight on some of the different emotions associated with jealousy. Some common, uncomfortable emotions that get confused with or are linked to jealousy include feeling disrespected, disempowered, overwhelmed, distrust, envy, insecurity, and a fear of abandonment.

Feeling disrespected

This is the most unrecognized feeling I see in my private practice. Often, I've witnessed a partner angrily shoot back with an accusation of jealousy after being called out for disrespectful behavior. This defense, like a blade, usually disables their partner and is followed by immediate emotional shutdown. It's mind-blowing to witness. Just make the accusation, "You're jealous!" and presto chango: Silence. Game over.

Why is this such a powerful accusation? Why is it so capable of making a strong person lose their voice? Sadly, many equate being jealous with being irrational, weak, an embarrassment, petty. So, even when the partner accused of being jealous is actually glaringly in the right—when they have been disrespected—as soon as they're accused of jealousy, they crumble in on themselves.

As Esther Perel, therapist and author of *Mating in Captivity*, says, "The majority of people don't have a conversation about jealousy because the feeling itself is taboo." One negative by-product of ignoring jealousy in a relationship is that it sometimes allows emotionally abusive and disrespectful people to get away with their bad behavior for years in a non-monogamous relationship, simply by hurling the J-word at their partner every time there's trouble. And it works. Shame shuts people down. At its worst, it can be a form of gaslighting.

What's even more brutal is that sometimes the wronged party will even describe themself as jealous when they have been disrespected. I've heard clients tell me tales of massive violations to their relationship agreements by a partner, all the while with their shoulders slumped and head down, and end by asking, "Why am I so jealous?"

In response to such situations, I often say, "You don't sound jealous. You just listed some huge violations to your relationship agreement, along with cruel words and actions by your partner. You sound like you feel disrespected."

If the client is using the three-stage approach we just discussed, they might discover that they have been disrespected on their own. Janel and Wolfgang, who came to me when they were new to non-monogamy, were such a couple.

These two felt they were ready to attend their first play party. First, they negotiated some limits: 1) they wouldn't actually play, 2) they would socialize in the common area and mainly stay together, and 3) if they got separated, they would check in with one another approximately every thirty minutes.

They got to the party and it was amazing: beautiful house, warm hosts, and a sexy, hip, smart crowd. They couldn't be happier. Soon, they were both swept up. (This happens; the flirty, fun energy is contagious.) Soon they were separated. Wolfgang was enjoying himself, flirting and chatting. But then he noticed that Janel was gone. He scanned the room. It was time to check in. It was past time. He assumed she was in the bathroom. He finally began to look for her in earnest and even asked a couple folks if they had seen her.

An hour later, he finally found Janel on the porch, looking deep into the eyes of another man. He joined them and listened to their conversation for thirty minutes, silently fuming, before finally saying to her, "It's time to go."

"But I'm having fun!" she protested.

He gave her the look. She glared back.

They said civil goodbyes to the hosts and guests and headed for the car. After minutes of silence, the yelling started.

"You are so jealous!" Janel accused. "I was having fun. And just because I'm talking to a hot guy, you pull the plug on the whole night. That was embarrassing. Everyone knew something was up. You're going to give us the reputation of being 'drama.'"

"We had an agreement!" Wolfgang said. "Don't you remember? Do you know how much time had gone by? I didn't even know where you were!"

"Whatever," Janel said. "You just can't tolerate me flirting with another man. I'm not even sure if you can really do this. Maybe you aren't cut out for non-monogamy."

What just happened here? It's the kind of fight that has happened a million times with countless couples. It shows up in my practice all the time. Is he truly jealous? If she had actually listened to his words, she would have heard that he was upset that their limits had not been respected. He was angry that she had disrespected him and hurt that she had forgotten about him.

If a couple can't recognize these kinds of distinctions, they will never resolve the true issues at play, and these fights will begin to feel like Groundhog Day in their relationship. If, however, the partner in Janel's place can recognize that the partner in Wolfgang's place feels disrespected, they can figure out how to improve things in the future.

In therapy, Janel and Wolfgang both worked on taking responsibility for the situation. The internal and external antecedents to Wolfgang's upset were sussed out. Wolfgang learned that it was not healthy for him to silently endure a situation that was uncomfortable for him. Rather than silently fuming for another thirty minutes, he learned that he should have said something like, "Sweetie, I just got an urgent text that I need to talk to you about in private," and then turn to the tall, handsome man and say, "Please excuse us." Now they could remove themselves from the situation to address the issue. As for Janel, rather than disavow that she broke a rule, she would learn to own her mistake—"Yes. Okay. I'm sorry. I got caught up. I lost track of time. I love you. I didn't mean to upset you."

When these scenarios unfold in my private practice, the partner in Wolfgang's role often has trouble accepting the apology and wants to continue to rage. This is when I'll pipe in to encourage both partners to have patience with one another and remind the person in Wolfgang's position that they're both new at this, and there will come a time when he'll make a similar mistake and hope for his partner's understanding and forgiveness.

The important thing is for both parties to take responsibility and find ways to communicate better going forward. Usually my clients move past these initial bumps in their non-monogamous journey quickly, but if they're left unchecked, Groundhog Day will inevitably come around again.

How to cope with feeling disrespected

Distinguishing between jealousy and disrespect is not always easy. The journal exercise we talked about earlier can help, however. As a reminder, these are the three steps:

1) Read your body. Write down sensations and corresponding feelings.

2) Define the antecedent to your somatic and emotional reaction as internal or external.

3) Get to the root of your struggle.

If the antecedent is linked to internal pain, you may be experiencing some form of jealousy. However, if the antecedent links to an external event, such as your partner breaking a relationship agreement, you may be experiencing being disrespected. It's also possible that both internal and external antecedents are present and both of you have some accountability.

If, after journaling, you are still not sure if you are being disrespected or are simply overreacting out of jealousy, ask some friends, join a support group, or see a therapist. They may not be firsthand witnesses to the behavior you're struggling to decipher, but even so, a third party can help you gain some clarity.

If you do decide that you are being disrespected, use the communication strategies found in Chapter 13 to help you express yourself.

Feeling disempowered

According to David Buss, professor of psychology and the author of *Dangerous Passion: Why Jealousy Is as Necessary as Love and Sex*, one reason jealous feelings are painful to admit is that they may be indicative of a power imbalance within your relationship: "It's a signal that your partner is higher in mate value or that you are generally threatened or fearful that your partner might leave, so people intentionally try to suppress the expression of jealousy." Such fears can be combated by working on your own self-esteem or talking to your partner about your abandonment fears.

However, feeling that your lover has higher mate value is not the only cause for feeling disempowered within non-monogamy. Role shifts within the non-monogamous relationship can create power imbalances as well. When your partner takes on a new lover, this shifts the homeostasis in your relationship and can dramatically alter power dynamics and even the roles played within a relationship. For instance, you may feel the new lover has yanked your role as the sexy, carefree, and captivating one. You may feel recast as the nag or parent who says yes or no to your partner's outings—a role shift that can feel incredibly disempowering. You didn't sign up for this, did you? Non-monogamy can test us in unforeseen ways.

These kinds of fallouts are most pronounced in a newly formed triad in which one partner (the V center or hinge) has two lovers (the two tops of the V), but the two V tops do not have outside lovers. For example, let's say the V hinge is Charlie and the two tops of the V are Skylar and Melisa. An ongoing competition for Charlie's attention and affection will ensue if dynamics are not addressed head-on from the beginning. It's common for one of the partners in either Skylar or Melisa's position in the triad to be cast as the "responsible" one. Usually, this is the partner who Charlie lives and/or parents with, or who already has more responsibility due to their profession or being a parent. In this triad, let's say this person is Melisa. Meanwhile, Skylar is a student who does not live with Charlie and does not share responsibilities with him. Skylar will therefore most likely get cast in the carefree sexual role.

This unconscious dynamic can be minimized by making it conscious. Set an intention to ensure that all partners get time to feel carefree and sexy. Encourage all parties to communicate their needs openly and negotiate reasonable agreements that are fair to everyone. And if you are the V hinge, if your partner expresses that they feel ignored or cast as the responsible one, please don't respond with, "Well, if you were more carefree and sexy, I'd give you more attention!"

Ugh—I've heard this reaction way too many times. That is a deeply self-absorbed response; it lacks empathy. And because it's often said to the partner who is the mother or father of the other's children, or who works eighty hours a week to support the family, it can breed resentment fast. Meanwhile, the one deemed sexy and carefree is often put on a pedestal despite the fact that they have little to no responsibility and thus have a very easy time being carefree and sexy.

A better course is for the V hinge to do everything in their power to avoid a power struggle between their two lovers. They can do this by keeping a pulse on whether their partners like the roles they find themselves in as the homeostasis shifts and giving both enough quality (carefree) time, attention, affection, commitment, and sex.

If the V hinge can't see the discontent from one or more partner, it's up to them to let that person know. Sometimes the person at the hinge is unaware because they have a lot to manage with two partners. When possible, it can be helpful for the V hinge's two lovers to become allies rather than adversaries, joining together to encourage change in their partner's behavior rather than turning against each other.

Unless everyone involved cooperates and is careful of everyone else's feelings and needs, it is easy for one person to feel disregarded and disempowered in any relationship. And no one should feel that way. So use your voice. Create the dynamic you deserve. Remember, it's your responsibility to teach people how to love you.

How to cope with feeling disempowered

If you are feeling disempowered after your partner has taken on a new lover, there are many ways to cope. But please take action quickly; don't ruminate and stew for too long. Unless you're talking about a consensual dominant/submissive power dynamic, a sense of disempowerment will quickly become toxic to the self and to the relationship as a whole.

Notice why you feel disempowered. Do you feel like too many changes are happening too fast? Are decisions being made without your input? Are there romantic adventures or sexual escapades that you thought were sentimental between the two of you—things only the two of you shared—but now they are happening with the new lover?

Use your voice. Assert yourself. Ask for what you need. There is nothing wrong with asking your partner to slow it down and to communicate more. There is nothing wrong with asking to keep certain things sacred between the two of you. This being said, you may not get your way; this request simply begins a negotiation. But hopefully you'll find a solution you can both agree upon.

Revisit, if need be. Sometimes one's first attempt to be heard is squashed. Sometimes we think we have been heard only to see patterns quickly revert back to the disempowering past. This can add a second layer to the pain that weighs upon you. Please don't fall into a helpless, hopeless place. Sometimes relationships have a bit of a power battle inherent in them. This is human nature. Just because your partner tests your boundaries doesn't mean they won't eventually hear you if you stand your ground as often as is necessary.

Assess the new role you find yourself in. If you don't like it, take your power back. If you feel like the boring one, ask for a weekly date night. Not spontaneous enough for you? Well, back when you were single, you didn't consider a date a spontaneity killer, did you? Ask any sex educator and they will tell you, the spontaneity happens *within* the date. And if you are attempting to reassert your role as a sexual god or goddess, remember Dan Savage's rule: "Fuck first." Don't fall prey to the trap of stuffing your faces with food at a lovely dinner and then wondering why you passed out afterward when you promised each other you would have sex.

If having a carefree conversation with your partner is challenging, choose an experience that is bonding and fun but doesn't require talking, like going dancing. Another idea is to choose a date that inherently shifts the conversation, like going to an art museum, so your conversation is channeled to art. Reclaim carefree time. Schedule that time in your calendar. It doesn't truly exist until it's on the books, as you know.

You may consider taking on a new lover yourself too. This suggestion isn't about a tit for tat, nor should the decision to do this come from a vengeful place. But I have noticed that for a lot of folks, the obsessive, anxious thinking dies down or ceases completely when they have their own other person to pour that energy into on the side. (That said, this coping strategy is only a superficial fix; you still need to address the root issues.)

A non-monogamous primary or nesting relationship ideally should be intellectually, emotionally, and sexually connected to be at its best. When this triple threat is optimized, a couple can withstand all sorts of stressors.

Feeling distrustful

You may trust your partner in so many ways. Perhaps you trust them to do their part financially. You may trust their dedication and love for your kids. You may know that if you were in the hospital, they would be right by your side. But that doesn't mean that you will automatically trust them within non-monogamy. This trust is completely new territory, and it has to be earned.

I've been talking about the fact that people new to non-monogamy are like little babies falling on their butts and faces in their first year of trying it out. Even those with good instincts will make mistakes, and when that happens, trust will likely take a hit. To a degree, this is normal. Having a heaping helping of forgiveness and compassion for your own mistakes and those of your partners will help you endure the beginning learning curve.

Remember, it's usually not the mistake that will have a lasting impact on a relationship, it's how you cope and communicate afterward. Intimacy and trust can be built during the post-injury repair if you treat these bumps as an opportunity to become closer.

How to cope with feeling distrustful

Let's assume you're already there—in a state of distrust. It's not a fun place to be, is it? The first step is to read your body and notice what you're feeling. The second step is to notice the antecedent. And then you need to figure out if the antecedent has an internal source or is caused by external factors. Here are some examples:

Internal Antecedent: Before Harry met Danielle, his previous wife cheated on him repeatedly, leaving him distrustful of women.
Feelings: distrust, suspicion, anxiety, paranoia

Internal Antecedent: Harry's parents both cheated on each other when he was young, which led to their divorce.
Feelings: sadness, anxiety, helpless, hopeless, abandoned

External Antecedent: Danielle and Harry have been corresponding with a married couple, Mark and Amanda, about a possible foursome. Danielle failed to disclose recently that Mark had texted her privately, when the texts previously had included all four of them.
Feelings: panic, anxiety, distrust, suspicion

In this case, because the source of most of Harry's distrust is internal, he has the tendency to project a story (women can't be trusted) onto Danielle. It may be that Danielle didn't have the chance to tell Harry about Mark's text before Harry intercepted it. Maybe he looked at Danielle's texts or emails without consent because of his predisposition to be distrustful.

When the source of most of our general distrust is internal, taking ownership is crucial. First, when having a distrustful thought, bridge back and notice if there's anything in your past that feels similar, whether emotionally or somatically. If so, notice how upsetting that past memory is and rate it from zero to ten. This rating system gives you an indicator of how triggered you may be. Then do a reality check around your original distrustful thought. Harry might ask himself, *Is it really true that Danielle is cheating on me? Is she being deceptive?*

Or he might ask himself, *Is this really true? What is my evidence? Could it be that I'm projecting a story onto my partner?*

Next, have a discussion with your partner. In this case, Harry might say, "I saw a text from Mark on your phone. Do you have something going on behind my back with him?" (This is not the most finessed way to address the issue, but it's at least to the point.)

"It upsets me that you'd look at my phone without asking me. I'm also mad that you don't trust me after five years of marriage. That said, no, I don't have anything going on with Mark. You might have noticed that I didn't respond. I intended to talk with you later tonight to discuss how to handle our boundaries with him and Amanda."

Upon hearing this explanation, Harry might be able to realize that, in this case at least, his unresolved past wounds were running the show. If he develops a practice of mindfulness, watching what is happening in his body, thoughts, and emotions, in a non-reactive, non-judgmental way, he will greatly reduce harming himself, Danielle, or their relationship. If this practice, along with reality checks, is not enough, Harry can also seek out an EMDR therapist to help heal these traumas that are getting projected onto his relationship. Again, unresolved trauma is the biggest intimacy block between couples.

And what if your distrust is built mostly on *external* factors? First off, if this is true for you, you likely feel like you're being deceived—and with that comes a lot of pain. It's hard to attempt non-monogamy when you feel you can't trust your partner.

There are many courses of action one can take in this situation. Maybe a break from non-monogamy is needed. It's hard to heal from the past if new stressors are currently unfolding. A break from non-monogamy can lower the stress level in the relationship, thus allowing the fog of overwhelm to pass. From this place of calm and clarity, healing can occur. This may not be ethically possible, or it may be difficult, if there are many loves involved—it's important to be mindful of couple privilege—but sometimes a break can be powerful.

Usually broken trust in non-monogamy is a by-product of broken relationship agreements. There are countless reasons a partner might break their relationship agreements. Instead of catastrophizing and going straight to "They're just a cheater; they don't give a fuck about me!" take a breath and unpack the possible reasons why.

Often, especially in the beginning, your partner may not understand relationship agreements or they may find them confusing. If this is the case, write a living, breathing document that you can change over time. Further help can be provided by a sex-positive psychotherapist or a sex educator who specializes in open relationships. Such professionals can help you come up with relationship agreements that are not carved in stone—that may, if necessary, even change from week to week.

Another reason for infidelities within your open relationship might be that your partner is being passive-aggressive. They may feel you are being too controlling. They may feel they are losing themself within the relationship, so they are quietly just doing what they want to do. If this is the case, then at least one of you has some work to do.

On your end, one thing to ask yourself is, "Am I an anxious person in general?" And I'm not talking about anxiety born from a partner's infidelities; I'm talking general anxiety. Partners of anxious people often feel controlled. Meanwhile, the anxious person rarely perceives themself as controlling. They usually are just attempting to manage out-of-control feelings, and they don't realize how their behavior comes off. If this sounds like you, then you may have some self-work to do—meditation, practicing mindfulness, or therapy—to reduce your anxiety. You don't want out-of-control anxiety to puppeteer your non-monogamous relationship. Regardless, your anxiety does not give your partner a hall pass to betray you.

Now, let's separate those of us who make a boo-boo, a true mistake, from those whose lying is more characterological. The first category of agreement violators can much more easily mend their ways. A relationship agreement may have been broken. Maybe the action that broke it was even a *bad* mistake. Perhaps the violator lied at first, but then came clean. If this is you, look into your heart. When you look across your life, have you been a pretty honest person? Such a person will most likely be able to recover and regain their partner's trust—mainly because their partner knows the mistake was out of character. It may slow down the adventurous journey, but if the injured party is given the time, love, and repentance required, the couple will move through the crisis.

If, in contrast, deception, hiding, and manipulation seem more characterological for the transgressing party, repeated injuries within their non-monogamous relationship may result in irreparable damage. But even in these cases—with the right help, commitment, and tenacity— there is still hope.

Take Gordon and Kylie. Gordon had hidden financial decisions, been caught cheating within their non-monogamous relationship repeatedly, and had put off telling Kylie about a major health issue, being diagnosed with diabetes, over the ten years that they had been together. He didn't seem to realize that this history of deception was a form of emotional abuse. Kylie had moved beyond heartbreak to simply feeling numb. She felt that trusting again would inevitably lead to the same cycle: hope, happiness, and then crushing disappointment when another lie was revealed. Eventually, she asked for a divorce.

Gordon was devastated, but he viewed this experience as a wake-up call. He knew that being accountable was measured in action steps, so he started individual therapy—and one night, he came back from therapy with a big insight. "We talked about how controlling my mom is in therapy today," he told Kylie. "Do you remember how I used to lie to her and tell her I was going to the library when I was really going to band practice?" His insight was that his mom never allowed him to pursue his interests, music and art; instead, she insisted that he become what she wanted, an academic. He had to lie repeatedly throughout his childhood in order to be true to himself. "She was such a narcissistic parent," he fumed, "only interested into shaping me into what she wanted. How was I supposed to develop a true sense of self?"

In therapy, Gordon realized that he'd unconsciously paired his desire to be authentic with dishonesty and having a secret life. Now as an adult, in his love relationships, he hadn't stopped this pattern—and over time, it had gotten to the point where an honest relationship was boring to him. He found eroticism only in secret affairs or hook-ups. Even when he became non-monogamous and found an amazing partner who gave him freedom, he still found reasons to rationalize his infidelities. He hung his head. "It runs deep in me." Then he met Kylie's eyes and said, "I want to break this crazy connection. I want to stop hurting you."

Gordon went to a men's emotional support group and started EMDR, a therapy modality designed to heal attachment injuries and trauma. Over time, he began to notice thinking, feeling, and behaving differently. Finally, he found a new way of life that allowed him to be true to himself and others simultaneously. Meanwhile, he made amends to Kylie, not simply by saying, "I'm sorry," but through acts of kindness and transparency.

In my professional and personal experience, for every person who has a secret life and who lies to a loved one to maintain it, there is a controlling parent in their backstory who punished them for individuation, authenticity, and the pursuit of their true self. And sadly, this is all too common. Non-monogamy is not a fix for wounds that run deep. However, I have seen such people, like Gordon, become heroes in their own journey by taking active accountability and doing the hard work in therapy for as long as it takes. Such courageous and humble people often repair their relationships and learn to love themselves and others better.

But remember, whether you simply made a boo-boo or whether you're more like Gordon, lying to yourself and deceiving others is a grave mistake. Also, expecting your partner to bounce back quickly after being lied to is unrealistic. Emotional wounds are invisible, but now we know that the same areas of the brain light up during heartbreak as when we are bleeding out or injured. And if lying becomes a habit within your non-monogamous relationship, healthy non-monogamous pursuits will be difficult to impossible for you and your partner(s) to achieve.

Once you have considered both your behavior and your partner's, determine how to heal. If you are generally an honest person who made a mistake, the communication model in Chapter 13 might be enough. And again, find a therapist if need be. Healing from broken trust is hard. Sometimes outside support is necessary.

Envy

First off, envy is not to be confused with jealousy. Have you ever thought, *I want what they have?* That is envy, and it's different from jealousy. I don't know if you can be non-monogamous and not eventually experience envy. Even with potential partners, you may catch yourself comparing yourself. One fine day, you might catch yourself thinking, *Damn, I really wish I was that . . .* fill in the blank. Smart, tall, hung, sexy?

Yes, this feeling sucks, but it's human. It's okay. Cut yourself a bit of slack.

Envy is a much more simplistic emotional reaction than jealousy. I'll give a personal example to explain. I remember a time when I felt envious of my partner's lover's amazing boobs. They were ginormous, firm, and perfect. I was also envious of Roxie's carefree nature. I wished I could be as consistently carefree and fun as her. That part hurt a little. But was I jealous of her? No. She was a lovely person, and I knew she wasn't any real threat to me. She had her gifts. I had mine.

And there you have it. Envy doesn't involve a sense of threat. If you feel threatened, jealousy is most likely on board as well—but if you're simply envious of the perfect threesome your partner had last night, or pouty that you haven't found the perfect lover like your best friend has, that's not the same as being jealous.

How to cope with envy

Coping with envy may be a relatively easy fix or incredibly diffi-cult, depending on the issue. Regarding my envy for Roxie's boobs, I could simply walk into Victoria's Secret and buy one of their super fluffer bras to give the illusion of big knockers for a night. But what if your envy runs so deep that it's painful to you? What if you don't feel good about your appearance—you don't like how you've aged or you're unhappy with your current weight? Or maybe it's not about looks at all. Perhaps you feel that you've failed yourself in terms of career goals or education.

These are more difficult situations.

And it can get even harder. What if you've had a mastectomy? Or perhaps you've suffered a back injury that doesn't allow you to have the primal, rough sex you know your partner wants? If your partner's new lover has what you deeply want for yourself, this will be painful—even heartbreaking. Clearly, envy ranges from a more superficial coveting to a deeper, more challenging issue.

With that said, let's start on the shallow, less challenging end of the pool. Let's consider Brad and Janet. Janet has just come home from a threesome, and Brad realizes he's having uncomfortable feel-ings. Is he jealous?

At first, he doesn't know. He's cranky with Janet and starts a fight over something dumb. He wakes up the next day wondering what's going on with him. Janet is equally confused and is trying not to catastrophize. After all, non-monogamy is relatively new for Brad. After a few days of mulling it over in his mind, he realizes he feels like Veruca Salt in *Charlie and the Chocolate Factory* when she covets the golden goose. Like Veruca, he wants *his* threesome and he wants it now.

This level of envy taps into a very young part of Brad. We all have that part of us that internally tantrums and wants things *now*. But that is the beauty of non-monogamy. You can get that bigger candy store you want if you act wisely, like Charlie.

So Brad has had this epiphany; what now? Well, he can ask himself in a more clarified way whether this is something that's simply a fantasy or something he truly wants for himself. If it's the latter, step two is to talk to Janet and discuss his feelings. Perhaps this is something that can be manifested for him, thus nullifying his envy. Or maybe he realizes that he is simply envious of a certain aspect of the threesome—maybe he's craving a cuddle party or a massage à trois experience. When explored in this way, envy can help us to discover, and then perhaps fulfill, unmet desires.

Here again we discover the healthy, positive side of uncomfortable feelings. So often, our uncomfortable feelings are like that annoying friend who knows us better than we do and can point out where we need to grow. We want to tell them to fuck off, but there they are, relentlessly tapping us on the shoulder, until we get a clue.

Now let's swim to the dark, scary deep end, where envy is painful. If it hurts this much, envy is merely a symptom and not the root issue. Take Samantha and her husband, Robert.

After years of being non-monogamous, Samantha found out that she had cancer. This diagnosis led to a mastectomy. Afterward, while happy and grateful to have survived, she experienced a deep loss of self. Before the mastectomy, she had been a vivacious, bold, sexy goddess. She loved her body and would often walk around the house naked. She always had sex with the lights on and loved to see her lovers' reactions when she rode them on top, her breasts bouncing and swaying. After the mastectomy, though other parts of her self-image were as strong as ever—she still felt confident professionally and she knew she was a good mother, wife, and friend—she felt bereaved. Her sexuality had always been a part of what had made her feel fierce and powerful; now she didn't know how to reestablish her sexual self.

In the past, Samantha had been more inclined to have lovers that came and went. She liked the variety and the adventure. Her husband, however, had had the same lover for years, Emily. Emily had been around for so long, she was part of the family. Usually, Robert played separately with Emily, but sometimes they had threesomes and sometimes Emily went out to events with them or just hung out at the house and watched movies with them.

Emily had giant doe eyes and beautiful, natural breasts. After her mastectomy, for the first time ever, Samantha caught herself feeling envious of Emily, a woman who had always been a good friend to her. She hated these new feelings, and she felt guilty for having them, yet she couldn't shake the feeling of salt being poured in the wound every time she thought of her.

As a therapist, this is a tricky situation to help navigate. Samantha had been traumatized by the cancer treatment process. The surgery had left her body forever changed, and had delivered a gut punch to her sense of self. My therapeutic instincts might have been to suggest that the couple take a break from non-monogamy if Robert also had partners who were not such deep connections. This break could create a time for him to focus on Samantha and thus speed along her healing process. However, in this case, casting Emily aside would be unethical—a golden example of couple privilege. Emily was not disposable.

This is a case where triggers both internal and external are at play. For Samantha, the internal antecedent is her sense of self having been deeply shaken; the external antecedent is how Robert and Emily behave—how the choices they make either lessen or heighten her pain.

Samantha has the responsibility to find ways to heal and reclaim a new version of herself, including her sexuality. She may change from having many hot lovers to finding one lover who sees her deeply—who perhaps sees her mastectomy scar as a badge of her strength. Or she may need to take a long break from non-monogamy and work on herself, going on yoga and spiritual retreats and/or joining a cancer survivor art therapy group. It's her journey, and she will have to find her way. Being assertive and voicing her needs with both Emily and Robert will be a part of this healing journey as well.

During this process, Emily and Robert have choices. Probably the first step is for both of them to talk to Samantha and find out how they can help her. This is a negotiation between three people, and all three people's needs matter. The hope is to find a middle ground that works for everyone, and for all parties involved to be kind and patient in the process.

Samantha may not be ready for discussions at first, but as her therapist, I would encourage her to have them sooner rather than later, because life goes on. If Emily and Robert are flying blind, without her input, the chance for increased injury skyrockets. Best to have the uncomfortable conversations that no one looks forward to. Perhaps Samantha decides she would rather talk to Robert one on one, as needed, and to also meet with Emily separately, over coffee. Meeting with each person individually may reduce her overwhelm or sense of feeling uncomfortable when two pairs of concerned eyes are looking upon her.

Perhaps Samantha asks them to take a break from seeing each other for a short while, or to cease sexual relations for a time, or to go on dates where she won't actually have to see them together. There are a million asks regarding logistics, behaviors, and verbalizations that Samantha may have. It's best for her to be honest about what she would ideally like rather than fear being seen as "bad poly," or needy. Why? Because Emily and Robert are adults and have a voice in this discussion as well.

For instance, perhaps Samantha asks for a break and Emily says, "Okay. I'm totally willing to give that to you." Now it's her turn to offer up how much of a break from Robert she feels she can emotionally tolerate. Then, together, they can all come up with a tentative plan (one that may change as needed).

In my practice and with those I know outside of my practice, some of these conversations go beautifully and are testimonies to compassion, empathy, and kindness. Others are train wrecks and illustrate what happens when egos lead, compassion is lacking, and no one is listening. With conscious intentions set, however, the former is possible.

Insecurity

Sometimes insecurity is a tiny sting that's easy to tend to, and other times it can rise up like a viper, biting quick and deep. Regardless, insecurity can make us feel helpless and hurt to the core. Often, several other painful accomplices come with it: a fear of having to endure the critical gaze of others, their potential rejection of us, and our consequent embarrassment and shame.

What are you insecure about? Maybe you think you are socially awkward. Maybe you don't like a physical feature. For men, often it's the size or shape of their dick. Or maybe you're embarrassed by the stretch marks you acquired after having a baby. Perhaps you think that you are not very sexually skilled and fear being called out on it.

These kinds of insecurities can be crippling. If we let them, they will rule us—and hamper our chances for an abundant, authentically non-monogamous journey. Like a toxic friend, they invite us to stay hidden in a tight little ball. How are we supposed to grow and express ourselves with this state of frozen restriction?

First, the good news. One might assume that being non-monogamous would press all sorts of insecurity buttons. It can. This is true. But—miracle of miracles—the opposite frequently happens as well. Being non-monogamous can be an incredible confidence booster. So often during this time, a positive transformation happens, especially if one is going to poly and/or lifestyle parties.

Before attending their first party, many women will say, "I was so nervous. Would I be pretty enough? Sexy enough?" But afterward, most of these same women report to me that not only did they feel embraced for their unique brand of sexy, their sexual goddess flame also got ignited. They felt sexy *and* more sexual in that atmosphere of positive sexual affirmation.

Many men, meanwhile, learn from the non-monogamous world

that they don't need to choose between two doors: 1) the asshole who gets laid or 2) the nice guy who is everybody's friend. There is a third door, and behind it is the noble slut—the man with the sex and love life of his dreams who is also kind to, and appreciated by, his partners.

I remember my first year of being a swinger in 2003. I was so self-conscious of my physical flaws. I assumed that in Los Angeles, a town infamous for superficiality, swingers would be hyper-focused on my flaws. Wrong. Instead, it felt like people of all genders merely saw my strengths and assets. Soon, I felt beautiful, sexy, and confident.

What contributes to this transformation? Primarily, the fact that this world is a slut-shame-free zone. There are exceptions, but in general, if you are behaving in a safe, sane, and consensual way, poly and lifestyle folks will embrace, reinforce, and even cheerlead you toward revealing your big, bold sexual truth. And when a person, regardless of gender, is not only allowed to be sexually authentic but is applauded for it, the whole psyche lights up with a fulfillment that goes way beyond sex.

Now back to the hard part. Just as the lifestyle can build up your confidence, it can also tear it down. The attention of attractive, charming people can truly boost your self-image. However, when you see your partner enjoying somebody new, it can test your strength. The assets of this new potential partner—this bright, shiny penny—will sometimes shine a harsh light on your insecurities.

How to cope with insecurity

Three effective methods for coping with insecurity are: 1) reframing your cognitions, 2) creating relationship reconnection rituals, and 3) creating your safety net.

First, let's discuss how to reframe our cognitions. Cognitive reframing is a technique commonly used by therapists that consists of identifying irrational thoughts, disputing them, and then shifting them to a more positive outlook that allows us to feel more mentally healthy and more grounded regarding our emotional experience.

Remember carefree Miss Boobalicious in the envy section? Although she was always kind and respectful to me, Roxie brought up some of my insecurities. My partner had a high need for play—some might call him a man-child. This was part of the reason I loved him. Often, he was just what the doctor ordered after a long day of work at the mental health clinic. However, at times, his need for play exceeded what I could offer. Being in love with a shrink can be taxing. We come home with some heavy stuff on our shoulders. Meanwhile, Roxie consistently offered fun. She just wanted to giggle, and go get ice cream with gummy bears—and my partner loved this. Sometimes I'd watched them run off with big smiles on their faces, and my heart would feel heavy. Was I fun enough often enough?

Eventually, however, I came to feel grateful to Roxie. She could provide something for my partner that I could not at times. She took the pressure off of me in that regard and was therefore a blessing: she helped meet my partner's needs. It wasn't all on me. I realized I didn't need to change. My job was to be me . . . the best version of me I could become. Trying to become someone other than *me* wasn't healthy for me. (And it's not healthy for you either!)

With such an attitude adjustment, working through insecurities is possible. Wonderful you, what do you bring to the table? Your metamour, how do they actually improve your life? You don't have to be them. They can actually make it easier for you to be authentically yourself by fulfilling needs for your partner that simply aren't part of your nature. And that's okay. You can't be all things to your partner. No one can. And when someone says, "You are beautiful; you are special to me," perhaps you don't understand why, but the non-monogamous journey often helps us to discover why. It helps us clarify what we are and what we are not.

If you choose healthy partners, each one will bring out and appreciate a different part of you. And sometimes they will see something in you that you didn't even know about. As Mr. Rogers says, "Knowing that we can be loved exactly as we are gives us all the best opportunity for growing into the healthiest of people."

So let's discuss the first method to cope with insecurities: the cognitive reframe. If your partner's love interest has a quality that stirs up your insecurities, and you are attempting to cope with these insecurities, ask yourself whether this trigger should be managed through inspiration or through self-acceptance, both of which are valid avenues to reframe your thoughts.

I know this sounds challenging, so let's talk about it. If this person is more muscular than you, more well-read than you, or more sexually skilled than you, inspiration could be at hand, because these are all things that might inspire you to learn, grow, and work on yourself. And if so, that's great. If you meet this challenge head-on, you might feel like a healthier, smarter, sexier you several months down the road. A little bit of competition can be healthy.

If, however, this person is taller than you, has a sexy accent, or has a higher IQ, self-acceptance is likely the better path. These are aspects that are difficult to impossible to embody. Self-acceptance includes acknowledging what you don't have even as you acknowledge what you do have. You're shorter, but you have a great ass. You don't have a captivating accent, but you have charm. You don't have a 130 IQ, but your artistic intelligence is through the roof. A cultivated and ongoing practice of gratitude for what you *do* have can slowly chip away at and eventually replace an inner monologue of self-criticism. And as we discussed in Chapter 5, thanks to neural plasticity, an active practice of self-gratitude not only shifts thoughts but also actually rewires the brain to notice the positive.

Self-acceptance is also needed when another lover embodies characteristics counter to your true nature. Maybe your partner's lover is a Zen-like yoga instructor who is always calm and self-possessed. Perhaps her calm presence triggers insecurities in you that you are a bit of a spaz. But maybe your high energy and exuberance is exactly what makes you such a stellar kindergarten teacher. You aren't meant to be Miss Zen yoga chick. You are you, and you're gorgeous just the way you are.

A second way to cope is to consciously create a reconnection ritual. A reconnection ritual is a powerful and effective way to increase a sense of security in your relationship and combat any insecurities your non-monogamous journey triggers. When your partner comes back from seeing their lover, what do you need? If the two of you have group sex, what do you need after you are both alone together again?

To cultivate relationship rituals, take a moment to ask yourself a few "what" and "when" questions. First, *what* words, behaviors, or rituals allow you to reconnect with your partner? And second, *when* is reconnection necessary for you? For instance, you might need cuddle time (what) after your partner comes back from a date (when). This is a thought process you can hash out together, or it can be a good journaling exercise. (Choosing the latter could allow you to be clearer when you express your needs to your partner.)

Rituals don't need to be a big to-do. Sometimes a small daily ritual, such as giving or receiving a hug upon waking next to your lover, can mean the world. It marks what we cherish, allowing us to sit with our gratitude while connecting with loved ones. A great one is the "last one home" ritual. This ritual might happen if you are coming home from work or coming home from a date. Regardless, if you are the last one home, within the first five or ten minutes (enough time to pee and change your clothes), connect with your loved one. Your ritual might only take a minute or two, and what it entails is between the two of you. But I suggest it not involve asking how the day went. This is an anti-connection question—one that will more than likely send you back into the stress of the day rather than connecting you with your love in the present moment. Eye contact and touch are better. A smile while holding one or both hands is lovely. You will know when you have found the right "last one home" ritual. Track your body. When you notice a felt sense of reconnection, a warmth in your heart, a sense of calm in your core, you'll know you've found it.

So why is reconnection a key to dissolving insecurities? To find the answer, let's go back in time and think of our childhood—or we can just imagine a child at play. When a small child toddles off to find a treasure or a seashell with the tide coming in, what does the child do when the fun turns to insecurity? They naturally return to home base to show Mom or Dad the sand dollar they found while reaching out for a hug. Once validation and security are reestablished, the child is ready for the next adventure once again.

As mammals, our need for attachment starts at birth. We were deeply connected to our mother in the womb. And our need to reconnect to loved ones continues across our life—some of us more often than others, depending on our attachment style (which we'll discuss in Chapter 10), but we all operate best when we feel connected.

A third way to cope with insecurity is to create your own safety net. A safety net is the tapestry of resources in your life: partners, friends, pets, support groups, or therapy. Perhaps right now you are fighting with your nesting partner, and the last thing you want is a hug from them. Times like this will happen. That is why it's important to have a safety net of resources to help you feel grounded when you feel insecure. Perhaps you need to have lunch with your BFF. Maybe you need to go on a hike with your dog. And there is always your online or in-person non-monogamous support group. Security-enhancing reconnection and grounding need not always come from our long-term relationship. If you feel it does, you might be in an enmeshed relationship.

In an enmeshed relationship, virtually everything is shared, including friends—which can result in an individual sense of self getting lost. Every spare moment is spent together. Your sole confidant and emotional support is your partner. This is not a healthy relationship model, especially if you are non-monogamous. Why? Because inevitably, your partner will hurt you. Even in the best relationships, the ones full of heaping helpings of compassion and emotional intelligence, feelings get injured. And sometimes the person who hurts you can't also be the person who heals you.

If you don't have at least a few people in place as extra supports, it might be time to expand your team. Build friendships within the non-monogamous community—at least one—so you have confidants who are not shared with your partner.

Also, build support resources just for you. Who or what makes you feel protected? Who or what makes you feel nurtured? Where can you go, real or imaginary, that makes you feel safe or peaceful? I encourage you to make a list. Some folks with hard backstories might say, "But no one has protected or nurtured me, and no place is safe. I only trust my partner." If this is you, have self-compassion. You are not alone. A great therapist can help you build a resource-filled life. But a therapist is not the only way forward. Sometimes a protector can be found in a dog. A nurturer can be found in a cat. A peaceful place can be found in your bed or your favorite nature spot. Peace, protection, love, and nurturance create a sense of security. Building a safety net of resources is not only important for non-monogamy but also for your entire life.

Loss and Abandonment

When it comes to relationships, loss and abandonment are the two biggest fears. Non-monogamy will eventually trigger any issues around abandonment, loss, or heartbreak that may still be tender within our psyches, so it's an important topic to unpack.

Within non-monogamy, we can sometimes feel that we have lost our partner even though they are sitting right next to us. Perhaps you're sharing the day with your partner. It's gorgeous outside and you are excited about your plans. But as they sit next to you in the car, they are texting other lovers rather than connecting with you. You may feel, in this case, that your partner has emotionally abandoned you. You may feel sad, angry, lonely, and hurt. And you may fear voicing this hurt due to the risk of being accused of being jealous, controlling, or insecure, so you're suffering in silence. Meanwhile, your partner is unaware that this beautiful day has been ruined for you. This experience is not one of literal loss, but it can land with a heavy emotional impact.

Those who have a backstory of abandonment, rejection, and related attachment injuries usually struggle much more with these kinds of fears. They may be prone to becoming triggered much more easily and frequently, and with greater force. These responses are nothing to be ashamed of. They are simply the neurobiological by-product of unresolved trauma in a human. And they are hard feelings to have. So let's consider what can help.

How to cope with loss and abandonment

Let's go back to our three journaling steps:

1) Read your body. Write down sensations and corresponding feelings.
2) Define the antecedent to your somatic and emotional reaction as internal or external.
3) Get to the root of your struggle.

Reading your body will help you avoid slipping into denial about your pain or intellectualizing away your pain, and it will also give you a sense of the degree of your pain. Once we connect to our body, we are better able to connect to our feelings and thoughts.

Defining whether your feeling of loss and abandonment comes from external or internal antecedents (or both) is a solid preliminary coping strategy that allows you to clarify your focus and more accurately get to the root of your struggle so that you can choose the correct coping strategies.

Let's take Mary as an example:

Internal: Mary's dad abandoned her at age six. Several of the boyfriends she had before Todd cheated on her, and one left her for another woman. She was left feeling she could only rely on herself and couldn't trust men to be emotionally supportive of her. She has a fear of abandonment, built by her life experiences.

External: Todd, her present boyfriend, has little empathy. He had incredibly controlling parents in his childhood and thus projects this narrative onto Mary, perceiving her requests for reassurance as controlling and manipulative. He feels in danger of losing his true self. When she attempts to assert her needs to reduce her triggers, he tells her she is being needy and pushes back. He tells her that she needs to use logic to override her issues. She is left feeling shamed, alone, and hopeless, with broken down self-esteem.

This damaging pairing of both external and internal antecedents is not rare, just as the pairing of these two personality profiles is also not rare. In this case, the person with unresolved abandonment issues is dating someone who is not emotionally available enough. These two types often find each other. Unfortunately, Todd will only etch deeper grooves in Mary's "men will never be emotionally supportive to me" story. And she, meanwhile, will reinforce Todd's "women are needy, manipulative, and controlling" narrative. Thus, the toxic relationship dance continues.

Now let's imagine that a magic fairy gives Mary a kind and assertive boyfriend, Sean, who has worked on himself. Mary's internal issues remain the same, but the external dynamic is much different now.

External: Although compassionate to Mary's abandonment issues, Sean is a true polyamorist who has two other girlfriends he loves deeply. He is able to adhere to many of

Mary's asks, such as a text check-in when he is out on a date, but when she pressures him to reduce his lovers down to just one other partner, he sets a limit.

At this point, Mary has to sort out her own issues and determine what, if anything, Sean can do to help with her abandonment fears. She decides to take responsibility. She finds a therapist who understands how the trauma of abandonment impacts her attachment style. She reads the book *Attached*, which helps her gain insight about her own behaviors. She realizes that part of the reason that she was able to attract Sean (besides the magic fairy) is that she has healed quite a bit through therapy and a practice of mindfulness. She becomes aware that she doesn't need Sean to cut down to one other lover. She realizes that ask came from a triggered place. But she does want to see him more often, get more texts from him, and spend more holidays with him. She proposes this to him. He counter-proposes that they move in together, with the understanding that he wants to see each of his other lovers once a week each.

Mary is ecstatic. This is way better than what she even asked for, and it gives her a stability that eases her fear of literal abandonment. These new agreements begin to break down her story that men will never be emotionally there for her. Sean has provided a corrective, healing experience.

As seen in this example, once we suss out what our responsibility is, we can take action steps to heal our injuries. And once we realize what pieces of the puzzle are our partner's responsibility, we can ask them for what we need and start a negotiation that can lead to a deeper connection. From here, a healthy non-monogamous relationship can be born.

Overwhelm, aka change overload

Too much change too fast in a non-monogamous relationship can be taxing. Imagine your partner jumps hard and fast into sexual escapades in their zeal to discover the splendor of non-monogamy. This breakneck speed doesn't allow the overwhelmed partner to process their feelings regarding the experience, whether it's a first date, request, or new lover, before the next date, request, or lover is brought to the table. And if the overwhelmed partner is also a non-assertive pleaser, the problem becomes compounded.

Another contributor to overwhelm is loving an unpredictable partner. It's hard to relax when your partner is always throwing you for a loop. Perhaps they've just found a new lover and you think they'll take some time to settle in—giving you, in turn, time to emotionally adjust—but instead they go right back out on the prowl, looking for a third lover. Overwhelm can occur when there is severe dissonance between what you expected and what actually happens—making you feel hurt, isolated, fearful, or resentful. But this overwhelm doesn't necessarily mean that you're not cut out for non-monogamy. It simply signals that you haven't learned how or when to negotiate self-care boundaries.

Let's say you and your partner agree to be non-monogamous, and a few weeks into the relationship, you see them making flirty eye contact with someone without running it by you. Immediately, your heart starts racing. You feel overwhelmed. You thought your partner would check in with you before flirting commenced. But perhaps you have just made an assumption. Has this boundary been clearly negotiated and agreed to?

When I ask this question in a couples therapy session, so often the overwhelmed partner will nod yes while the other partner adamantly shakes their head no. This is why your relationship agreements have to be crystal clear to both of you. And if you know you are prone to memory or perception differences, put all agreements in writing and change them as needed. Clear relationship agreements reduce overwhelm.

When you're overwhelmed, unprocessed emotions stack up like anvils on your chest. When you have to absorb unexpected emotional changes too fast or too intensely for your psyche, your autonomic nervous system's response to threat (fight, flight, or freeze) begins to kick in.

Say the speedy partner finally comes in for a pit stop, notices something is wrong, and asks, "What's going on with you?"

If the overwhelmed partner is in a mild freeze state, they might lose their voice or experience thought blocking (fuzzed-over thinking) and simply mumble, "I don't know." If they're in fight mode, they might launch into a flurry of subjective accusations regarding their partner's lack of consideration. And finally, if they are in flight mode, they may storm out and simply avoid the subject or ask to shut down the idea of non-monogamy entirely. Any of these responses may be so intense that it seems non-monogamy is outside of their true nature—but this assumption is often false. The person in question likely just needs a slower and/or gentler experience.

Good decisions rarely come from a place of overwhelm. If your partner is overwhelmed, it's not that they can't handle non-monogamy; rather, they can't handle the speed, intensity, or twists and turns of the ride. My advice to you—and I say this with love—is to chill the fuck out.

You're probably thinking, *But what about me? Don't I have a say in this?* Of course you do. However, in a healthy pairing, a middle ground can be found between keeping the integrity of our true self and making our partner feel that we have their back. Both must coexist.

How to cope with overwhelm

My scope here will be limited to overwhelm caused by speed, intensity, or unexpected turns. (Overwhelm due to triggers is covered in Chapter 12.)

As always, let's look at both internal and external factors. When our partner is going faster, harder, or more erratically than our preference, we need to start by examining our own responsibilities and internal world.

Have you been educating yourself? Reading up on non-monog-amy? Listening to podcasts? Information is an emotional anchor. And it gives us a framework to cope.

Have you made friends or found mentors within the non-mo-nogamous community? Such resources can help you process through your feelings. And they are a second anchor to help you withstand tidal waves of overwhelm.

Do you have a self-care practice? Are you getting enough sleep, healthy nutrition, and exercise? Are you moderating your intake of booze or drugs? If not, you may simply be overwhelmed due to your own lack of self-care. You have to take time out to love yourself well.

Finally, are you communicating often and in a grounded man-ner? When communication is lacking, issues build up, leading to overwhelm. Don't lose your voice.

Now let's look at your external world, including your part-ner. Whether you're new at non-monogamy or an old-timer, your partner's desires and needs will throw you for a loop at times. Let's consider an open couple, Tasha and Crystal, who encompasses all three in their relationship: too fast, too hard, and too erratic.

Tasha and Crystal are a burner couple who've been non-monog-amous for three years. Both have gone to Burning Man many times in the past, but their recent experience was only their second burn together. The first time together, last year, was lovely. They managed to stick together. They looked at the art by day and danced all night. A little bit of MDMA made everything all the more beautiful and connected. They stayed up to watch the sunrise, cuddled up in each other's arms. They never felt so in love.

But a lot had happened since the previous year, and at this year's burn, Crystal was ready to have an entirely different experience. She wanted to be able to venture out on her own part of the time, do drugs when she pleased, and have the freedom to be sexually sponta-neous, whenever, at will. After all, this was Burning Man. She shared these desires before they left, but Tasha had a hard time taking the information in and didn't think Crystal really meant it; she was hoping for a repeat performance of the previous year.

Meanwhile, Crystal had been feeling stifled in their relationship over the last few months. Resentment had built up. She hadn't verbalized any of this to Tasha, however; she simply asked for what she needed at Burning Man.

On their five-day trip, Crystal did more drugs than she ever had in the past and Tasha witnessed her making out with many of their camp mates. Each day, she was more unavailable to Tasha than the last. On their second to last night at the burn, Tasha watched Crystal take the first drugs that came her way, and then more after that. Within an hour, they'd been separated.

By 2:00 a.m., Crystal was inside Orgy Dome. She stumbled back into camp at sunrise, the exact time that had been so special to Tasha the year before, and climbed into their tent. Tasha was wide awake under the covers, with puffy, teary eyes. Crystal collapsed onto the bed with a thud, mumbling something about Orgy Dome being epic, and soon passed out, snoring loudly, oblivious to the deep sadness next to her.

The fight that ensued the next day was not pretty, and the trip back home was equally cold, quiet, and icy.

Upon their return home, they eventually scheduled some time to talk.

"You know," Tasha said, "you were way too much for me this time. Too much drugs, too many sexual partners. I didn't know where you were, and I felt left. I had a horrible time. I felt betrayed by you."

At this point Crystal could have chosen to fly into a rage, but instead she simply said, "You realize that you agreed to give me freedom before we ever left, right?"

"Yes," Tasha admitted, "but I didn't know what I was agreeing to. I didn't think you would really do all that. I thought I was being tested."

Crystal was able to hear that. "Well, we can't undo the past, but we can figure out what will work going forward. The truth is, I want more freedom—not just at Burning Man. So let's talk this out."

Tasha was willing to engage and she started the conversation, beginning with stating that Crystal had moved too fast, too hard, and too erratically for her comfort at the burn.

Crystal asked her to break down exactly what she meant by that—so Tasha did. She was able to verbalize how Crystal could dial back to a level that was okay for her. It was a great starting point for further negotiations.

I should note that these two had a lot of healing to do related to the injuries incurred at Burning Man. But because they started both the healing process and the negotiation process from a place of compassion—and used the communication techniques we'll discuss in greater detail in Chapter 13—their chances of moving forward into a place that worked for both of them were high.

Through this example, you can see how external factors that impact your overwhelm can be delineated and addressed. Please, don't take on what is not yours.

Chapter Seven

COMPASSION FOR PARTNERS

The view from the floor-to-ceiling window of my sixth-story office reveals a perfect, beautiful California day. The palm trees are sunlit and caught in a soft breeze. The sky is a pristine, cloudless blue. But Casey and Drake don't notice. As Casey tearfully expresses the pain she's feeling as a result of Drake's inconsiderate actions, Drake cuts her off and launches in, exclaiming, "Your pain?! What about my pain? What about all the times you haven't thought of me?" And he runs through examples just to drive the point home. As a therapist, this is a common dynamic that plays out in my office: both members of a couple begging for compassion but stubbornly withholding it. It's troubling to watch, even when I'm confident I can improve their connection.

If you want to be successful at non-monogamy, you must learn to give and receive compassion in equal measure. Compassion even surpasses communication in importance. If you have ever watched a brilliant politician speak eloquently while completely lacking heart, you can understand why compassion is so essential.

According to the Dalai Lama, "Compassion is the wish for another being to be free from suffering." When compassion leads, we have more of an acceptance for where our partner is emotionally in a given moment and our inner child—that part of us that wants immediate gratification, pronto—takes an appropriate back seat.

In Chapter 13, we will discuss communication techniques to convey caring to our partner, but before we get there, let's talk about the resistance that may get in the way of truly feeling and emoting compassion.

Buddhist spiritual teachings address resistance at great length. A central tenet of the Buddha has been melted down into a mathematical formula by dharma teacher Shinzen Young as:

Suffering = Pain times Resistance (S = P x R)

When we add resistance to pain, that manifests suffering. One of the primary reasons one resists having compassion for their partner is a fear of emotional pain (such as guilt or shame), but in resisting they create a heightened and debilitating suffering within the relationship. So let's discuss how to overcome our resistance and courageously face our partner with compassion and love.

A wise friend once said to me that the experience of pain is not an excuse to continue the cycle of suffering—that instead the experience of pain should inform us, leading to greater compassion for another's suffering. There are many dynamics that can block compassion and consequently sabotage an attempt to be non-monogamous.

At the heart of this chapter are fifteen blocks to compassion that I've witnessed in my practice.

1. Delaying Asserting Yourself until You Explode

I address this powder keg first for a reason: because it's so freakin' common. Harmony keepers who avoid unpleasantness, ironically, almost always have the most chaos in their lives. I will give you an example to illustrate.

Ethan and Dominic had been in a non-monogamous relationship

for over a year. They loved each other, but their communication skills were less than stellar. As a result, sometimes they avoided hard topics altogether. Ethan's original upset happened at a sex party. It wasn't a huge deal, maybe a four on a scale of one to ten in terms of upset. Ethan thought it over and decided, *Ahhh, it's not worth it. I don't want to seem like a whiner; plus, we are in such a good place right now.* So he stuffed his upset under the rug.

But then another upset happened during a date with another couple, and when Ethan woke up the next day, he realized he was still angry about it. As he began his morning routine, he thought, *This isn't the time. The kids will be late to school if I bring it up now.* So he shoved this unhappy feeling under the rug as well.

Finally, another bump happened two weeks later, during a foursome, and Ethan thought, *Dominic isn't going to change. There's no point in even addressing this. It'll just make things worse.* And under the rug it went.

Six months went by and Ethan noticed he was experiencing a low-level anger almost all the time and didn't know why. But we do, right? By this point there was a mountain of fiery, combustible stuff packed under the rug. So it wasn't shocking when one day Dominic tripped over Ethan's rug and blew it all sky-high, setting their living room on fire—to Dominic's complete surprise.

Ethan had his reasons for keeping mum. He thought, *The offense isn't bad enough,* or *The timing is off,* or *There's no point, because my partner will never change.* But these were all excuses to avoid dealing with something he found emotionally challenging. Perhaps he feared rejection, invalidation, or belittlement—but regardless, if he'd faced his fears and addressed the upsets when they were small, he would have been calm enough to express himself in a compassionate and respectful way instead of turning into a fireball.

Another reason for a pattern of avoidance is a fear of being perceived as unkind or controlling. It's not surprising that when we make choices from a place of fear, we often become exactly what we fear.

In Desiree and Eli's situation, Desiree often wished that Eli was more emotionally accessible. They'd been together for several years, she loved him, and she had sympathy for his backstory: he'd grown up with a rageful dad and an alcoholic mom. From a young age, he'd learned that if he made himself invisible enough, he'd get less wrath from Dad. And if invisibility was not possible, being the congenial, charming, good kid who didn't make waves had at least kept the chaos to a minimum.

As an adult, Eli's jovial nature—by this point grooved in deep—helped him to be a success in his career. He could manage and finesse the most difficult of clients with ease. But when he and Desiree decided to start going to non-monogamous parties, this trait of his got him into trouble.

They went to the first party just to check out the vibe. Once they got there, Desiree was decidedly flirtatious. This bothered Eli, because she hadn't asked him how he felt about flirting, but he didn't say anything.

At the next party, Desiree was even more flirtatious and even made out with a couple of people while Eli chatted with others. Eli was angered by this too. She never asked him if it was okay for her to make out with other people. But he didn't say anything.

At the third party, Desiree left Eli's side to make out with their friend Max, who later pulled her into the back bedroom without Eli knowing. She had been gone for fifteen minutes when Eli excused himself from his conversation to look for her. Upon entering the bedroom, he discovered Max between Desiree's legs; her breasts were exposed, and her back was arched in ecstasy. His heart sank and his eyes hardened. His fleeting feeling of heartbreak was quickly pushed down and replaced with a quiet rage. He whispered sternly in Desiree's ear, his tone shifting Desiree's blissful expression into one of panic on a dime, "Desiree, what the fuck do you think you're doing? Get your things. It's time to go."

On the car ride home, he exploded, going through all of her

misdeeds across several months of parties as he perceived them. Desiree was completely blindsided.

"I thought you were okay," she said. "At all the parties you've been laughing and talking. You seemed fine. Why didn't you let me know?"

He fell silent. She cried.

It wasn't until their therapy session the next day that Eli was able to admit that he hadn't been letting Desiree know when he felt jealous, disrespected, or uncomfortable. "I don't want to ruin your fun," he said, looking down.

In therapy, Eli learned to verbalize to Desiree when his discomfort was at a two rather than at an eight or a nine. It was way better than pushing his feelings down into a box, only to have it explode at a nine or a ten at some unexpected time. Desiree, in turn, felt safer and more trusting. She no longer felt she was walking on eggshells and trusted that Eli would let her know if something bothered him. As a consequence, she felt more loved by Eli. She made a point to express her appreciation.

Desiree and Eli are another example of how compassion is lost when we avoid confrontation for too long and let anger take over. Compassion comes from a place of calm. Our partners will feel lucky to have such a compassionate partner if we always choose to discuss grievances from a calm state versus a reactive one. They will trust us and in turn feel relaxed in our presence. This self-control can be achieved if we address issues when we see them rather than wait until it's too late.

2. Not Feeling Heard

Sometimes I point out to my clients that they're making a passionate plea for compassion even as they're refusing to give it. When I shine light on this irony, the client's response is often, "Why should I empathize with them if they don't care about me?" When the other partner is operating from the same logic, you have a stalemate.

If you and your partner find yourself at this block, I suggest you make a deal to do a compassion reboot. This reboot means you both agree to practice the communication skills in Chapter 13, with the intention of deepening your connection.

In the case of Mack and Dahlia, Mack was a kinky mother-fucker. If kink had ski slopes, Mack would be cascading down the black diamonds. When Mack met Dahlia, her submissiveness in the bedroom couldn't have made him any happier. However, outside of the bedroom, Dahlia was a strong, assertive woman and an expert in her professional field—and after the two moved in together, their responsibilities began to clash with their kink.

Three years into their relationship, they were dating their fourth submissive girlfriend, Clarice, and Dahlia felt Mack was focused more on her than he was on Dahlia. In therapy, things became heated fast.

"I just wish you would initiate sex with me at least some of the time," Dahlia said, her voice tense. "You're always focused on Clarice. And you never make love to me. I don't feel connected to you anymore."

"Well, maybe if you were sexier, I'd focus on you more," Mack snapped. "And you've completely let go of our kink dynamic. You know that normal sex has never done it for me."

"Well, it's easy for our girlfriends to be sexy because none of them work the long hours I do," Dahlia shot back. "You have no sympathy for how hard I work."

"Excuses, excuses," Mack muttered.

You hear how they are both screaming for compassion without hearing each other or showing a willingness to offer that same compassion in return? Chapter 13 will explain how to combat this dynamic more fully, but in the meantime, when you catch yourself lacking compassion because your partner isn't listening or showing compassion for you, you can choose to attempt to break this vicious cycle. Slowing down and simply listening to your partner is a good first step.

3. Compassion Fatigue

We all have a compassion gas tank—and its levels fluctuate. After a hard day at work or after taking care of the kids, we may be emotionally exhausted. Many of my clients make the honest mistake of introducing a hard discussion about non-monogamy in this very moment: when their partner's gas tank is on empty.

This is an easily avoided mistake. Before introducing a conversation, simply ask, "Where is your compassion gas tank right now on a scale of zero to ten?" If the answer is three or less, your partner doesn't have the psychic mojo to have this discussion now. The follow-up question should be, "When do you think we can have a check-in?" Then set up a time to talk. These simple steps can help avoid unnecessary fights and unpleasantness.

Lena was a VP of a Fortune 500 company and traveled to a different country every week or so. Her girlfriend, Hayley, was an actor who hadn't had work for a couple of years and was often at home alone. Needless to say, Hayley, who had too much time on her hands, tended to spin on what was wrong with their relationship while Lena was away. Lena, meanwhile, had little time to think about their relationship.

Hayley often hit Lena with questions as soon as she came through the door. One afternoon, Lena got news that her company might be merging with another company and her job might be in jeopardy, and she came into the house sullen and burdened. Hayley, in her anxious exuberance, didn't notice and launched in, "Can we finally discuss opening up our relationship? There is a woman that I'd like to get coffee with. I've been trying to talk to you about her for weeks. Can we discuss her now?"

Without a word, Lena glared at her, slammed down her briefcase, stormed to the bedroom, and shut the door. Hayley was left alone in the kitchen, wide-eyed.

Now let's imagine that after that Lena and Hayley came to therapy, where they learned how to handle this another way. Now, if Lena texts that she's on her way home, Hayley might text back, "How are you feeling?"

Lena may respond, "I'm hungry. You know how I get hangry when I don't eat. Can you jump in the car when I pull up? After I get some food in my belly, I'm sure my emotional gas tank will go from a five to an eight, and I'll be ready to hear anything that you'd like to talk about."

Hayley will no doubt be amazed by how much better that exchange is than their usual clashes.

4. Narcissistic Traits

See Chapter 11 for more information on how narcissistic traits can negatively impact a non-monogamous relationship, but I'll give a quick overview here. Those with narcissistic traits don't experience much, if any, empathy and are incredibly self-entitled, with a lot of grandiosity. They rarely change, mainly because their behaviors are ego-syntonic, meaning they don't think anything is wrong with them. My clients who lean toward narcissism but aren't quite diagnosable, however, are often capable of change, especially if they can be helped to see how behaviors that indicate compassion for their partner actually serve them as well. For instance, I might help them see that if they actually listen to what their partner needs, they might be able to go on that date with their other lover without complaint. Their behavioral shift may be initially selfish. But once they see the positive feedback loop, sometimes they can begin to develop a true and natural compassion that is healthy for their partnership.

I personally dated a few diagnosable narcissists in my earlier years of non-monogamy. In my naivete, I thought that my affection and knowledge of psychology would slowly shift them into more empathetic individuals. Back then, I was guilty of being an over-giver. Unfortunately, non-monogamy and narcissism is a nasty combo. If you discover that you are in a non-monogamous relationship with a narcissist, it's better to back the truck up and find a partner who's already cultivated compassion and empathy. They are worth the search.

5. Lack of Shared Experience

Research shows that humans have trouble empathizing and having compassion for someone if they haven't experienced the same things the other has. For instance, it is not uncommon for me to hear about a Dom who has many submissive lovers but doesn't allow his submissives to have other lovers, and who lacks empathy around jealousy, insecurities, or his submissives disrespecting each other. He doesn't get it because he's not experiencing a similar struggle.

In the same vein, if one person in a couple is more experienced in non-monogamy than their partner, they may lack empathy for their partner's jealousy until their partner gets going and the tables are turned. Then, now that they are having a similar experience, the light flicks on; they come into therapy and say, "Ohhhh, nowwww I get it!"

Empathy and compassion often come from a place of firsthand knowing. If a person has been cheated on, they have all the empathy in the world for someone who is going through the same thing. Why? Because they know that pain and have compassion for it.

6. If I Give Compassion to My Partner, I Will Sacrifice My Own Needs and Wants

This need not be true. You can stick to your guns while providing compassion to your partner. You can give compassion and assert your boundaries. When you begin a discussion about non-monogamy, set an intention. One example might be: "My intention for this discussion is that we are both heard. We find common ground. And we both feel healthier as a couple as a result."

Sid came into therapy with Mirabelle reluctantly. He was not interested in non-monogamy, but he loved Mirabelle. He expressed in therapy that he feared that if he even entertained Mirabelle's interest in non-monogamy, Pandora's box would fly open. He feared their relationship would inevitably lose any semblance of what he wanted or needed.

"This whole notion of non-monogamy terrifies me," he told Mirabelle in one session. "I'm scared of losing you. I don't want or need anyone else."

"I hear you," Mirabelle said. "But what about kink that doesn't include full-on sex? Would you be willing to co-top me with another person? Or would you be willing to have side by side sex with another couple without swapping partners? Wouldn't that be fun?"

"Oh," Sid said. "I thought you were only interested in having other lovers without me. This is still scary, but yes, I'm willing to discuss some of those ideas."

Do you see how quickly Sid discovered that there was room for his needs and wants once he was brave enough to hear out his partner? Compassion need not run tandem with losing your own wishes.

7. The Need to Win

Many coupled people operate as if love is a war. You can see it in their communication patterns. When the heart feels tender, the battle armor is on. Difficult discussions usually sound like, "You hurt me!" "Really?! Well, you hurt me worse! And let me explain how!" The fiery tennis ball bounces back and forth, with no resolution or kindness in sight.

If this resonates for you, ask yourself: *Is this the story I want to keep living?* Remember, if there is a winner in any argument within a love relationship, you have both lost. The true goal is compassion, communication, and finding common ground or compromise, if possible.

Jade and Luke had been together for two years, and Jade had been a top porn performer for three. They were new clients, and as they closed my office door and sat down, the energy in the room became tense. Jade looked at her lap. Luke had a furrowed brow, staring and me, then the floor, and then back again.

"Welcome," I said. "What should we talk about today?"

Luke said, "I'd like to talk about boundaries. I don't mind Jade being in porn, but I don't want to hear the details. Lately, she's too tired to have sex with me, and yet I hear her talking to girlfriends in the industry about which talent she prefers to work with—who makes her squirt, etc. I don't want to hear those details."

Jade looked up from her lap. "Well, how do you think I feel about you always pushing for a threesome with my coworkers? You complain about not having sex with me, but it seems like all you want is other women."

"Well," Luke shot back, "it's my way of leveling the playing field."

"But that's my work," Jade said. "It's not the same."

Once I step in, I ask them to let go of the need to win or be right and focus instead on the need to connect. In therapy with a couple like this, we focus on empathy, validation, and creating boundaries, one issue at a time. (I'll break down the steps related to communicating compassionately more fully in Chapter 13.)

8. The Need to Blame

With the need to win often comes the need to blame. The Buddhist monk Pema Chödrön says, "We blame in order to ground ourselves." Once we determine blame, we no longer have the discomfort of spinning in the chaos of our feelings. We can focus on punishing, shaming, or acquiring justice, but what we need to do instead is find our compassion for ourselves and others. And the path to compassion includes sitting with our uncomfortable feelings and letting go of our attachment to blaming.

Em sits before me. She identifies as non-monogamous, submissive, and pansexual. Although she comes to me for individual therapy, she has a couple of partners at home who have both been voicing needs she feels overwhelmed by. She looks at me with slumped shoulders. "I suck at this. I'm failing them. I'm not good at poly. I don't know why they stay with me. Rosa wants to start dating Sam. And Mica wants to see Frankie. I'm just so overwhelmed right now. I can't do this." She begins to cry.

In this case, Em is blaming herself. The only way to attempt to makes sense of all her feelings is to oversimplify and shift all the blame onto herself. This self-blaming pattern goes way back to her childhood, but we aren't diving that deep today. Together, we problem-solve, and she begins to see the core issues at play.

Once we unpack the details, the overwhelming cloud of self-blame begins to dissipate. We can begin the heavy work of sorting through each issue, seeing how they interrelate, and identifying who is responsible for what. As that happens, the overwhelm begins to melt away.

9. Withdrawal

Often emotional withdrawal is our self-protective response to our partner overwhelming us. When our partner has an angry, harsh tone, a loud voice, or big, fast movements, we may experience emotional overwhelm that leads to a withdrawal. Tragically, the withdrawal often inspires an even bigger response from the partner, who feels ignored.

The emotionally demonstrative partner in this situation will often say, "I can't figure out how to get my partner to hear me, so I yell louder, cry harder, etc." But let's face it. It's hard to hug a porcupine. Few people will come forward with love when their partner is prickly. Regardless, so often, I've had upset clients say, "When I'm angry, that's all I want. I just want you to hug me. I just want to know that everything will be okay." They are often in tears when they express this. Meanwhile, their partner is confused and overwhelmed by the combination of tears and anger. Their impulse is to back away, as one might back away from an agitated wild animal.

So, what's the solution? In this case, work needs to be done on both sides.

Sue Johnson talks about this dynamic in her book *Hold Me Tight.* The intense person in the relationship needs to dial things down. And this may go way beyond monitoring yourself when pissed or hurt. This shift may be a lifestyle change. Dialing down can show up in many ways: refraining from texting your partner all day, which may feel incessantly to them; making sure your tone, volume, and body language aren't too much for your partner; pulling back from asking for sex throughout the day if your partner has asked for a break; filtering out unkind words that your partner has expressed are hurtful; and more. In other words, no matter how upset you are, it's never okay to assault your partner's sense of self. Saying things such as, "Only a dick would come home at two a.m.," is not alright even if it was clearly agreed that midnight was the time to be home from a date. Why? Because calling them a "dick" implies that they are bad. Instead of shaming, pointing out how the behavior was hurtful is a better way to go. A sentence like, "I'm really hurt by the fact that you were late coming home from your date" will lead to a more constructive, calm conversation. And when you're upset, the grounding techniques you'll find in Chapter 12 can help you find ways to increase your calm and self-control.

The one who tends to withdraw has their work cut out for them as well. They need to make a point of coming forward more often. Examples of coming forward might be to spontaneously ask your partner how they're doing, give hugs, initiate sex, or set a structured time for weekly or monthly check-ins. This proactive behavioral change will yield a calmer partner who sees that their emotional escalation is no longer required in order to get your attention.

10. Catastrophizing

New and/or scared couples lovvvve to catastrophize. It's one of the most common dynamics that I witness in my private practice.

Catastrophizing is irrationally blowing up a simple fear into a worst case scenario. Catastrophizers will often take something their partner said or did, whether it be voicing a fear or making a hurtful mistake, as hard evidence of a much larger problem they have imagined. Catastrophizing's impact can be incredibly damaging to a relationship if it becomes a reactive pattern. Luckily, I find it's one of the easiest communication hurdles to overcome.

Karen and Mark had been dating for five years. Both were young, in their twenties. Before Mark, Karen had mostly had long-term relationships with women. Recently, she had discovered Dan Savage's *Lovecast* and become an avid listener. Within a few weeks of listening to his advice about non-monogamy, she decided that being open was her destiny. One morning, while she and Mark were eating breakfast before work, she excitedly said, "When I fell in love with you, I fell so hard. I was sure that I just wanted you alone. But now, five years later, I can't deny that I'm bisexual any longer. I miss girls. I want to open up the relationship."

She was wide-eyed, smiling, and hoping for a well-received reaction. She was met with Mark's furrowed brows.

After a pregnant pause, Mark expressed first that he couldn't believe she was bringing this up right before work, and second that he was full of fear that if they opened up the relationship, Karen would fall in love with another woman and leave him. His heart was racing. He knew this was not what Karen wanted to hear. But he was still hoping for her compassion.

Sadly, Karen met his vulnerability with rage. "You're never going to let me be my true self!" she spewed. "You are determined to keep me in a cage. I'm dying in this relationship, and you will never be capable of letting me meet my needs."

At this, Mark's face turned to stone. He coldly grabbed his car keys, crossed the kitchen, and slammed the door behind him. As Karen heard his car start up and tear out of the driveway, she burst into tears, her head in her arms on the kitchen table.

Karen was catastrophizing. It doesn't have to go down like this. But as I said, I have found it relatively easy to break this reactive pattern with most couples. Once the client couple learns to be present with their partner rather than leaping to fictitious, bleak future scenarios, they are better able to find their compassion. Once compassion is found, the couple can begin to define flexible rules and boundaries that can be utilized to reduce anxiety. A fear that was synonymous with doom is now the springboard for creating a new relationship model. Let's look at a couple that inspires more hope.

Glen turned Helen down for sex yet again. He'd been hugging her less and staring at his phone more. Her mind was a hamster wheel, spinning with assumptions and fears. *He doesn't love me anymore*, she thought to herself. *He's lost his sexual desire for me. He's texting Lori more. They must be sexting. Is he going to leave me for her?*

Finally, as Glen sleepily typed on his phone before bed, Helen burst out with a litany of her pent-up fears: he clearly no longer desired her or wanted to touch her, and perhaps he didn't even love her anymore. "Why do you even stay?" she exclaimed. "Why are we even together?"

Glen just stared at her for a moment, wide-eyed and shell-shocked. But then he gathered himself, took a long, deep breath, and explained that since he'd gotten his promotion two weeks earlier, he had been working twelve-hour days. "I'm exhausted," he said, "and even when I get off work, they text me at home telling me about something I need to handle now." He admitted that he knew that it had impacted their sex life and his ability to focus on her. But he went on to promise that once he learned the new job, things would get easier; asked her to please be patient until then; and, finally, said, "But tell me, what are you upset about exactly?"

Helen fell silent, feeling sheepish but also relieved. She realized that she had been catastrophizing. Once she realized this, she was able to calm down, and they resolved her issues quickly.

Catastrophizing is a common psychological process for those who are scared. It's a misguided form of self-protection. If you think of the very worst devastation that could occur in your relationship, then at least you're emotionally prepared for that dire future.

But sometimes catastrophizing can be an unconscious means to manipulate our partner into behaving as we want them to. I often see catastrophizing when a couple first opens up their relationship. Often, one person is eager to dive in, while the other is more hesitant and fearful. As the fearful partner begins to unpack their fears within the therapy session, sometimes it's the more eager partner who starts to catastrophize, proclaiming, "See, there is no way that you are ever going to be able to do this! You've never been truly non-monogamous. You're just doing this for me." Now, the eager partner may simply be scared that their differing relationship needs may lead to growing apart or splitting up. But when catastrophizing comes from the eager partner it can be manipulative, callous, unloving, and pushy. If you know you're prone to this, you are at risk of seeming unsafe to your partner. And if the recipient of this shaming is a pleaser, they may say yes to something that is not a true yes to avoid the catastrophizer's accusations.

Healthy non-monogamy does not blossom in toxic soil, whether it's truly toxic or simply perceived as such. Dialing back the catastrophizing and reactionary behavior can help the more nervous partner gain confidence and bravery.

Catastrophizing is the most common thing in the world when you're attempting something hard like non-monogamy. Notice your thoughts and ask yourself, *Are my thoughts definitely true?* So often, they are not. Instead of thinking the worst of your partner, talk to them. Believe in their desire to love you well. If you have a loving and compassionate partner, they should be able to calm your fears using the communication skills outlined in this book.

11. The "Shame Spiral"

The shame spiral occurs when one person cannot tolerate hearing that their partner's pain is a result of their actions. Instead of listening, they launch into an even larger emotional display than their partner's, stating things like, "I can't believe I'm so horrible. Only a worthless person would hurt you like this." This overwhelm hijacks their ability to listen and they become the center of attention, stealing the focus away from the original injured party. In a bizarre turn of events, the injured party usually finds themself caretaking the shame spiraler.

We may feel this self-flagellation is our method of atonement. However, it's not what the hurting partner asked for. They need you to be present—to hear them, validate them, empathize, and ask them what they need. You can't do any of this if you're gone, deep in a shame hole.

Consider Bill and Vanessa. One Sunday morning, Bill walked into the bathroom as Vanessa was toweling off from her shower and said, "I need to talk to you. It's about our threesome last night."

"I'm listening," Vanessa said, immediately tense.

"You didn't look at me at all last night," Bill said, staring at the bathroom tiles. "You just looked at him. I felt so ignored. You kept telling John how gorgeous and handsome he is. I even left to go get a drink in the kitchen at one point, and you didn't even notice I was gone." He teared up. "I felt so betrayed by you."

There was a moment of shock on Vanessa's face, followed by recognition—then she immediately spiraled down. She burst into tears, collapsed onto the toilet seat, clenched her towel around her, and cried, "I'm such a disappointment to you. I fucking hate myself. Why do you even stay with me? You're such a good man. I wanted last night to be fun for us, but I can't get one goddamn thing right."

At this, Bill's angry face softened. "Sweetie, you know I love you. Don't cry. It's going to be okay. We will figure this out."

Do you see what happened here? Bill was holding the emotional baton until Vanessa's shame spiral ripped it from him, and now there was no way for him to get it back.

This was not an isolated incident for this couple, unfortunately. Vanessa's shame spirals had been a pattern in their relationship for years. There wasn't much room for Bill's feelings. When confronted about this unhealthy imbalance in therapy, Bill said, "But Vanessa is the one who has had the harder life. She's more emotional than me. I don't mind giving her what she needs."

That sounds sweet, but is it healthy for him? Is it healthy for the strength and longevity of their relationship? Absolutely not. Shame spirals block a person's ability for compassion because they're collapsed in their own pain.

So what's to be done about a shame spiral? Your first reaction might be to perceive it as a manipulation. If the shame spiraler in your life has narcissistic or sociopathic tendencies, this might be true. If that's the case, they might need to be called out. But usually those who experience heightened shame spirals come from traumatizing backstories in which they were made to feel bad or insignificant. The shame spiral is a reaction not only to the present but also to the painful past. Vanessa wasn't just reacting to Bill's feelings about the threesome. Her old wounds were also being triggered.

If you tend to fall into shame spirals, I invite you to ask yourself what self-care you need to engage in and what you need from your partner in order to stay grounded in such moments. Do you need to ask them for a short time-out to regroup and reduce your feelings of overwhelm? Such a break can be used to do some positive self-talk, some slow, deep breathing, or perhaps some journal writing. Then, once you're in a calmer state, you may be able to recognize what is triggering you. Perhaps memories of a critical parent? If you aren't able to find a method to ground yourself, going to a therapist who practices EMDR can help reduce triggers associated with shame so that the next time you feel your integrity is being called into question, you will be better able to stay grounded.

12. Shaming Partners

It should be noted that a triggered backstory is not the only possible antecedent to a shame spiral. A shame spiral can also result from listening to an upset, verbally assaultive partner. Remember, slut-shaming and other forms of emotional abuse are never okay, even when you feel you have been poorly treated or disrespected.

Even for the most Zen of us, being verbally attacked can heighten the challenge of staying present. And no one should have to attempt to cope with such unacceptable treatment anyhow. Instead, the shamer needs to take responsibility for their part in contributing to the shame spiral.

There is a much more constructive approach to verbalizing injuries within a non-monogamous relationship than lashing out. A kinder, more centered partner is capable of containing themself enough that they don't become verbally abusive. Touch, such as a hand on a knee or shoulder, is an effective way to ground your and your partner's nervous system during a difficult conversation. This simple non-verbal addition can be the difference between a productive outcome and a screaming match.

A second smart strategy is to front-load with positive affirmations before verbalizing the injury. Kind words as a preamble to hurt words increase the chance that the receiver may be better able to stay present and hear their partner's pain rather than become lost in a shame spiral.

Let's consider Anthony and Tabitha. Tabitha had always loved her birthday and was really looking forward to celebrating her thirtieth with Anthony. They had been planning the weekend, especially her birthday play party, for months. Thirty guests had RSVP'd, including Tabitha's boyfriend, Javar, and Anthony's new love interest, Stacy. It was shaping up to be a fabulous weekend. But during the party, Anthony got caught up with flirting with Stacy for way too long, forgetting to make the birthday girl his priority. And although

Tabitha had Javar with her, as well as the attention of many guests, she felt hurt by Anthony's behavior.

After the last guest left, Tabitha raged at Anthony, yelling, "You were such a dick tonight! I can't believe I'm in love with such a total asshole. Was it Stacy's birthday or mine?"

Although it's understandable for her to be righteously angry, such shaming language will always backfire. Let's imagine instead that she were able to say, "Anthony, I know you're usually incredibly considerate of me [affirmation], but when you focused on Stacy more than me on my birthday night, I felt unloved and disrespected by you. It was my birthday. You know how important that night was to me."

When Tabitha leads with "I know you are usually incredibly considerate," Anthony will be more able to own his behavior and stay grounded and present for Tabitha.

Now, asking Tabitha to be this "mature" is asking a lot. It's asking a lot of anyone. We are human. We won't always be able to lead with an affirmation when we feel our partner is being an ass. We may want to shame or punish them. In our anger, we may want to make them feel that, they, not their actions, are bad. But just know this will not work out for you in the end. So if you are in a rage, take some time away to center yourself before you talk to your partner.

13. Leading with Affective Empathy Rather Than Compassion

In the article "Compassion is Better Than Empathy," Dr. Tara Well writes about "affective empathy," which refers to the sensations and feelings we get in response to others' emotions, such as feeling stressed when we detect another person's anxiety. At times, utilizing affective empathy can deplete us to the point of being too drained to be supportive to our partners. Compare this to compassion, which is a positive emotional state that leads to action, such as volunteering or helping others. Compassion motivates. Affective empathy tends to emotionally drain us, while compassionate love tends to fuel us.

Liza and Bette were married and had two-year-old twins. Bette worked as a public defender, and Liza stayed home with the boys. There had been a lot of drama in Liza's family recently, and her sisters had been calling and texting her all day as she attempted to manage the twins. She tended to feel everyone's pain. This made her a loving and responsive mother and a kind, caring sister, but it also drained the bejesus out of her at times. She dreamed of a vacation with just Bette.

Bette's days were demanding as well, but she had always been able to separate herself from taking on the emotions of her clients. Perhaps her practice of meditation and running three times a week helped. So when their shared girlfriend, Susie, left a distressed voice message for Liza saying she wanted more time with both of them, Liza immediately put it on speaker so Bette could hear the message, during which Susie, crying, said the once-a-week visits weren't enough anymore and explained that she was lonely.

Liza looked at Bette and shook her head. "I just can't handle this. I've absorbed everyone's stuff all day. I'm tapped out."

Although Bette dealt with emotional cases all day, she said, "Don't worry, sweetie. I'll call Susie and work things through. Do you feel like we could see her a couple more times a month?"

Relieved, Liza agreed that one or both of them could fit in a couple more dates.

You might be thinking this sounds like some next-level emotional ninja stuff. But it doesn't have to be that complicated. If you track your body and stay grounded, you will be more likely to keep proper emotional boundaries rather than make your partner's emotions your own. Consequently, you will have the fuel to help them when they need your support.

14. Feeling Controlled

Why does the fear of being controlled elicit such a primal, visceral response? The answer is simple: fear of being controlled often feels synonymous with the fear of losing oneself. Frequently, I witness someone in my practice who is overly angry with their partner as a result of fears related to their open relationship. Their anger response can be so large that it obliterates any compassion they might have for their anxious partner, who is merely verbalizing self-care needs. Sometimes these clients remind me of cornered, feral cats. It's as if, in a subconscious way, they are fighting for their lives.

Jeremiah and Layla had been in the lifestyle for several years. Although Jeremiah was a congenial guy, there were a few people in the lifestyle community whom he didn't like. One was Kevin, who had always been competitive with Jeremiah, and whose "bro" demeanor didn't help matters. An artsy guy himself, Jeremiah found Kevin's alpha-male behavior abrasive and off-putting.

One night at a play party, Jeremiah rounded a corner to find Layla making out with Kevin in the hallway. Such behavior was within their relationship agreement and normally would not faze him one bit, but it was *Kevin*—so, the next morning, he spoke to Layla about his feelings. He was calm and even-keeled but made it clear that he didn't like Kevin and that it was hurtful to see her making out with him. He didn't go into the details of the times he'd felt disrespected by Kevin, because he felt this disclosure should be enough and trusted that Layla would respect his wishes. She seemed to understand, and so he felt the issue was resolved.

The next party that they were invited to, Jeremiah was busy but told Layla, "Why don't you go alone? There's no need for you to have a dull weekend just because I have to work."

He didn't have to tell her twice. Layla excitedly got ready and left.

The next morning, Jeremiah asked her, "How was the party?"

"It was great," Layla said. "I just hung out and talked. I flirted a little bit, but that was the extent of it."

Jeremiah smiled and said he was glad she had a great time.

Several days later, a close friend sent some texts to both of them that included a few pictures from the party. In one, Layla was passionately making out with Kevin, her dress pulled halfway up her thighs.

Jeremiah was pissed. "How could you do that?" he demanded. "You know how I feel about him. Are you purposely trying to sabotage our relationship?"

"You don't own me," Layla snapped. "I have a deep connection with Kevin. I love how he makes me feel about myself. When's the last time you made me feel like a goddess?"

Jeremiah was speechless.

In therapy that Monday night, we talked about Layla's childhood. She disclosed that she had controlling parents and had been taught way back that if a loved one discovered what was dear to her, it would be taken from her. To Layla, the issue with Jeremiah and Kevin just confirmed this belief.

Through therapy, Layla was able to see that rather than trying to control her, Jeremiah was trying to exercise self-care. And with this reality check in place, she was able to see all the freedom she actually had within her relationship with Jeremiah.

Once Layla was able to verbalize her understanding, Jeremiah was able to say, "Hon, I'm sorry I haven't been making you feel like a goddess lately. I didn't know you felt that way. I've always thought you were beautiful. Talk to me."

What followed was a heartfelt discussion about how she felt they had grown apart and their joint desire to fix things.

At one time or another, your partner is going to attempt to set a limit within your non-monogamous relationship. In that moment, you may feel that your partner is being controlling—but avoid being reactive and defensive. Staying grounded is key. Their request is just the beginning of a negotiation of needs that may lead to some adjustments to your non-monogamous relationship agreements.

You might also want to share with your partner any still-raw emotional injuries from your backstory that non-monogamy might poke. Such vulnerable disclosures to your partner may be hard, but with a compassionate partner, they can truly pay off. They will be more aware and so you will you. With awareness comes a heightened capacity to be in tune with and compassionate toward your partner—key ingredients for successful non-monogamy.

15. Witnessing Your Partner's Grief for an Ex

Non-monogamy brings up unique issues when there are breakups within any given relationship configuration. This might play out in any number of ways. For instance, one configuration may be a primary couple that has separate partners, and one of the couple breaks up with their secondary partner. While suffering the loss, the grieving partner may struggle with how much to reveal to their primary about their sadness. They may choose to hide their pain, knowing that full disclosure might bring up fear-related questions about whether their great sadness indicates that they loved the secondary partner more.

Conversely, other people make their long-term partner their go-to for emotional support. In such cases, the supportive partner will often want to be caring but will also have discordant feelings of their own that get in the way of providing full emotional presence.

As a general rule, you'd do better to choose a good friend who identifies as non-monogamous or is non-monogamy friendly to be your main shoulder to cry on when you grieve. In this case, your partner doesn't need to be your foremost emotional anchor—and during a breakup like the one I've just described, they are going through their own emotional process (one that likely isn't complementary to yours). So find someone else to confide in. The effort will be worth it.

Bella and Trish were married. Bella's girlfriend of one year, Anne, had just broken up with her. Anne was marrying a man who had asked her to be monogamous, so she'd cut off all contact with Bella abruptly, per his request. Bella was crushed, angry, and wanted to scream to the heavens. She was regularly bursting into tears without warning.

Bella and Trish had kept their non-monogamy very private and had never connected to any non-monogamous communities or made any non-monogamous friends. Consequently, Bella felt that Trish was the only one she could go to for comfort.

Over the course of a week, Trish absorbed all of Bella's pain. At the end of that week, in therapy, Bella expressed that she felt incredibly grateful to Trish and felt blessed to have such a supportive partner. Then she spent the first twenty minutes of their couple's session talking about Anne and grieving.

After processing with Bella, I turned to Trish. "I'd like to hear how you're doing. But before you respond, I'd like to point out that the head and the heart exist on different planets. I don't want to hear what your logic asks of you. Instead, what does your heart say?"

Trish immediately broke into tears. "My heart is broken. I didn't know her feelings for Anne ran so deep. I've always been the only one she loved." She looked at Bella. "Do you love her? And what does that mean for me? Do you still love me? I feel like I have less of you."

Now, Bella and Trish had always known that one or both of them might fall in love with another partner. However, they had never actually had to contend with it before, and now Trish felt blindsided by it. In actuality, Bella may just have been going through a natural grieving process that was heightened by how abrupt and jarring the circumstances were. And because Trish had to absorb all of Bella's pain, Trish became destabilized as well.

This illustrates why it's so much better to have at least one non-monogamous friend; solely relying on your main partner may be insensitive and could have negative consequences for your relationship.

Balancing Self-Compassion
and Compassion for Our Partner

Now we have discussed both compassion for ourselves and our partner. However, balancing the two can be tricky. Couples are at their healthiest when there is a strong sense of connection to the self and to one another. Both connections take work and effort.

Why isn't a philosophy of self-work enough? For instance, you work on your issues and your partner works on their issues; your couplehood should be strong then, right?

I've often heard this philosophy voiced along with the phrase "Not my circus, not my monkeys." But such a stance opens the door for trouble. At its worst, self-work alone, without considering what responsibility your partner has, is a framework that allows those with narcissistic tendencies to game the system. This kind of dynamic fuels gaslighting and allows those who are manipulative to continually shift emotional labor onto their partner. It creates an atmosphere in which people can behave badly without taking accountability.

Nikki and Chet had been non-monogamous for a while, mostly as swingers. Recently, Chet had said to Nikki, "I want to start playing separately. I want to take on Georgina as my lover."

Nikki's heart fell. "But Chet, she's my cousin and good friend. She comes to all our family gatherings. I've known her since I was a child. Plus, she's your business partner's wife. Does he even know? Please choose someone else. She's too close."

"You really need to work on yourself," Chet said angrily. "I shouldn't be subjected to your jealousy. This is your issue. Don't put it on me. Her husband is fine with it. You're just being anxious and paranoid. You've always been this way."

"Please," Nikki pleaded, "we need to talk this out. I just need some empathy. I need you to understand where I'm coming from."

But Chet just walked out, muttering under his breath, "You need a shrink."

Chet has narcissistic tendencies (he was an over-taker), and partners like him will often ask their partner, who tend to be over-givers, to "just be logical" when they have uncomfortable feelings that may thwart the over-taker from doing what they want to do. But not everyone is a Chet. Many of us can balance compassion for self with compassion for our partner, and thus work things out effectively as a couple.

Solely doing couples work without self-work isn't sufficient either. When one partner has a lot of self-work to do but refuses to do it, an unfair burden lands on their partner.

Remember this model from the beginning of this book? To set yourself up for success within non-monogamy, your investment and connection to 1) yourself, 2) your partner(s), and 3) your community must be present and strong. When you feel emotionally connected and in tune in these three areas, your relationship will be far more likely to thrive.

So yes, it's important to know that you are responsible for your own happiness. And we should all have an ethic of coming from a place of love, compassion, and empathy for our partner—always. Or at least as much as possible. We should seek support from community when need be. Then we may reach a place of fulfillment, connection, and contentment within ourselves, our relationship, and our community.

Chapter Eight

STARTING ON
THE RIGHT FOOT

As you begin your non-monogamous journey, your first steps should be chosen wisely. Setting yourself up for success will build confidence that you and your partner(s) can do this. Key components of starting off well include your speed of entry, transparency, and healthy boundaries. Let's talk each in turn.

Adjusting Speed of Entry

In Chapter 6, we discussed how the speed of a non-monogamous relationship can impact relationship stability. Specifically, through the example of Crystal and Tasha, we saw how speed can lead to one partner's overwhelm.

Couples who are at an equal level of exuberance as they consider non-monogamy are a rarity in my office. When Bruce and Victor walked into my office, for example, Victor was grinning from ear to ear while Bruce, though polite, was clearly stormy and pensive. As I fleshed out the work I do with couples, Victor's smile glowed brighter; Bruce's brows, meanwhile, just furrowed even more.

"I just don't know," Bruce said. "I'm afraid that if we explore non-monogamy, I'll lose Victor. I don't even know if I'm wired that way. I'm happy just the way we are, but I love Victor and I know he feels trapped. For him, I'm willing to explore this, but it's really hard for me."

Victor's smile crumbled.

In their eight years together, they had always been monogamous. They had two children and had an ideal life in many ways. Bruce was the breadwinner, working long hours in the entertainment industry. Victor stayed at home with their children, ages five and seven. They had many shared friends, but Victor often felt trapped. Back before they became fathers, Victor had been part of an art community and led an actively pansexual existence. Now his days were spent at home, except for when they were able to hire a babysitter to see mutual friends. Victor craved Victor time. He also missed having other partners. This left Bruce feeling underappreciated.

"I work so hard for our family," Bruce said, "but clearly it's not enough. I can't keep up with Victor and all his new ideas."

Going at the pace of the more fearful or uncomfortable partner is a guideline and not a rigid rule. It doesn't mean that the more uncomfortable partner should always be catered to over the other partner. It does mean, however, that the fearful partner's feelings need to be unpacked. Once they're defined, the fears can be validated with compassion even as a distinction between real fears and unwarranted fears or distorted thinking is made. As a sense of safety is cultivated, the more fearful partner often gains steam and is able to either experience adventures or hear requests with less anxiety.

In our second session, Victor launched in. He had recently heard about a naked pool party that happened on a monthly basis. He explained that he had asked Bruce if he would be willing to go as they drove to their therapy session. He went on to say that he was so excited about it but then felt so deflated when he saw Bruce's reaction.

Now I knew why Bruce had looked so unhappy when he walked through my office door.

"This is overwhelming," Bruce said. "It feels like too much. But what are my options? I don't want to lose Victor. Maybe I should just force myself to go." His body posture collapsed as he brooded.

I jumped in. "The naked pool party sounds fun. And maybe one day, Victor, Bruce will be the one dragging you out of the house to go—but perhaps this isn't the best starting point. Instead, maybe both of you could listen to a talk on non-monogamy." I told them about an upcoming talk by Tristan Taormino regarding opening up a relationship. "She's a wonderful speaker and knows the topic both professionally and personally. Afterward, you two can walk to the bar across the street and talk about what you experienced over a drink. How does that sound?"

Bruce brightened. "I could do that! I'm totally down for that."

Victor smiled. They had taken their first step.

Emotional Processing Speed

Down the road, Bruce and Victor realized that fear of the unknown was not the only thing creating dissonance in their new non-monogamy. They also had very different emotional processing speeds. That may not sound like a big deal, but this one is a doozie when it comes to non-monogamy; it's a relationship dissonance that can be at the root of many fights within open relationships.

Emotional processing involves your whole compass: thoughts, feelings, and somatic reactions. We all experience somatic changes in our bodies—tension, breathing, heart rate—in both stressful and exciting situations. Our ability to track our somatic changes helps us home in on our true feelings, whether they are happiness, lust, bliss, sadness, or anger. Our somatic and emotional reactions engage our mind, which in turn attempts to make sense of what we are feeling and sensing. Ideally, this process allows us to make logical and healthy decisions.

Speed of emotional processing simply refers to how long this process takes. And it doesn't count if you are moving around and not through your feelings, as so many of us are guilty of doing.

An event requiring emotional processing could be as difficult as the death of a loved one, but in the context of this book, it's more likely a new experience or challenge within your non-monogamous relationship.

Imagine you are the Mario Andretti of emotional processing: you can experience a new lover, party, or adventure and zoom through your emotional experience, ready for the next thing. Now imagine that your partner takes much more time than you to do this. The speed demon within such a pairing often becomes frustrated and resentful in short order. Meanwhile, the slow processor may feel guilt, anxiety, and confusion, all of which can lead to self-criticism. Their guilt may lead to thoughts such as, *I'm holding my partner back. I feel horrible. I wish I was better at this.* Their anxiety may fuel thoughts such as, *I'm freaking out. I can't sleep. I just spin on my thoughts.* Thought blocking or confusion can lead to thoughts such as, *My brain feels fuzzed over; I can't think and I don't know what I want,* or self-criticism, such as, *I'm not good at non-monogamy. I'm failing.*

The fast processor may come off as a bully at times. The slow processor, meanwhile, may be perceived as passive-aggressive, subtly sabotaging any steps forward within non-monogamy. It may be that neither is true. The truth may be that both parties are doing the best they can—full of good intentions and trying to live with integrity.

So what can be done in this situation? First, insight is powerful. A game-changing insight is a simple one: *We are operating on different speeds.* The second necessary insight is: *Catastrophizing is inaccurate, unhelpful, and dysregulating.*

In the case of Victor and Bruce, Victor needed to realize that the safer Bruce felt, the faster they could both move through their emotions and get to the fun, adventurous stuff. Being patient, calm, and nurturing always helps.

Meanwhile, Bruce needed to avoid taking advantage of Victor's patience. A wise, Yoda-like therapist once said to me, "Confusion is a defense. Decisions will never be made while frozen in confusion." The takeaway here is that being slow is fine, but being frozen is not. It's not healthy for you. It's not good for your relationship. If you find yourself spinning on emotions, consider meditating, talking to non-monogamous identified friends, or seeking out individual or couples therapy.

Your needs are important. So are your partner's. The speed of your non-monogamy will vary, but as a couple you will be best served if you find an in-between speed that is healthy for both of you. Of course, this speed will vary.

Transparency and Boundary Crash and Burns

It seems counterintuitive. Why wouldn't someone be transparent within non-monogamy if they have a partner open to this journey? Surprisingly, a lack of transparency is a common problem and typically plays out in the form of:

- A partner in the midst of an infidelity who thinks that non-monogamy is the golden solution that will allow them to keep both partners.
- A partner who decides to research non-monogamy on the sly before introducing the idea to their partner. They may even go as far as choosing another partner. When they disclose their interest in non-monogamy, this introductory conversation is comingled with their potential lover that they would like to proceed with.
- A couple who discusses playing separately but one partner hides information about the new lover they choose— for instance, the fact that the new lover is a coworker or friend, or someone who identifies as monogamous.

In all of these cases, the lack of transparency, coupled with poor boundaries, creates a powder keg. Healthy boundaries within a non-monogamous relationship are especially important when you're new at it and don't know what you're doing. If you choose an additional lover with whom setting certain boundaries is difficult to impossible, the chance for pain is amplified.

A perfect example of this is a coworker. Your partner cannot ask that you only see the other partner once a week if you work with that other lover five days a week. This dynamic often leaves the original partner feeling disempowered and upset.

And of course, asking your partner to open up the relationship at the same time you disclose that you have been having an affair is a double whammy that does not bode well for your relationship—especially if you would like your affair partner to be your other lover within non-monogamy. This double punch of poor boundaries and deception will likely leave your partner so overwhelmed, blindsided, and traumatized that opening up the relationship will lead to a crash and burn.

Here are some ways you might make the journey easier:

1. Choose your first partner(s) wisely

When you are new to non-monogamy, you are like a little baby falling on your butt and on your face. Why choose another newbie to hold you up? They can't. They haven't learned how. Entering the world of non-monogamy can be likened to entering a new and foreign culture. So why not find a seasoned non-monogamous partner or couple who would like to share their knowledge, their mistakes, what they have loved, what they have hated? You need not reinvent the wheel. There are other people who have made mistakes that you can learn from.

Many non-monogamous people love to share their knowledge and will enjoy bringing you into the fold. However, sometimes seasoned non-monogamous people steer clear of the newly non-monogamous because newbies are notorious for causing drama, since they have not yet learned how to manage their feelings within non-monogamy or clarify what their limits and boundaries are.

Those who have been non-monogamous for some time are more likely to know how to be respectful to you and your partner, which will reduce your chances of running into ego-driven competitiveness from someone who hasn't learned how to share nicely.

In the beginning, while you're still learning, avoid choosing a lover who has always identified as monogamous until meeting you. Someone who is used to looking through a monogamous lens will not understand the etiquette and intention behind non-monogamy. And their ignorance can have a dire impact on your relationship.

Consider Chelsea and Howard, who had been married for eight years and had two gorgeous children, an amazing house, and a picture-perfect life. Recently, they'd decided to open up. Howard found a few girlfriends to have light, fun relationships with. Chelsea tried that and just didn't find it satisfying. Then, one night out at a bar with girlfriends, she met Roman, a dark, handsome man with captivating exotic features to whom she felt incredibly attracted. They exchanged numbers.

The next day, she told Howard about Roman. Howard just wanted Chelsea to be happy, and he trusted her, so he gave her the go-ahead to move forward with Roman. What Chelsea didn't tell Howard was that Roman had never been non-monogamous—and Howard didn't know to ask, new as he was to non-monogamy.

Chelsea had three scorching hot dates with Roman, and on the third date, after an incredibly passionate lovemaking session, he said breathlessly in her ear, "Your husband doesn't love you. If he loved you, he wouldn't let other men have you." He told her that she should be with him and him alone, that she would be his everything. "I will cherish you in a way that you have never known," he promised. "I love you."

Chelsea, brimming over with new relationship energy, thought to herself, *I've never felt like this. I feel so alive.* She thought of her life with Howard and all of a sudden it felt so stagnant, so routine.

One month later, she asked Howard for a separation.

What went wrong? One, Roman's monogamous lens drew him to wildly incorrect conclusions. Howard, in fact, *did* love Chelsea—so completely that he trusted her even with something she had not learned to manage. He didn't know that she'd been feeling stuck in her life or that Roman had entered into the mix when she was the most vulnerable.

Could something similar have happened if Chelsea had chosen a man who had identified as non-monogamous for years? Sure. But non-monogamy is playing with fire, and the aim is to keep it contained. Choosing an already non-monogamous man would have been one more safety valve; it would have heightened the chance that he would understand Howard's point of view, respect him, and honor the greatest gift Howard could give: trusting him with the woman he loved.

2. Choose your first setting wisely

Depending on whether you are an extrovert or an introvert, your ideal setting will vary. What makes one person completely nervous and on edge is another person's slice of heaven.

To figure out what's best for you, ask yourself a couple of questions. Are you a highly sensitive person who is impacted by the five senses in addition to your emotional environment? For instance, is a department store with blaring fluorescent lights, an overhead loudspeaker, and people bumping their carts into you a special kind of hell for you? If your answer is even a maybe, then you should probably steer away from a full-tilt play party for some time. A dinner with a couple or an individual for a chemistry check date will be much less overwhelming and more controlled, and make for less emotional drama.

On the flip side, are you overwhelmed by deeper conversations and opportunities for emotional closeness? If so, you might feel more relaxed in a party setting. House parties, gatherings at bars, and hotel takeovers might all be your happy place.

When choosing your first settings, knowing yourself well is key. Especially when you are new at non-monogamy, choosing a setting that is comfortable for you will set you up for success. Starting on the right foot is an important way to build confidence.

Chapter Nine

BREAKING DOWN CULTURAL PROGRAMMING

Cultural norms are like our heartbeat: ever-present and often unnoticed. What we don't notice, we don't question. However, I invite you to grab the horns of your self-awareness. Steer your own course, starting now.

Society tells us that if our partner truly loves us, they won't want another sexual partner—won't love anyone but us—and that we are all destined for our perfect attunement, our one true soul mate. Ahem. If this were true, Ashley Madison wouldn't have close to sixty million members. The notion that if our partner loves us, they won't love or want another—or, similarly, that if we truly love our partner we won't love or want another—is heavily woven into the fabric of our culture.

Now let's consider what these culturally imposed belief systems do to us. When our partner has an affair, we think to ourselves, *I failed them as a lover, I'm not enough*, or *They never loved me*. All of these thoughts cripple our self-esteem, incapacitate our ability to take action, and create soul-crushing jealousy.

From the time we are old enough to be influenced by our environment, our cultural, religious, and family norms begin to shape us. These norms tell us who we should be and how we should act. One dear and wise friend once told me that as adults, our healing journey is remembering who we were as little children. This resonates for me. What is your personal truth, separate from what has been programmed into you? Many of us have been told that we should look for our "forever person," get married, and be with this one person until one of us dies. But what if you simply are not wired for monogamy? What might this plan ultimately do to a person's self-esteem if they repeatedly fail at monogamy simply because it's not part of who they are?

Let's take a look at Cyan. In our first session, she disclosed that she had always been a cheater. "I'm just worried that I'm a bad person," she said. "Why can't I just be satisfied with one man?"

She went on to say that she'd grown up in a restrictive and tight-knit religious community that had made it clear that, as a woman, if you wanted more than the missionary position with your husband, you were bad. Sexuality outside of a monogamous marriage was seen as sinful, and free thought was considered baiting the devil.

"Recently, I realized that I just can't be in my marriage anymore, and I asked for a divorce. I know it's the right choice. He's my best friend, but we need different things from life. I know I'm doing the right thing, but I still hate myself for all the times I betrayed him. And he would hate me if he knew."

This deep self-loathing is a common by-product of our monogamous culture. It's not uncommon for a couple to redesign their relationship to something less rigid and discover that infidelity becomes a problem of the past. But the transition isn't easy. Books like *Sex at Dawn* tend to crack open the psyche and allow the mind to open, but a person who's new to the idea of non-monogamy will often swirl in confusion in the beginning, fearing whether it's ethically right and "good" to pursue this path.

The first thing I attempt to do for a client like this is to separate shame from guilt. I explained to Cyan that she was not a bad *person*. She did, however, have some bad *behaviors*: she'd broken her relationship agreement. But I reassured her that this is a common thing that people do, and I invited her to have compassion for herself. "You can't change the past, but you can learn from it," I said.

"How?" she asked. "I don't know what to do."

"You need to begin by clarifying a relationship model that is in keeping with your true nature, one that you can adhere to," I explained. "Finding this truth will take educating yourself, along with trial, error, and revision. But as you step out of your current confusion and begin to discover and accept a relationship model that is a better fit for you, that model will be more likely to set you up for success. Once you begin to date again and form new relationships, this model will be a work in progress with any current or new partners. This model is not carved in stone; rather, it is fluid and will shift whenever revisions are made."

Cyan's mouth dropped open. "Wow."

In the next weeks and months, she read books on non-monogamy. She went to sex-positive and poly meet-ups. As she met people who were successfully non-monogamous, her old cultural norms began to break down. She connected to a new community of non-monogamous friends—a community that allowed her to let go of the components of her cultural backstory that did not serve her.

I encouraged her not to "throw the baby out with the bathwater" regarding her restrictive religious upbringing, but rather to notice what aspects of her culture she wanted to discard and what she wanted to keep.

"One thing I know I want to keep is my love of community," she said, lighting up. "I loved that about my childhood, and I want to rebuild that sense of community." Within a few weeks of connecting with her new community, she felt she was already on her way.

A couple months into therapy, I asked her, "How do you feel about yourself right now?"

"I've never liked myself more," she shared. "I feel alive. I've never felt so hopeful, excited, and happy."

Once a person steps into a more authentic life, they often discard the shame inherent in believing that they are bad. They realize that they no longer need to fear a future filled with ethical failures. As we embrace a life that is suited to our true nature, kindred spirits find us, opportunities come to us, and life gets better. This blossoming self-esteem brings excitement and hope for the future.

Fluidity and Identity

As we open to non-monogamy, we often blossom in other ways too, including gender fluidity and identity. We may begin to play around with our dress, method of seduction, and more. With this process, we might connect to feminine energy or switch to masculine energy or even feel agender, depending on the moment. We all have masculine and feminine energy within us. Allowing this authenticity within ourselves and others is part of loving well and is part of opening deeply.

Some of the sexiest and most confident people I know embrace both what is deemed masculine and feminine. They optimize both energies. And isn't it advantageous to explore both? How will you know your authentic truth and become well-balanced if you don't?

In addition, the non-monogamous exploration process, which often exposes the journeyer to unique sexual situations and sexually open-minded people, may also be a catalyst that encourages sexual fluidity and a reevaluation of sexual orientation and identity; a person might go from being heterosexual to bisexual to pansexual. For others, of course, sexual orientation won't change a bit. However, breaking down rigidity around one's relationship model can lead to a reevaluation of other areas of your life. Don't be shocked if this happens to you. It's common and often just part of the journey.

And finally, the non-monogamous journey often leads to relationship fluidity. I invite you to let go of the notion that you will always be monogamous or non-monogamous. Or that someone in your life will always play the same role in your life (friend, lover, spouse). A person might identify as non-monogamous but be monogamous in practice for finite periods of time—when a baby is born or when a partner is in graduate school or has an illness, for example.

Breaking down relationship rigidity can result in having a friend turn into a lover and back to a friend again, and then later to a spouse. Allowing this fluidity in our relationship with any given person can allow relationships to be healthier, richer, and more resilient. It ups the chance that such a person will be in your life ten years or twenty years later.

So if you find that you are shifting in terms of gender, sexual, or relational fluidity, I invite you to embrace these shifts. A more complex and authentic version of yourself is emerging, and that's beautiful. These changes may be scary, but growth often is. Lean into discovering your truth.

Polynormativity Concerns

Polynormativity, as portrayed in the media, features a hetero, cis couple—cute, young, and white—who takes on a girlfriend. Typically, they have a hierarchy, along with a lot of relationship rules and boundaries. This stereotype can lead people to believe that non-monogamy can only look a certain way and that only certain people are welcome within its bounds. However, the reality is that there is much more diversity in the non-monogamous sphere than this. With this in mind, let's address the concerns of two diverse groups that also practice non-monogamy: those who identify as transgender or genderqueer and people of color.

Non-monogamous people who are transgender or genderqueer

The queer community is a hotbed of non-monogamy. Regarding the question of joining largely cis, non-monogamous communities and associated parties, however, some genderqueer or transgender people report feeling excluded, while others say they have felt fetishized or dehumanized by cis partners. Still others have felt demeaned by people's ignorance related to gender identity and transgender physiology, which can dampen the joy of connecting to potential partners. Consequently, many have chosen to exist in genderqueer and trans polycules, where they report being treated with more dignity.

This is a call to action. If you are cisgender, please take the time to learn how to be considerate of genderqueer and transgender people. Learn how to respect others' pronouns. And by all means, avoid fetishizing. Non-monogamous communities should be safe bastions of sex positivity and gender exploration. No one should feel excluded due to their gender identity or expression.

Non-monogamous people of color

People of color have expressed similar issues and concerns to those raised by genderqueer and trans non-monogamous folks. Some report feeling fetishized or unwelcome in predominantly white non-monogamous communities. They have expressed to me that often they are the only non-white people in the room, and that at some events they've sensed a racist vibe. When I've asked what might help create more diversity and inclusion at parties, the most frequent answer I've received is, "More people of color need to be party promoters and included in the organization of events." In the absence of this shift, the predominant choice among folks I've spoken to is to attend parties or form polycules exclusively composed of people of color.

Obviously, people of color are not a monolith, and experiences vary. Regardless, there is much room for improvement.

The larger white, cis non-monogamous community needs to be consciously inclusive. Only when white non-monogamous people are willing to do outreach and have uncomfortable conversations will change take place. From there, we could have a much more diverse and wonderful community.

Feminine Norms and Concerns

Those who identify as women struggle with their own culturally imposed fears when considering and exploring non-monogamy. One heavy hitter is the fear of being labeled a slut. The good news is that slut-shaming is less frequent within the non-monogamous community, and those who are not non-monogamous won't know unless you tell them. However, this is something to think through in advance.

Another concern women often voice is, "Will I be safe?" Regardless of gender, the fear of physical boundaries being disrespected is common. Clients sometimes ask me, "If I go to a play party, will people just touch me? Will I be expected to have sex?" Women-identified clients are typically more fearful of having their physical boundaries violated.

The more you vet the settings you are attending (and the attendees themselves), the safer you will be and feel. Vetting can be increased by asking seasoned non-monogamous couples which parties they think are the safest. Some swing lifestyle parties are online with RSVP'd couples listed. If this is the case, you can often click on their profile and see what others have said about them—get a sense of whether they're viewed as respectful. Putting safety measures in place, like periodic check-ins, with a friend or partner is another way to feel safe. And while this may be a lot to ask, staying sober, especially when you are new, is a great way to keep your awareness acute so you can notice if someone's behavior is off. Finally, the more trustworthy your adventure buddy is, the more your chances of safety improve.

Entertaining the prospect of non-monogamy can be overwhelming. Many women fear being disrespected. However, women usually report to me that they feel much safer within non-monogamous communities. They tell me that consent and boundaries are more readily discussed and honored there than they are outside of non-monogamous circles. This, especially when one is initially connecting to non-monogamous communities, can be healing. It can be a corrective experience to feel so safe while being unabashedly flirty or, perhaps, scantily clad.

With all this said, there are exceptions to this experience of feeling safer within non-monogamous settings, and you do need to cultivate a strong assertive voice when entering into non-monogamy. It should also be noted that as non-monogamous and kink communities have gone more mainstream, there has been a greater influx of those who don't know or don't respect non-monogamous rules and boundaries. So please, keep your radar up, vet your setting and partners as well as possible, and create guidelines with your partner or date to keep both of you safe.

Masculine Norms and Concerns: Can I Be a Noble Slut?

Those who identify as men often feel they have two options in terms of sexuality and gender. Behind door number one is the asshole who gets laid a lot and isn't respectful of women's boundaries. Behind door number two is the nice, honorable guy who has a lot of platonic girlfriends but little sex, and who certainly would never consider non-monogamy. I'm here to tell you that there's a third door. You can be a noble slut. And this is something available to all gender expressions. That said, I'm addressing a particular male struggle. Men will say to me, "If I allow myself to go down that rabbit hole of having many lovers, I'm afraid of what I'll become. I'm afraid that I won't treat women well. I'm afraid that I'll become a creep or an asshole with an out-of-control ego. I don't want to be *that guy.*"

Where do these fears of lack of control come from? I believe they are culturally programmed in. Despite the fact that a man who has many lovers is applauded in our culture, many men who don't want to be part of the problem choose the opposite extreme. It's not shocking that they aren't happy there.

In the brilliant documentary *The Mask You Live In,* this damaging process is explained in great detail. If a boy is sad and seeks comfort from a parent or mentor, too often they are told to "be a man" or that "boys don't cry." By age thirteen, words that are deemed "feminine," such as compassion and empathy, drop out of boys' vocabulary. It's at this point that the suicide rate for boys skyrockets. Even worse, this emotional neglect, for many boys, is coupled with entitlement. Society tells them, "You are a man. Take what is rightfully yours."

Men who are aware of negative cultural programming often fear that their sexual authenticity will reveal that they're a creep. And what price do men pay for internalizing this toxic message? A massive one: their sexual truth. When a man suppresses his sexuality for fear that he's a monster, he never learns to control his urges. He never truly learns who he is. He doesn't learn how to kindly and ethically gets his needs met. And he never learns how to talk about sex with his partner. All of these deficits can fuel the fear and associated message that men are unable to sexually control themselves or are monsters.

So how can a man embrace his inner noble slut? The first step is a man realizing that he can, in fact, drop into his primal, sexual masculinity without losing ethical control. The second step is committing to lead with honesty and transparency. The noble non-monogamous slut starts, out of the gate, with truth. On his dating site profile, he admits to being non-monogamous. If dating, he discloses non-monogamous dynamics. The partners he has are not in the dark regarding one another. If he sleeps with someone, even if he isn't interested in pursuing something further, he doesn't ghost them the next day; instead, he sends a thank-you text for the date. These higher levels of transparency, courtesy, and kindness are the building blocks for constructing solid non-monogamy and a cultivated noble slut.

Consciously breaking down cultural programming is difficult work, but it's worth it. Through this work, you will likely crack through layers of programming that block you from finding your authenticity and happiness. It's a large part of finding your truth regarding non-monogamy and so much more.

Chapter Ten

ATTACHMENT THEORY'S CRUCIAL ROLE IN NON-MONOGAMY

Understanding the basics of attachment theory will support your non-monogamy. Why? Because non-monogamy pokes at our attachment injuries way more than monogamy ever could.

An attachment injury can occur when there is an abandonment or a betrayal of trust during a critical moment of need. It can also occur when needs for comfort, closeness, and security are not adequately met. Its worst form is abuse and neglect from someone who is supposed be loving, protecting, and nurturing. Childhood attachment injuries are usually the most psychologically damaging, since we are so vulnerable and dependent on others in our early years.

Attachment Styles

By adulthood, our attachment experiences, both good and bad, have shaped us. These experiences influence the way we attach in our adult relationships and thus become our attachment style. Our attachment style can shift over the course of our life—especially if we work on ourselves or are impacted by later-life experiences—for good or bad.

These styles are a reflection of our feelings of security, the personal meaning given to our relationship experiences, and our ability to develop and maintain intimacy with others. According to Dr. Diane Poole Heller, there are four main attachment styles in adulthood: secure, ambivalent, avoidant, and disorganized.

Secure attachment

Securely attached adults were raised in a consistent, reliable, and caring way. They benefited from a parenting style that taught them the world is a safe and accessible place, and thus they regard people as generally dependable and supportive. Such children grow into adults who feel able to love, and to feel lovable. They are compassionate and responsive to others. They are flexible thinkers, able to explore options and ask for advice. They are accepting of differences and trusting in love.

Because of this security, this type of person often finds non-monogamy easier. They have less fear that they will be betrayed, or that their partner will leave them for someone else. If their partner does leave them for someone else, they still know that they are lovable and will find love again. They tend to be calmer during tough discussions regarding non-monogamy because they don't have an underlying fear that they will be left or betrayed. And because their nervous system tends to be calmer, their thinking during an uncomfortable discussion regarding non-monogamy tends to stay clear and flexible—a mindset that allows for an exploration of options within relationship agreements and allows for a higher chance that all parties involved in these types of negotiations will end up happy with the decisions made.

Ambivalent attachment

Caregivers who are inconsistent in their attention and attunement often cultivate anxiously attached children. Such parents might be nurturing and attuned and respond effectively to their child's distress part of the time, and then they'll be intrusive, insensitive, or emotionally unavailable at other times. When parents vacillate between these very different responses, their children become confused and insecure, not knowing what kind of treatment to expect. These children often feel distrustful or suspicious of their parent(s) and thus act clingy and desperate. They learn that the best way to get their needs met is to cling to their attachment figure, thus cultivating a preoccupied state of mind with respect to attachment.

In adulthood, this attachment style often gives up their own self-care needs to please and accommodate their partner. Furthermore, they often do not speak up or assert either self-care boundaries or needs as often as they should. This loss of voice leads them to all sorts of problems within non-monogamy, such as agreeing to things they don't really want and enduring things that aren't truly working for them. Such a person is often preoccupied with the relationship and highly attuned to their partner, which leads them to do too much emotional labor within the relationship.

In non-monogamous relationships, this style often tries to be "good poly." When their partner voices a non-monogamous desire, they are more likely to overextend themself and say "yes" when their answer is really "maybe" or "no." When their partner has a new partner or there is a change in the non-monogamous agreement, this style is more likely to fear the change will have a detrimental impact on the relationship and might become a hoover pilot—hypervigilant and scanning for danger or threat.

If an ambivalent attachment style person falls in love with a secure partner, they may experience anxiety or even withdraw from their partner's consistent love if they have not yet gained the positive affect tolerance for such steady love. But if this person learns to lean in and build a tolerance for being loved well, they can slowly heal. Within non-monogamy, ambivalent attachment types may find that having more than one partner can create an extended security net. Furthermore, connecting to good, solid people within the non-monogamous community can give them the security and con-sistency they might not have gotten as children.

Avoidant attachment

People with an avoidant attachment tend to have been raised by parents who were frequently emotionally unavailable or unrespon-sive to them. As children, these people were disregarded or ignored, and perhaps especially rejected when hurt or sick. In adulthood, this attachment style avoids intimacy and close affective involvements. When faced with threats of separation or loss, they are able to focus their attention on other issues and goals. They tend to withdraw and attempt to cope with the threat of loss in a solitary manner. It's also common for this type of person to deny their vulnerability and use repression to manage emotions that activate their attachment needs. Avoidant adults are uncomfortable with closeness and intimacy. They are emotionally distant and uncomfortable expressing needs or asking for help. They avoid conflict and tend to be passive-aggres-sive. They don't want to rely on anyone, fearing dependency.

In a non-monogamous relationship, this style can be great when the relationship is light or new. However, the relationship can take a brutal turn when love deepens. This style is at its worst when their partner feels, angry, hurt, or betrayed by the avoidant: instead of providing empathy, the avoidant often shuts down emotionally, withdraws, and goes silent. This withdrawal and refusal to give com-fort is often more traumatizing than the initial injury.

If you are in love with an avoidant, know that yelling louder or nagging more will not stop the emotional withdrawal; it will only make it worse. In a love relationship, your job is to move back and make room for them emotionally, and their job is to attempt to come forward emotionally. Both parties have to be on board and do this work—but if you are and do, you may succeed in breaking old, harmful patterns.

In her book *Hold Me Tight*, Sue Johnson is all about breaking the pursuer/withdrawer dynamic. Pursuers need to become more responsible for themselves and distancers more responsible to their partners. The result is a more secure, interdependent relationship. Such a partnership is much healthier than either a codependent relationship or solitude with a false sense of self-sufficiency.

If your avoidant refuses to own their issues and work on themselves, I advise you to keep the relationship light or avoid making them your primary or nesting partner. If less is expected of them, they are less likely to get triggered by closeness and intimacy—and thus less likely to play out their childhood pain with you.

Disorganized attachment

Parents or caregivers of this type are often abusive (sexually, emotionally, or physically), neglectful, abandoning, and inconsistent. Consequently, their children learn that the parent, who they love and who is responsible for their safety, is also someone to fear. Disorganized adults often run very hot and cold in relationships. They're afraid of genuine closeness and see themselves as unworthy of love and support. Many lack empathy or remorse. If left bereft of healing modalities, they may be selfish and controlling, refuse to take personal responsibility for their actions, and disregard rules. Their experience of severe attachment trauma makes emotional, social, and moral problems more difficult for them to navigate.

If you see yourself in this style, then life probably gets painful for you. You may have a long healing journey ahead of you. The first step is to read the following two sentences more than once: *I am not bad. Bad things happened to me.*

Repeat.

I am not bad. Bad things happened to me.

The next step is to take responsibility for your present life and your part in the dynamics of your existing relationships. Practices of meditation, mindfulness, yoga, and running can reduce PTSD symptoms and calm the nervous system. Therapy modalities such as EMDR and somatic psychotherapy can help heal profound attachment injuries caused by abuse and neglect. All of this work will lead to a more grounded you who will be more capable of navigating life and loving well.

If you are in a non-monogamous relationship with someone with a disorganized attachment style, your experience will be dramatic, to say the least, and more than likely painful. If you have a secure attachment style, your unflappable nature will be calming to them. However, even an oak tree with deep roots will take some damage in a tsunami. Your own self-care is crucial.

Attachment Injuries

The common theme throughout the last three attachment styles we just discussed is the impact of attachment injuries on the human psyche. Attachment injuries are the biggest hindrance to deep intimacy between two people—and profound attachment injuries are trauma. When I say "trauma," I'm primarily talking about past histories of abuse (physical, emotional, or sexual) or neglect. Neglect can be just as damaging as abuse, and need not be as obvious as leaving one's child starving. Often, the neglectful parent simply isn't physically or emotionally present enough to protect their child from potential threats. Trauma can also include loss, such as death, abandonment, or divorce. Past, unresolved trauma not only impacts how we connect in a relationship but also has a heavy impact on our ability to cope within non-monogamy.

We all have some level of attachment injuries and/or trauma. This does not mean we'll all fail at non-monogamy. What it does mean is that part of our responsibility is to be aware of our own tender underbelly, as well as our partner's. One indicator that our attachment injuries are being triggered is if we have a response that seems bigger than what is appropriate for the situation. When we are triggered, we may become incredibly elevated—get angry or anxious, or yell. Or, in contrast, we may shut down, dissociate, become numb, withdraw, or check out.

Let's talk about two specific attachment injuries that greatly impact non-monogamy: the controlling/engulfing parent or culture, and the abandoning or deceased parent.

The controlling/engulfing parent or culture

If you had an emotionally engulfing and controlling parent, or if you came from a culture that made you feel heavily controlled, you may get triggered by the requests your partner makes in an attempt to get their basic emotional needs met in a non-monogamous relationship. You may see their requests as an attempt to control you.

Such moments will require you to be extra mindful, lest you become reactionary. It will be easy for you to tell yourself that your partner is attempting to manipulate you. But perhaps they are merely expressing true needs. Give them the benefit of the doubt.

Any of the following and more can be emotional need requests: 1) "Please send a check-in text while you are on your date"; 2) "Please don't date that one person who I feel disrespected me"; 3) "I'm not ready for us to play in separate rooms, so please stay with me"; 4) "Please don't take on a third lover—I already don't see you enough."

I could go on forever with examples, but it's not the examples themselves that matter—it's how you react. I'm not asking you to refrain from asserting your own needs if they are counter to your partner's. However, I am asking you to mindfully watch for whether your partner's requests are triggering you—and if they are, I'm suggesting that you take time to calm yourself before you enter into a negotiation or discussion with them.

The abandoning or deceased parent

If you had a parent who died or abandoned you in your childhood, you will likely be triggered when you feel left or abandoned in your non-monogamous relationship. For instance, if your partner shifts their level of focus from you to hunting for non-monogamous events or a new lover, you may feel a jarring emotional spike or you may feel numb, withdrawn, or shut down. Such moments will require you to use all the coping skills in your toolbox, lest you slip into telling yourself that they aren't into you, they are going to leave you, or some other, similar, catastrophizing story.

In Chapter 12, I will discuss triggers, and how to ground yourself and your partner once triggered, at length. For now I'll just say, the bottom line is, it's important to try to exercise compassion for both your own triggers and those of your partner. With your increased awareness will come a heightened ability to track the impact of those triggers.

Healing Attachment Injuries and Rebuilding Trust

Harville Hendrix states in *Getting the Love You Want*, "When you experience trust in a relationship, then you can take back disowned parts and become whole, thus reconnecting to the universe." The power of a trust-filled relationship is a healing experience indeed. In this section we are going to go through three ways to heal old wounds: 1) corrective experiences, 2) a gratitude practice, and 3) building positive affect tolerance.

Corrective experiences

Harville Hendrix states that one reason we choose a particular partner is that they reflect the negative and positive traits of caregivers in our childhood. Now, why would we choose someone who embodies the negative characteristics as well? Why not just the good? Because we are attempting to have a corrective experience—to heal our childhood wounds—with someone who mirrors our childhood as closely as possible. If we are still very traumatized, we will tend to pick someone who mirrors the past too much, a mistake that will lead to retraumatization. But if we have healed a bit, we will be more likely to pick a better partner, or assert boundaries and self-care needs sooner, or at the very least leave a toxic relationship sooner.

Our unresolved attachment injuries and trauma impact our ability to feel safe with partners, and certainly within non-monogamy. People with extreme trauma may choose one person, often their partner, to trust, and if that partner asks to open up the relationship, it can be a completely terrifying and overwhelming request.

As a child, Sarah's alcoholic father was cruel or neglectful when he was drunk, but mostly kind when sober. At age eighteen, she married Corey, who after a year of marriage began cheating, lying, and staying out all night, but was usually kind and attentive when he was at home with her. When she cried, saying, "Why are you treating me this way?" he responded, "Are you being paranoid again? You know I had to work late last night."

Now let's suppose that somehow Sarah got up the strength to leave Corey. She moved to California, got some great therapy, began meditation, mindfulness, and yoga practices, and met some great, supportive friends. She began to heal. In therapy, she realized that Corey had been emotionally abusive like her father. Her therapist helped her to realize that she was drawn to inconsistent men because of her upbringing. She strove to meet a more present, secure man.

Then she met Shaun. Shaun was sometimes moody, but he had worked on himself, like Sarah had. In particular, he had become more even-tempered and empathic toward his loved ones due to his daily meditation practice.

One night, after a couple of years of being together, Sarah and Shaun began to discuss the idea of non-monogamy. Maybe it could be fun? Maybe it could add to their relationship? Sarah launched into a series of fears. She asked, "What if you fall in love with someone else? What if you start hiding things from me? What if you can't tolerate the big emotions that non-monogamy might bring up in me?" This went on for some time, and Shaun did find himself overwhelmed by her anxious energy and a few implications that felt a bit insulting to him. But he also realized that she was a little triggered. Her fears weren't about him; they were about her past getting projected upon him. She was making up stories that fit the narrative of her life.

Due to tools he had learned in his own therapy work, he was able to say, "I need to go for a jog. I love you, but I need to calm down. I'll come back in about an hour, when I feel able to answer your questions from a good place."

Now that, my dear reader, is a corrective experience. Instead of treating Sarah how her dad or Corey had treated her, Shaun made her feel respected and cherished. And yes, waiting that hour was hard for her anxious soul, but before he left he reminded her that he loved her and that he'd come back in an hour, and those two statements made all the difference in the world.

As you travel your own non-monogamous journey, noticing what your partner's default attachment style is, what triggers them, and how you can help them move to a more secure attachment style will be key to your relationship's success.

Gratitude practice

In a new relationship, having a gratitude practice is easy. Most of my clients fall in love with their adventure buddy. They're so grateful that they have found a fun-loving, kindred spirit to romp through life with. Shared adventure is their love language. Many of my clients feel loved when their partner gives them freedom, but also when that same partner shares carefree, life-embracing adventures with them. This adventurous gusto is a big part of what draws them to non-monogamy.

But then, one day, one person has to turn to the other and say, "No, I'm not ready for that. I don't know if I ever will be."

"That" could mean any number of things, such as group sex or playing separately. When the time comes to assert self-care boundaries, a danger zone has been entered. If this moment is not handled well, it can begin a dynamic turn in which the one setting boundaries falls into the role of a fun-blocking, restrictive parent and the one receiving the boundary is pushed into the role of denied, tantruming child—and it's a shift that can happen fast and without conscious awareness.

How does gratitude shift to resentment so quickly? Well, as always, attachment styles and triggers come into play. Your coping skills to combat these difficult moments can join the ball game too, however—specifically, your practice of gratitude for your partner.

Our brain and nervous system were originally wired to keep us alive against threat. These days, most of us are pretty damn safe, but our brain still scans for threat, especially if we have a trauma history. In the modern-day psyche, this often translates to a self-critical mind. And within a relationship, it translates to scanning for what is wrong with our relationship and our partner.

For many of us, this is our default. Therefore, scanning for what we are grateful for in our partner has to be an active commitment and practice. In moments like the one we just talked about, in which Sarah is panicking and scanning for anything that could go wrong in her relationship with Shaun if they become non-monogamous, the relationship will be even more likely to fall into the restrictive parent/tantruming child model if she becomes reactionary and shuts the whole discussion down on a dime. But when we can remind ourselves to be grateful for the fun-loving, adventurous partner we originally fell in love with, we are more likely to keep a grounded prospective as we initially consider non-monogamy.

As we touched on earlier in the book, being adventurous is a trait. The good side of that trait is that such a partner will make life amazingly fun for you. The negative side is that they will sometimes scare the bejesus out of you. I'm merely asking you to remember and have gratitude for the positive side of this trait. In doing so, you will be better equipped to get through tough moments related to non-monogamy.

In *Getting the Love You Want*, Harville Hendrix asserts that one reason people choose a particular partner is because they embody the positive parts of ourselves that got disowned in childhood. "The only way to achieve oneness," he says, "is through rediscovering the positive discarded parts of yourself."

So, how does your partner help you reach your human potential? Why did you originally fall in love with them? Why are you grateful for them? Your consistent gratitude and appreciation will help heal their attachment injuries, thus making them more capable of enjoying the relationship model the two of you have agreed upon.

Positive affect tolerance

Your gratitude practice is part of building positive affect tolerance. Strong positive affect tolerance is another key to healing attachment injuries and being successful at love and non-monogamy. In a broader sense, positive affect tolerance is simply about an individual's ability to tolerate positive feelings.

We all want to feel good, but the harder our backstory, the more feeling love or happiness can be too vulnerable to bear and too risky to allow. We all know someone who sabotages great business opportunities, tosses away a good, kind romantic partner, or blows up previously healthy relationships. There are many reasons that such a person behaves this way, but part of it is low positive affect tolerance. Exposing their heart is too scary.

Lack of positive affect tolerance in a love relationship translates to an inability to tolerate the positive feelings of love. Such a person might pull away, either literally or emotionally, when their partner attempts to show affection.

In a non-monogamous relationship, a person with poor positive affect tolerance may use non-monogamy to create distance rather than enhanced love with their partner(s), leaving the other party feeling lonely or disposable. Building positive affect tolerance is like building a muscle at the gym. On a personal level, it might mean engaging an active practice of gratitude regarding life, simply saying "thank you" to a compliment, or countering a critical thought with positive affirmations.

Within a love relationship, building positive affect tolerance may include cultivating an active gratitude practice for your partner and responding positively to their attempts to connect to you. Renowned couples therapist and researcher John Gottman labels these positive responses to our partner's attempts to connect with us as "turning toward" behaviors. His research revealed that at "a six-year follow up, couples that had stayed married 'turned toward' one another 86% of the time. Couples that had divorced averaged only 33% of the time."

Turning toward your partner's bids for affection or attention simply means responding positively to their attempts to connect to you. Within non-monogamy, this dynamic will be tested constantly. When your partner has a need or a fear related to non-monogamy and voices it, will you provide empathy and validation, or will you discredit them? Will you sit down and listen, or will you stomp out? Will you have patience and compassion, or will you become impatient and frustrated? Your choice will greatly impact whether or not your relationships and your non-monogamous journey have longevity and health. Furthermore, turning toward behaviors are a great way to help heal any remaining attachment injuries in your partner's psyche.

Chapter Eleven

HOW PERSONALITY AND MOOD DISORDERS IMPACT NON-MONOGAMY

Approximately one in five adults in the United States will experience mental illness in any given year. Given this, the chance that someone's psychological suffering, perhaps your own, will impact your non-monogamous relationship is very high. I can't imagine talking about any form of relationship model without looking this bear straight in the eyes. And it should be noted that one need not be diagnosable for psychological unrest to impact a relationship. Because of this fact, this chapter addresses personality and mood disorders through the lens of symptoms and traits rather than diagnoses.

First, let's talk about symptoms related to two of the personality disorders I've seen impact non-monogamy the most: narcissistic and borderline personality disorders.

Narcissism Defined

Narcissistic personality disorder (NPD) is a mental disorder in which people have entitlement, grandiosity, a deep need for admiration, and a lack of empathy for others. But behind this mask of ultra-confidence lies a fragile self-esteem that's vulnerable to the slightest criticism. Based on psychologist Elinor Greenberg's research on narcissistic disorders, in terms of attachment injuries, narcissists often come from families who focus on winning at all costs with the continual threat of devaluation, and who do not teach, give, or reward empathy. Thus, the child never develops a healthy sense of self. The child's worth is only as good as their last performance.

People with narcissistic traits are often "over-takers" with an avoidant attachment style. They often dominate the relationship, greedily holding ownership of the metaphorical talking stick while denying their partner consistent love or a voice in the relationship. Often, they emotionally deplete their partners, sometimes to the point of emotional instability.

Over-takers almost always date "over-givers." Over-givers give to the point of forfeiting self-care, enmeshed and hyper-focused on the over-taker, thus creating a codependent relationship. Although people of any gender can be over-givers as a result of attachment injuries, our patriarchal society overwhelmingly conditions women to be over-givers.

How narcissistic symptoms impact non-monogamy

I am a recovering over-giver. A lot of therapists, nurses, and healers tend to be over-givers in their private lives.

Here's a metaphor for the over-taker/over-giver dynamic: The over-giver attempts to walk across a desert barefoot for ten miles to bring the over-taker a glass of water. In the ninth mile, due to sunburn, bloody feet, heat exposure, and dehydration, the over-giver falls, unable to complete the task. The over-giver, crestfallen, feels like a bad person, a selfish failure. The over-taker agrees wholeheartedly, escalating how badly the over-giver already feels about themselves.

The over-giver's psyche can be likened to someone with body dysmorphia—but instead of a distorted body image, they have a distorted sense of self, often seeing themself as selfish. They give until they deplete themselves emotionally just as the anorexic depletes themself nutritionally.

Despite their self-sacrificing nature, the over-giver will at times assert themself. At this point, the over-taker usually employs a response called gaslighting. If the over-giver says they feel abused by the over-taker, the fault or responsibility will be switched back onto the over-giver with a fair share of wrath. Gaslighting can include remarks on the over-giver's emotional "issues" and displacing blame of abuse as the over-giver's fault. After an over-taker has an abusive tantrum, they will frequently use defenses such as, "You provoked me," "You're too sensitive," "I never said that," or "You're taking things too seriously" to gaslight the over-giver into thinking that the abuse is indeed their fault, or that it never even took place. And since the over-giver's psyche often believes that they fail at giving enough, they can be easy to manipulate.

Now let's imagine how couples with this dynamic going on engage with non-monogamy. You might be thinking, *Well, they don't. It must be a complete crash and burn.* But you'd be surprised. This brand of horrible dysfunction can continue in both monogamous and non-monogamous couples for decades. The injuries become greater in non-monogamy, however, because there's a candy store involved. The over-taker is always asking for more lovers, more experiences, more, more, more.

Why does the over-giver have such a hard time asserting themself or setting a self-care limit? That runs deep. They believe that if they assert themself, their identity will be shifted into something intolerable—that it will make them: 1) a nag, 2) bad at poly, 3) a controlling jerk, or 4) a selfish failure. They would rather fall on their sword and give until an emotional breakdown ensues than become any of these things. Of course, with this psychological makeup they are a lamb to the slaughter, completely vulnerable to the over-taker's whims.

It should be noted that those with narcissistic tendencies rarely go to therapy or seek help of any kind. Why? Because their behavior is ego-syntonic. In other words, they don't think anything is wrong with them. As I have become a bolder therapist, I have been able to break down grandiosity and self-entitlement and build empathy with the rare narcissist who is willing to emotionally grow, but it's tough.

Over-givers, meanwhile, are generally much more willing and able to heal because they want to break patterns, which leads to a much better future. There is a ton of hope for them. For me, once I realized that I was an over-giver, I began to take steps to change my patterns. Soon, my physical health got better, my girlfriends became closer because I was no longer ashamed to disclose the intimate details of my life, and my mental health improved. I literally felt ten years younger over the course of a year.

For the over-givers out there, I say to you, it is *so* important that you assert yourself. You are not bad for taking care of yourself. You are not selfish if you look out for your own emotional health—in fact, in the long run, your relationship will be healthier if you do. Oh! And if an over-taker walks away because you valued yourself, well, that's the sifting process, darlin'.

Borderline Defined

Borderline personality disorder (BPD) is a condition characterized by difficulties regulating emotion. Typical symptoms include frantic efforts to avoid real or imagined abandonment by friends and family. It's typical for those with BPD to have an insecure attachment style with unstable personal relationships that alternate between idealization and devaluation. In terms of attachment injuries, they often have childhoods filled with abuse and neglect, unstable parenting, and abandonment.

Most often, an individual with BPD intensely wants and fears the same thing: love. Since they often have severe attachment injuries (neglect and/or abuse) in their backstory, healthy love is something they crave more than anything, and yet their experience has taught them that when they get too close to love, pain follows. So being in love with someone with BPD often feels like being caught in an ocean current; there is a constant push-pull within the relationship.

Early in the relationship, your BPD lover will usually put you high on a pedestal, idealizing you and adoring you. This is not manipulation. It's truly how they feel in that phase of the relationship. The sex is often epic—through the roof, in fact. It's not surprising that the receiver of all this yummy intensity feels like they're on the best drug high ever. Every cell in their body feels the formidable passion and love. The receiver is in sheer bliss.

But then the wave pulls back—hard. Once the partner with BPD senses that true love and connection is afoot, unconscious panic ensues. They must retreat before risking being left or hurt. When this happens, they might vilify you before fault can be found in them. They may lash out in a rage. Or they may abruptly withdraw with iceberg coldness.

Within non-monogamy, this can show up in many ways. The partner with BPD may sabotage the relationship by purposefully breaking a crucial relationship agreement. They may have sex with the one person that their partner has said is off-limits. And when their partner walks in on the forbidden sex session, the heavenly bliss instantly shifts to evisceration. It's time for their love to crash down from the pedestal.

After a settling process that may include not talking to their partner for a couple of days, they will eventually come back around when they feel a safe level of intimacy distance has been reestablished. At this point, they will prop you up, stitch you up, and send you right back to your pedestal.

Why on earth would you get back on the pedestal? Well, people do it all the time. And the reason is that the attention of a partner with BPD in the pedestal phase can make the receiver a heroin addict for their intense love, chasing the next hit, the next pedestal phase. And the partner, often an over-giver, will say to themselves, *If I heal them with my love, I'll get to live in this epic, blissful space with them forever, right? RIGHT?*

Nope. That's not how this thing works.

Love can soften BPD symptoms, but it's not a cure. It's better to get a partner with BPD symptoms to a therapist who can do DBT, EMDR, somatic psychotherapy, or other kinds of therapies that have an impact on those with borderline symptoms. They need to heal past traumas that may have created their symptoms. Otherwise, their partner will likely become very worn down over time. Those diagnosed with BPD are deeply wounded people. They suffer deeply, and their partners suffer right there with them. But with the right therapist, those with borderline symptoms can heal.

If you are in love with someone with BPD and they have committed to therapy, the best thing I can advise is to love them gently while maintaining strong self-care boundaries. Loving them fiercely with love bombs of romantic poetry, sweeping romantic gestures, etc. can actually make them swing harder. Poor boundaries will result in negative behaviors running the show. A gentle, consistent love will be healthiest for both of you. And if they blow out of your life because you set a self-care limit, then again, that's the sifting process, baby. If your partner is unwilling to treat you kindly, it's time for a change.

I have all the compassion in the world for both those with borderline symptoms and those who love them. Let's face it, by age twenty we have all experienced some sort of abandonment or loss via heartbreak, parents divorcing, or the death of a loved one. However, not everyone with abandonment issues has a pattern of idealizing/vilifying. This extreme pattern comes from a painful past.

How borderline symptoms impact non-monogamy

Most therapists who come from a monogamous lens might say that non-monogamy would be horrible for someone with BPD. Such logic is reasonable. Someone with extreme attachment injuries needs consistent boundaries and secure love to heal. That's monogamy, right?

Well, yes, but it's a bit more complicated than that. For some—generally those with light, more manageable BPD symptoms—non-monogamy may actually be a better fit than monogamy, although it will be hard for them. Let's look at the positives and the negatives.

Positive #1: Multiple partners can create a safety net of resources for someone with BPD, reducing the fear of complete abandonment.

Positive #2: For those dating someone with BPD, having other partners creates an alternate support system that softens the impact of their partner's mood swings, thus reducing burnout.

Negative #1: If someone with BPD feels their partner is choosing another partner over them in any way, it can trigger rage or a dramatic withdrawal. Thus, nonhierarchical non-monogamy will most likely be too emotionally triggering for the them. They may need more security than that to feel safe.

Negative #2: When someone with BPD becomes triggered by other lovers, flirting, or perceived threats to their relationship, it can leave their partner walking on eggshells. This fear of upsetting the partner with BPD often leads to allowing them to have more lovers, freedom, and leeway in an effort to appease them. For obvious reasons, this dynamic often feels unhealthy and unfair.

What's the solution? A simple, less changeable, more predictable, hierarchical form of non-monogamy with a relationship model that changes slowly or stays fixed for long periods of time.

Symptoms Indicative of Mood Disorders

According to the National Institute of Mental Health (NIMH), just under 10 percent of US adults have a mood disorder. Anxious, depressed, or manic symptoms need not be diagnosable for them to impact a non-monogamous relationship. And it should be noted that the reverse is true as well: a non-monogamous relationship can impact anxious, depressed, or manic symptoms for good or bad, either by soothing or exacerbating them. Consequently, such symptoms should not be ignored. They will more than likely impact you at some point on your non-monogamous journey.

Let's take a look at some of the most common symptoms associated with mood disorders—how they impact a non-monogamous relationship and how to cope with them when they do.

Anxiety

Managing anxiety is a formidable challenge within non-monogamy. Even those of us who are cool cucumbers may experience fear or anxiety as a result of the stressors involved.

Anxiety tends to make a person desire simplicity, rigid rules, and predictability—things that will make them feel calmer in their body and safer in their heart. None of these desires easily blends with non-monogamy, which is a relationship model that lends itself to flexibility, change, and complexity.

If you struggle with anxiety, you may find that you worry excessively about—well, almost everything. This worry may be challenging to control. You may also struggle with some of the following symptoms:

- Edginess or restlessness
- Fatigue/tiring easily
- Impaired concentration or poor focus
- Irritability (which may or may not be observable to others)
- Increased muscle aches or soreness
- Difficulty sleeping

Impact of anxiety within non-monogamy

Anxiety might make big and small issues within a non-monogamous relationship more challenging. If your partner said that they would be back from their date at 2:00 a.m. and it's 2:30 a.m., you might be in a panic. Or perhaps your partner suggested a big change, such as shifting from one lover that you share together to suggesting frequent group sex at sexual play parties. Such a change can be extremely challenging to even a relatively calm person, but for you, the prospect is daunting indeed. And yet folks with anxiety choose to be non-monogamous all the time.

If this is you, for the sake of your mental health, please don't overextend yourself. Your "yes" should always be a true yes. Boundaries, clear agreements, and defined expectations around predictability can be operationally defined in your relationship agreement. This agreement can be amended at will, but keeping to these agreements is crucial to managing your anxiety and making non-monogamy a possibility. Taking breaks, if ethically possible, within your non-monogamous journey may occasionally be helpful as well. And if your anxiety continues to plague you, you might consider a therapist, a psychiatrist, more calming partners, or a more calming relationship structure.

Impact of one's anxious symptoms on partners

If you are the partner of an anxious person, their anxiety may sometimes come across as controlling, which can make it easy to forget that they struggle with anxiety and inspire a growing resentment in you. And yes, those riddled with anxiety can have a lot of requests. I suggest that you mindfully watch your relationship. If you are caretaking your partner, so much so that you are losing yourself, you are slipping into codependency and becoming an over-giver. You have to suss out a balance between relationship health and individual health. Relationship health requires that you listen to your partner's requests for structure and reassurance. Individual health requires that you don't cater to those requests and needs so much so that you feel squished under the elephant's weight of their impact. You deserve some semblance of balance.

Depression

I haven't witnessed depression stopping someone from being non-monogamous if that's how they identify. While it's true that a person suffering from depression might find it difficult to meet all their lover's needs when their emotional gas tank is close to empty, that doesn't mean they're bound to fail at non-monogamy. Depression can make a person withdraw or isolate. It can also make a person have a short fuse. But it does not hinder people from living their authentic truth if that truth is non-monogamy.

Impact of depression within non-monogamy

Being non-monogamous and struggling with depression can be a daunting combo at times. Why would anyone struggling with depression choose such a complicated relationship model? I would say because they are choosing what feels right for them. Just like the artist with a mood disorder doesn't choose to give up on their creative pursuits to be a tax accountant simply because it would be an easier life, for some, non-monogamy feels not like a choice but like an orientation. It's who they are, and they won't walk away from that.

That said, the stressors of non-monogamy can be an extra weight on a psyche that already feels too heavy.

Let's look at a few positives and negatives of the non-monogamous experience when depressive symptoms are in the mix:

Positive #1: Non-monogamy can be a blessing of extra love, resources, and support that may help pull the depressed person out of a depressive episode. Having a large safety net of resources—love, support, and community—is a key piece of managing depression, and at its best, non-monogamy can provide that.

Positive #2: A person with depressive symptoms needs to fight the desire to isolate too much. A little alone time is fine, but depression tempts people to take it too far. Non-monogamy comes in handy here by providing more partners who are encouraging you to engage with life.

Positive #3: So often in monogamous relationships, the depressed person feels guilty for leaning too heavily on their love. Having more than one partner means the depressed person has more than one person to lean on, thus easing the feeling of being a burden to any one person.

Negative #1: With more lovers comes more potential breakups. The grief associated with a breakup might compound depression, leading to greater struggle.

Negative #2: Non-monogamy can be difficult to manage at times. This complexity can lead to feelings of overwhelm that may exacerbate a depressive episode.

Coping well as a depressed person practicing non-monogamy might include being honest about your depression and its current impact. For instance, during good times your depressive symptoms may lift, and therefore coping with non-monogamous stressors may be easy as cake. However, in times of depression, the stress of changes in the non-monogamous routine, like a new lover, might be too much. You may need to request that your primary take it easy, especially when you are in a rough patch. Now, your partner will have their own needs, but it can't hurt to make the request and see what can be negotiated.

Coping may also include simplifying your non-monogamous relationship. The more lovers you have, the more responsibility you have. If these responsibilities cut into self-care basics crucial for mood stabilization, your relationship model needs to be reevaluated. Self-care basics, like exercising at least three times a week for fifty minutes, getting enough sleep, and proper nutrition, should not fall to the wayside due to attending to a needy lover or taking on a third lover when one truly doesn't have enough time or emotional bandwidth for that.

The impact of one's depressive symptoms on partners

When depressed, the effort required to manage the internal world leaves little room to notice the external world. Thus, those suffering from depression often miss cues from their partners. Consequently, their partners often feel neglected and helpless. Concerned partners of people with depression often struggle with being supportive without over-giving to the point of their own burnout. Finding a balance between loving support and self-care is key. It is important for both partners to be heard, seen, and have their needs met. Such an intention may be difficult within difficult discussions regarding non-monogamy, but with kindness, gentleness, and patience, it's possible.

Mania

Mania is one of the two poles of bipolar disorder, the other pole being depression. Those with bipolar disorder swing from the lofty highs of mania to the debilitating lows of depression. Manic symptoms may include racing thoughts, grandiose beliefs, inappropriate elation, euphoria, irritability, increased sexual desire, increased talking speed or volume, and/or markedly increased energy. Bipolar disorder not only creates shifts in mood but also changes energy and activity levels, impacting one's ability to carry out day-to-day tasks.

Impact of mania within non-monogamy

Since successful non-monogamy needs to be set up with a thoughtful, grounded approach, the impulsiveness that comes with mania creates serious challenges. If you struggle with mania, your responsibility is to see a good therapist and psychiatrist while building a practice of self-care.

Within non-monogamy, I would encourage you not to make big decisions or go to non-monogamous parties when feeling manic. (This advice will run counter to your instincts while in a manic state, I know. You feel so alive and capable. But you will be much more likely to damage your relationships with partners—who are undoubtedly experiencing your mania much differently than you—if you do.)

The impact of one's manic symptoms on partners

As a partner of someone who struggles with mania, you might frequently feel blindsided when your partner breaks a relationship agreement while in a euphoric frenzy. You might also find that when you attempt to exercise self-care and assert yourself to them, they react with irritability and accusations that you are being unfair or perhaps controlling.

Again, if this person is receiving proper care and is properly medicated, all of these troubles may fade away and become a non-issue, which is why getting help is key—both for the sake of the individual and the relationship.

As you can see, cultivating awareness of the impact personality and mood disorders can have on your non-monogamous relationship is crucial for your health and your partner's health. But taking action steps that address adequate self-care, proper boundaries, and structuring your non-monogamous relationship in a healthy way given these extra stressors is a must as well. Please don't be afraid to assert yourself when necessary. Non-monogamy can only thrive when all parties involved are cared for and respected.

Chapter Twelve

SETTING THE STAGE FOR COMPASSIONATE, CONNECTED COMMUNICATION

As we've discussed already, it's common for me, in my practice, to have a couple sit before me, both individuals begging for compassion from the other even as they reveal themselves to be unwilling to give their partner that same compassion. I watch as one "lawyers up," pronouncing their defense while countering their partner's argument with the perfect, logical soundbite in the hope of winning the debate and ending their discomfort.

Here's an example:

Benjamin, in a deeply hurt state, might say, "Every time we go to a play party, you forget I'm even there. At the last one, I literally didn't see you for two hours and you didn't even notice. I was devastated."

In response, instead of empathizing, Kelsey coolly lawyers up with her defense as so many of us do and replies, "Actually, it was only twenty minutes, and you have ignored me many times too."

Benjamin stares at her, his mouth open, then throws up his hands and stomps out.

These dynamics are a recipe for a complete crash and burn in any relationship, including a non-monogamous one. This chapter is about setting a couple up for success before an uncomfortable discussion regarding non-monogamy even begins. Such preparation will up your chances for a grounded, focused, compassionate, and successful communication.

Overreliance on Logic

I remember the first advice I got as a struggling non-monogamous newbie: "Just reason through your discomfort. The discomfort is just your lizard brain overreacting and being irrational. Mind over lizard brain, baby!"

Since then, I've heard countless non-monogamous people repeat this seemingly simple advice. But the truth is, attempting to use reason alone to work through problems leads to shame spirals and broken-down self-esteem. When you over-rely on logic to the detriment of the other two aspects of your compass, emotions and bodily sensations, you end up feeling internal shame and confusion. You will be much more likely to say yes when it's not a true yes.

For example, Sunny asks Ryan, "Do you mind if I go to Big Bear with Ken?"

Ryan thinks to himself, *Sunny has been dating Ken for a year. He seems like a good guy, and I'm always away on business trips. I should let her go.* So he ignores the sinking feeling in his gut and says, "Yes. Go ahead. Have a great time."

While Sunny is away, Ryan feels anxious and upset. When she comes home, giddy from a great trip, she discovers him brooding and silent.

"What the hell?" she demands.

An argument ensues.

Now let's do a redo. This time, Ryan notices his emotional

discomfort, owns it, and is able to say, "I know I travel for work all the time, but you and I haven't taken a real vacation in years. Let's finally go to Hawaii, like you've always wanted. When we get back, I'm sure I'll be able to get on board with you going to Big Bear with Ken."

Sunny grins. "That's even better! Deal!"

This is the difference between making decisions based solely on logic versus letting our body and emotions guide us as well. Some people go for years using logic as their only guide, and then they wonder why they have generalized anxiety or anger as they move through their day, or they wonder why they don't have sex with their primary or nesting partner anymore. Take the time to sort out what you notice in your body and how you feel. For some people, connecting to feelings and sensations is hard. If that's true for you, talk to friends to help you process. Give yourself alone time. Don't pressure yourself to understand your feelings immediately. Go for a walk. Exercising allows emotions and sensations to process as well. And, of course, don't forget the heavy hitter: meditation. Meditation is the secret to so many things in life. It allows epiphanies to surface.

If you are the logical one in your relationship(s), begin to break your habit of overreliance on logic now, even if only within your non-monogamous relationship(s). If you over-intellectualize your partners' feelings rather than validating and empathizing with their emotions and sensations, you will create distance between you.

Those with an avoidant attachment style will frequently prefer cognitive coping because they are often subconsciously attempting to keep distance within their intimate relationships. Deep connection is an itchy sweater for them. I would invite loved ones of the Spock-like to call this behavior out instead of colluding with them. Intellectualizing has its place—it's a third of our compass—but it's not the end-all be-all. Let your body sensations and emotions play a part as well.

Lawyering Up

Before beginning our discussion of compassionate communication, let's toss out this need to "lawyer up." Despite its inherent dysfunction, it's incredibly common, especially with the highly intelligent and/or educated (which describes the majority of my clients). So many people, when faced with a disagreement, set an intention to *win* instead of setting an intention to find a middle ground. And when one person wins, no one wins.

Graham and Mia have been together for ten years. Graham says to Mia, "I'm really upset with you. I feel like you were flirting with John for way too long at the party. I felt like a chump, just sad and hurt."

Lawyering up, Mia replies, "We arrived at nine p.m. I checked my watch. I stopped talking to John after twenty minutes and came to check in with you. You are incorrect. I was not excessive."

Graham's shoulders slump, and he shakes his head and leaves Mia alone to eat her cereal.

Mia smiles to herself and thinks, *Well, that was easy.*

Meanwhile, Graham is thinking, *I don't even know why I tried. She never hears me. She doesn't give a shit about me. She never has.*

Okay! Now let's do a redo . . .

Graham says to Mia, "I'm really upset with you. I feel like you were flirting with John for way too long at the party. I felt like a chump, just sad and hurt."

"Wow," Mia says, "I had no idea. So the amount of time I was flirting with John left you feeling that way? You said sad and hurt. Help me understand. Is there anything else?"

"Yes." Graham looks away. "I felt unloved by you."

"I can see why my flirting made you feel sad, hurt, and unloved. We are new to all this. You don't know John well. And this is the first large party we've gone to. Does that feel true? Is there anything else that left you feeling that way?"

"Yes, I wish you had just stayed with me for the first hour of the party," Graham says. "It was new, and for you to just take off like that hurt."

"I can totally do that next time," Mia says.

Do you see how much better that went? Now, Mia may need to hold the metaphorical talking stick as well, and that may include explaining her experience of that incident, but she didn't lead with that reality check. She led with mirroring what she heard, empathizing with Graham's feelings, and validating the logic behind his experience—three steps key to Harville Hendrix's "Imago Dialogue" (we'll delve deeper into this in Chapter 13). This response is way more constructive then lawyering up with evidence aimed at discrediting our partner's emotional experience.

Sometimes clients will say, "But what if I can't validate because I don't agree?" or "What if by empathizing, my partner just sees warmth as an opportunity to take advantage?" These questions and more will be addressed in Chapter 13, but for now I ask you to make a pledge to yourself and your relationship to let go of the need to win. Instead, set an intention to emotionally understand your partner. And ask your partner to do the same for you.

Accept That Self-Awareness Is Limited

Humans tend to project their partial experience as the whole truth. It may be disconcerting to own that our self-awareness is limited. However, humility and acceptance are the first steps toward higher enlightenment and self-knowledge.

A great framework to encapsulate the human experience is the Johari window as seen here.

THE JOHARI WINDOW

	Known to Self	Unknown to Self
Known to Others	**OPEN** Things that you and everyone else knows	**BLIND** Things that you are unaware of but others know
Unknown to Others	**HIDDEN** Things that are known by you but unknown to others	**UNKNOWN** Things that are unknown by you and everyone else

This technique was created by Joseph Luft and Harrington Ingham to help people better understand their relationship with themselves and others:

- Quadrant 1 represents what we know about ourselves and what others know about us as well.
- Quadrant 2 represents things others know about us but we are clueless about, in denial about, or unaware of.
- Quadrant 3 represents what we know about ourselves but is hidden from others.
- Quadrant 4 represents things both we and others are unaware of.

How is this knowledge helpful? With this awareness and humility, when our love wants to discuss something regarding our behavior that is troubling, we will be less likely to shut them down before they even get started. We will be more likely to acknowledge the possibility that they are seeing something in us that we are unable to recognize.

If you have a partner who has earned your expression of vulnerability, I invite you to step into this gift they have given you. An open heart, a grounded body, and a present mind are key requirements for constructive and successful conversations regarding challenging issues within one's non-monogamous relationship. Own that you are not aware of everything within. The wisdom of the Johari window stresses that our friends, and especially our loved ones, can give us the gift of heightened self-awareness.

Don't Discredit Perceptions and Feelings

If you had a color-blind friend and they said, "The sky looks gray to me," would you argue with them? Hopefully not. Their perception is their experience. And yet we invalidate our partner's perceptions and feelings all the time in our relationships.

To illustrate, consider the following communication between partners Tameca and Cameron. Tameca says to Cameron as they are driving home from their date with Josh and Kimber, "You embarrassed me tonight. Just when I was getting over my nervousness, you cut me off in the middle of my story about how we got into the lifestyle and had a tone with me. All my anxiety immediately came rushing back. Now Josh and Kimber probably think I'm a pushover. Why did you do that to me?"

"I didn't have a tone," Cameron says. "You're just trying to start a fight. Josh and Kimber think you're great. Don't be insecure."

Now, Cameron has his perception of the vocal volume and tone he used during their date. He believes he spoke calmly and kindly.

But Tameca has her own perception—and it's that he had a tone and was being pissy. Instead of invalidating her in this moment, Cameron might do better by saying, "I didn't hear my tone, but right before I spoke I was thinking about how we were staying out too late and that I had to get up early." Why is this a better response? Well, first, when we hear a tone in our partner's voice, we often fear that they're upset with us. This fear is frequently followed by feeling angry, if we believe they're treating us unfairly. If Cameron chooses not to invalidate Tameca's perception and instead shares what he was thinking about, he very well may avoid a huge fight.

Perception differences happen all the time with couples. Metaphorically, there will be many times when you will believe that the shirt was blue and your partner will believe it was red. You can argue over that difference in perception for years and never agree. An approach to love as war and an overreliance on evidence over empathy will allow this to go on and on. You're not in court. There's a better way. And it's found in being attuned to our partner.

You might have also noticed that Tameca mentioned her nervousness and anxiety. Oftentimes when our partner makes a comment about our tone, voice level, or body language, they are letting us know that our demeanor is dysregulating them. When our partner gets dysregulated, they may experience any of the following: poor focus, heart racing, tension in the body, an inability to speak eloquently or even to speak at all. And none of these experiences lead to a constructive conversation. So the next time your partner says, "You have a tone" or "Your voice is too loud," check in with your compassion. Realize that they are probably letting you know that you are overwhelming them; then you can choose to dial it back.

Just as invalidating perceptions is counterproductive, so is invalidating emotions. Let's try a more compassionate approach. To illustrate, consider Rebecca and George, who have been together for seven years and dating other partners for two. Rebecca's upset because George failed to text her during a date, despite having agreed to do so.

"I'm sad that you didn't text me while you were on your date with Jessie," Rebecca says.

Now, George could respond with his defense: "You can't be sad. You didn't text me during your last date either. So you don't get to be sad." But while George may have a point about her also breaking their agreement to check in, can he tell her that she did not experience sadness? No.

With that in mind, a better response might be, "Alright. Yes. I get that you were sad. I was sad when you did the same thing to me. Maybe I was being passive-aggressive when I didn't text. I was getting back at you. But let's both try to do better. I will definitely text you next time."

Do you see how he resisted becoming defensive and instead responded with empathy and validation for Rebecca and himself? That's an approach that will lead to a much more harmonious non-monogamous experience.

Invalidating other people's feelings and perceptions often triggers old childhood wounds. Many of us have memories of saying to a parent, "I feel sick; I don't want to go to school," only to have a parent reply angrily and aggressively, "You aren't sick. You're just trying to get out of going to school. Put your clothes on before I give you a spanking."

What did we want in those moments? Empathy and validation. Perhaps something like, "Oh, sweetie, I'm so sorry that you feel sick. Come here. Let me give you a hug and take your temperature." As adults, we aren't any different. If anything, we might need empathy and validation even more due to accumulative childhood attachment injuries. Validation and empathy are easy, beautiful ways to love your partner better.

Set an Intention

We have spoken of letting go of an intention to win, but what replaces this intention? Some examples include:

- Finding a common ground or solution you can both agree on
- Attempting to make your partner feel loved and heard

- Comforting your partner
- Kindly asserting your needs even as you hear theirs

Setting an intention will help you hold yourself accountable and committed to operating from your higher self. You can form your intention within your own mind, but it's even better to set your intention out loud so your partner can hear it. This verbalization has the added bonus of positively impacting your partner. It helps them relax and know that your intentions are good. In turn, they will be more willing to let down their defenses, set an equally benevolent intention, and operate from their higher self.

Make Sure You're in Your Resilient Zone

Your autonomic nervous system is responsible for your response to stimuli—whether that's Zen-like calm or a catlike startle reaction. One of the main functions of our autonomic nervous system is to process, interpret, and respond appropriately to sensory input, but that doesn't always mean we get to feel peaceful, now does it? In fact, part of the autonomic nervous system's job is to help us go into some degree of a fight, flight, or freeze response if under attack, whether physically from a tiger or verbally from our partner.

The autonomic nervous system has two parts: the sympathetic and the parasympathetic nervous systems. The sympathetic nervous system is like the gas in your car, while the parasympathetic nervous system is like the brakes. Not surprisingly, the sympathetic nervous system is responsible for your fight-or-flight response. But if you can't run or fight, the parasympathetic nervous system takes over, eliciting a freeze response.

Now, this may seem counterintuitive. However, the freeze response is the body's last-resort protective measure because it greatly reduces your experience of pain and fear. And, as previously noted, the parasympathetic nervous system is usually a place of calm.

As taught by the Trauma Resource Institute, when the nervous system is in balance, we feel like our best self. We make better decisions and communicate more clearly and kindly. If you are in your Resilient Zone, you might feel any variety of emotions: mad, glad, or sad. Even if you're demonstrably emotional, your nervous system, body, and mind are still grounded. Thus, you're still able to hear your partner, think clearly, and make better decisions—which means you are less likely to have regrets about what you said or did in a disagreement the next day.

However, if you are in the high zone (panic attack, road rage, screaming, out of control) or in the low zone (dissociated, checked out, daydreaming, or numb), you are likely to be so overwhelmed that your prefrontal cortex, the part of the brain that is responsible for judgment might not be working so well—which means your decision-making abilities may be impaired.

Some evidence that your prefrontal cortex is on the fritz due to overwhelm is when you wake up the next day and have regrets. *Why did I call her a fucking bitch? That was so vicious and mean! Why did I overreact and threaten to move out and end our relationship? That must have been devastating to hear.*

When the prefrontal cortex isn't working well due to overwhelm, we might do and say things that could have lasting damage to our relationship. Even if the next day you say, "I'm so sorry. I didn't mean it. I was just mad," it might not be enough. Your partner's head might understand that you were just upset, but the head and the heart live on different planets. Their heart may not understand at all—and may continue to hold the pain weeks or years after those cruel things were said. Because of this, it's better to stay grounded and thus in your Resilient Zone.

Ways to stay grounded or in your Resilient Zone

Breathe

Deep breathing is one of the simplest ways to move from fight, flight, or freeze to a grounded place of calm. You are much more likely to communicate from your higher self, a place of love and connection, when in this state. Your partner will feel that and love you for it.

Be mindful

Mindfulness is a mental state achieved by focusing one's awareness on the present moment. Being aware of the present moment may include noticing what your five senses perceive. It may also include tracking, acknowledging, and accepting your thoughts, feelings, and sensations from a place of compassion. Develop a practice of watching yourself, your own unfolding reality show. Compassionately watch your psychological and emotional patterns, the stories you tell yourself about your relationship, and reactionary body sensations that occur during an emotionally difficult discussion. This practice is a crucial step toward remaining grounded during uncomfortable moments in your non-monogamous relationship.

As I got better at mindfulness and watching what I now affectionately call *The Kate Show*, I could observe and say to myself, for example, *Oh! This is the part where Kate goes into tough-chick mode rather than stepping into her vulnerability.* Once I developed a habit of watching *The Kate Show* as an outside observer, I became better able to give myself what I truly needed, and to ask for what I needed within my relationships.

As you begin to watch your thoughts, feelings, and behaviors, you might notice the antecedents that occur right before you step out of your window of tolerance, such as: 1) racing thoughts, 2) a feeling of hopelessness, helplessness, or despair, 3) a desire to walk or run away, 4) raising your voice, 5) feeling tension in your gut or chest, and/or 6) a fear of being abandoned, to name a few. Once you notice these antecedents you will be better able to make changes before becoming reactive and flipping out of your Resilient Zone.

Let's take a look at Sally and Landon. Sally says to Landon, "I'd really like to have a male, male, female threesome with you. Would you be up for that?"

He nods, and she continues.

"In my fantasies, the other man is tall—over six foot four, muscular, and super alpha—but in real life, I'm not sure who I would choose."

Landon mindfully watches himself. He notices his heart rate spiking. He notices the tension in his chest and heat building in his cheeks. He notices the thought: *She's just trying to humiliate me.* And he notices feelings of anger coming up fast.

"I'll be right back," he says. He gets some water in the kitchen and uses this as an opportunity to take ten slow deep breaths. Once his body feels a bit calmer, he asks himself, *Is this story really true? Is she really trying to humiliate me?* He concludes, *No. She loves me. She always has my back. This just hurts. I wish I were taller. I wish I could get more muscle on this skinny frame of mine.* Once he is able to track his body, thoughts, and feelings with compassion and lack of judgment, he is able to return to her and say, "I'm definitely open to having an MMF with you. But let's choose the guy together. I need to be comfortable with him too."

She replies, "Of course! That sounds like fun!"

Now that's a way better outcome than if he simply took his thoughts as truth and let the corresponding rage rule the show. Mindfulness allows us to see the big picture.

Connect to resources while using somatic (body) tracking

A resource is anything that, once mentally conjured, brings on positive emotions, such as peace, or positive bodily sensations, such as relaxation. Resources can be internal or external. Examples of internal resources are a spiritual belief that provides comfort, or a self-belief that inspires confidence. Examples of external resources are a favorite vacation spot or a heartwarming relationship with a friend, lover, or pet. For me, a positive resource is being on my porch on a sunny day with my three kitties as I watch the hummingbirds zoom around amongst the trees. When I imagine this scene, I can check in with my body and notice tension melting away and a smile coming over my face. This process of checking in with the body is somatic tracking.

The word "somatic" comes from the root word "soma," or body. Therefore, somatic tracking is awareness of physical sensations and can be a part of your mindfulness practice. It's a key practice and powerful tool for keeping your cool during a discussion. This tracking includes noticing shifts in tension or relaxation in the body, energy shifts, and changes in breathing and heart rate.

Have you heard the American Indian story in which a wise elder tells the boy a tale about a benevolent wolf and a destructive wolf? The boy asks the elder, "Which wins?" The elder says, "Whichever you feed." Our body works in a similar manner.

Next time you feel heightened love for a friend or partner, notice what part of your body knows about this love. Perhaps you notice a warmth in your heart area. Focus there and you might notice that warmth expanding across your chest. And if you want to be a somatic Yoda, I invite you to ask your heart space to let every cell in your body know about this warmth and love. At this point, you may notice a warmth extending further into your body. Lovely, right? Yes. And you can use such techniques in the bedroom to enhance arousal and connection (especially when verbalized to your partner), but I digress.

During an uncomfortable discussion, focusing on the part of your body that feels the most calm and relaxed will enhance groundedness, as will focusing on long, deep breaths. But sometimes we tend to unconsciously do the opposite. Why? Because scanning for what's wrong is part of our survival instinct. However, our survival instinct sometimes shoots us in the foot. Noticing the tension in our body, or our heart beating faster, often escalates those feelings, leading to more emotional and physical upset. If you are feeling a panic attack coming on and you focus on your racing heart, guess what? Your heart is likely to race even more. But if we make somatic tracking a conscious and mindful choice, we can increase our control over our state of being.

That said, sometimes we will not catch things on time. So let's consider moments of heightened dysregulation and how we can help ourselves or our partners become grounded again.

Understanding Triggers

First, let's consider the correlation between negative body sensations and triggers. As a starting point, since "trigger" is such a popular word these days, I need to be sure you understand a psychotherapist's definition of both a trigger and being triggered.

A trigger is a psychological stimulus or combination of stimuli that prompts the somatic and emotional recall of a previous traumatic experience. The stimulus can come from any one or more of the five senses (a visual, a texture, a taste, a sound, or a smell). It could be a phrase that we associate with a negative emotional memory. It could be an anniversary of an upsetting event, like a death. You get the idea.

When we experience a trigger, and thus become triggered, our body may react as it did when the original trauma happened, which likely means that we switch to our autonomic nervous system's threat response: fight, flight, or freeze. This switch is biological and not a conscious choice. At that point, we may shift to the "high zone," which may include experiencing anxiety, panic, rage, or hypervigilance (to name a few), or shift to the "low zone," which may mean feeling numb, checked out, disconnected, exhausted/fatigued, or dissociated. Some people vacillate between these two extremes.

I'll give you a somewhat extreme example for the purpose of clarity. Maggie has been in a polyamorous relationship with her girlfriend, Lana, for five years. Tonight, she is on her second date with a potential new lover, Omar. Omar and Maggie have been sexting for months and both have been excitedly waiting for this date. Both love spontaneity and ravishment fantasies. They know each other's turn-ons, kinks, and hard nos. They both know that tonight might be the night they seal the deal.

They go back to his place. Omar makes her a cocktail, but before she can even take a sip, he glides her to the bedroom, puts her drink on the bedside table, throws her down on the bed, and starts aggressively making out with her.

Now, Maggie likes it rough, and she really likes Omar, but suddenly her heart is racing and she can't breathe. She pushes him away and starts gasping for air.

What's happening to Maggie? Well, as it turns out, Omar's Old Spice cologne is a trigger, because Maggie was mugged by a guy wearing that scent two years ago.

When triggered, a stimulus or stimuli, such as the scent of a certain cologne, can unleash a past traumatic body memory, such as Maggie's mugging, as if the past trauma is happening *right now*. Notice the term "body memory." Obviously, the details and thoughts around the mugging are much different than the date with Omar. But the "body memory" has enough similarities, including smell and how Maggie felt in her body when Omar pinned her on the bed, to trigger her.

Triggers will vary in intensity. We can be just slightly triggered or we can be so triggered that we have extreme responses, such as having a panic attack, shouting, or shutting down in a dissociation. Anytime we have a reaction to a person or event that seems, in hindsight, like an overreaction, it might be wise to ponder whether we were triggered at some level.

Getting triggered within a disagreement with your loved one is as common as birth and death, love and hate. Not understanding how to cope with triggers in yourself and others puts you at a severe and profound disadvantage if you would like to have a positive relationship with anyone, let alone a deep, intimate, trust-filled love.

I'd like to share another example of how getting triggered can play out in a partnership by sharing the story of Ben and Angie.

When Ben was a child, his parents frequently screamed at each other. These shouting matches often got redirected at him, even though he was a defenseless child. He coped the best he could. He learned how to be almost invisible and to avoid their wrath. He tried to be a good boy. As an adult, he promised himself not to be like them. But rather than joining an anger management group or pursuing other effective choices, he bottled his anger up.

Then he fell in love with Angie, who comes from an emotionally demonstrative family. They smile big, hug hard, talk loud, and, yes, sometimes they argue loud, but then they let it out, resolve the conflict, and move on. Angie has always felt loved by her big, boisterous family.

Not surprisingly, when Ben gets upset with her, Angie gets loud, as her family taught her to do. When, for instance, Ben gets mad because she texted a couple on a dating site without waiting for him to join her, she shouts, "We don't have any relationship agreements about that. I didn't do anything wrong!"

Immediately, Angie's tone, volume, dramatic facial expressions, and body language trigger Ben. He feels small, trapped, defenseless, angry, and scared, as he did as a boy. From a body memory level, he is right back in his childhood, defenseless. But then a wrath rises up in him and he bursts out in anger, "I feel so disrespected by you! You aren't considerate of me! And you're always yelling! You remind me of my parents!" Then he stomps out, slamming the door behind him. He is in the high zone.

You might have memories of being just slightly triggered in a more subtle way than the Ben example. But hopefully you can see how easy it is for old traumas to show up in your current relationships in big or subtle ways.

For a final example, let's look at Claudine and Ralph, who've been together for nine years but are newly non-monogamous. Claudine's childhood was filled with abandonment and feeling neglected by those who were supposed to love and nurture her. When she attempted to reach out for her parents' love, she was often yelled at and told to quit being a needy brat.

In a discussion, Claudine says to Ralph, "I know that you've been dating Jax for three months and your relationship with him hasn't changed the way you treat me at all. But I still feel terrified. I'm so scared I'm going to lose you."

There is a long pause from Ralph, but then he lets his pent-up frustrations out, saying, "This has got to be the thousandth time we've discussed this. I've been patient, but this is ridiculous." And then, with a tone, his piercing eyes stabbing a hole in Claudine's heart, he bellows, "Will you just get over it!?"

Claudine's shoulders collapse. She looks away and falls silent. Inside, her heart literally hurts and she feels overwhelmed. Her body quickly shifts into a state of feeling both floaty and numb at the same time. Her thoughts become unfocused and she can't find her words. She's in the low zone.

As a reminder, triggers happen with most couples to varying degrees. You don't have to be a war vet or survivor of a crime to experience getting triggered to a greater or lesser degree. This incredibly common phenomenon is another reason not to argue when your partner verbalizes a perception, such as saying, "You're yelling at me." Instead of arguing with their perception, assume that they're getting overwhelmed or even triggered, and simply lower your voice, smooth out your tone, soften your face, and slow your body movement. These adjustments will help a triggered partner move back into their parasympathetic nervous system and have a real conversation with you.

The fawn response

If you or any of your partners has an abuse history, you should be aware of the fawn response. Unlike the autonomic nervous system's physical response to threat—fight, flight, freeze—the fawn response is psychological, and is characterized by immediate attempts to please a person to avoid any conflict. This behavior is usually developed as a response to childhood trauma, where a parent or an authority figure is the abuser. Children go into this pleasing response in an attempt to avoid physical, emotional, or sexual abuse. This behavior may manifest as being overly agreeable—saying what they know the parent wants to hear—suppressing their personal feelings and desires, and/or doing anything and everything to prevent the abuse.

In adulthood, this behavior pattern may continue in friendships and love relationships, not only during a fight but at any time that tension is felt. And while the fawn response likely helped this person survive in childhood, in adulthood it does not contribute to a healthy relationship. Why? Because fawning means abandoning self-care. Within non-monogamy, this response can lead to agreeing to sexual experiences or relationship changes when the answer is actually a no or maybe, and such agreements can lead to the fawner feeling traumatized, even though a yes was given. Often, the partner assumes all is well; meanwhile, unresolved emotional material, and even trauma, is mounting.

Happily, this behavior pattern can be overcome. Through healing trauma, choosing safe partners, working on staying grounded, and learning assertiveness skills, a person can shift from the negation of self-care that comes with fawning to active self-love—but it's a process that will take time and compassion.

If you suspect that you or your partner shifts into the fawn response in moments of tension, please avoid making agreements about your non-monogamous relationship when either of you feels triggered or upset. Encourage assertiveness within the relationship. And remember, being assertive is light years easier when you are grounded and in your Resilient Zone.

Tone, volume, and non-verbal triggers

I'd like to talk about some forms of communication that many of us have little to no awareness of but may be greatly impacting our relationship. This may include tone, volume, body language, and facial expressions. It took me a while as a therapist to realize that certain tones and/or volumes can be triggering or dysregulating to the body. The words, themselves, if typed up, might be benign—but the tone can land on the recipient like a thousand angry snakes. Or the vocal volume may be as booming as the snarl of a ferocious bear. For every action, there is an equal and opposite reaction. So it should not be shocking to find that when you lash out in a primal way, in terms of your partner's own primal, physiological reaction, you *are* one thousand angry snakes. You *are* a ferocious bear. And your partner's primal reaction may be a fight, flight, or freeze response: they may yell back (fight), storm out (flight), or fall silent and shut down (freeze).

It's possible that you're completely unaware of your tone and volume. In that case, regardless of fairness, the ball is in the receiver's court. If the receiver says, "You're yelling at me!" or "You have a tone," the accused will most likely defend themself, proclaiming, "I'm not yelling," or "I don't have a tone." So you have to learn a better way to respond.

The receiver can stay more centered than this, of course. Instead of saying, "You're yelling at me," or "You have a tone," a better communication would be, "Your volume is upsetting me and making it hard for me to listen. Can you please lower your voice?" or "The tone of your voice is making me tighten up. I could listen better if you softened a bit." Upon hearing this, even if the partner feels their tone and volume is on par with the Dalai Lama, they can choose to try to speak more softly. Over and over, I've witnessed this latter approach pay off. In contrast, I have never seen a defensive partner's reaction be met with anything short of frustration or anger.

Triggering language

I bet you know the perfect thing to say that really sends your partner over the edge. You might know the exact sentence that will get a "rise" out of them or shut them down. Maybe at times you've been upset enough to pull that sentence out of your arsenal.

This doesn't have to be as extreme as calling your partner a bitch or an ass. It may simply be demeaning language, such as, "I feel like I'm your mother," "You're stronger than this," "I thought you were cool with poly, but maybe you're not as cool as I thought," or "The way you're acting just isn't hot to me." Emasculating, disempowering, insulting, or desexualizing comments often elicit an emotional shutdown. And so many people are guilty of interpreting their partner's shutdown as a victory. They believe they've won; their partner has admitted defeat!

Nope. This confused soul has mistaken their partner's quiet seething, shame, or hopelessness for a win, when in fact no one wins in the long run in the case of this kind of shutdown, especially if it's a pattern within the relationship.

So let's consider how to restructure potentially triggering language. Take the belittling phrase "I feel like your mother." How can we replace the attacking language with something more vulnerable and honest?

Let's say Margaret is upset because 1) her partner forgot to text while on their date per their check-in agreement and 2) nagging him makes her feel shoved into a role she doesn't want: the desexualized mother figure. What might she say in this situation? She could try an honest approach: "One of my requests is that if you are out on a date, you send me a text at some point in the night. The last three dates, that hasn't happened. I want to give you a sense of freedom, but I also want to believe that you enjoy making me feel loved. When you don't fulfill this small ask, it feels like you regard loving me as, well, a burden."

Now this may be an incredibly hard message for her partner to receive, but it doesn't include shaming language, and a compassionate, mature partner will likely be able to hear it.

How about those other two triggering sentences: "I thought you were cool with poly, but maybe you're not as cool as I thought," and "The way you're acting just isn't hot to me." I've heard these a lot in my years as a therapist, and they're both incredibly demeaning. Usu-ally, they come on the heels of one partner voicing a concern about non-monogamy. If a concern is met with either of these responses, even a secure person may for a moment take pause and ask themself if their concern is worth being perceived as "less cool or sexy" in the eyes of their partner.

It may seem counterintuitive, but if you want the cool, confident, sexy partner who loves freedom, both for themself and for you, then you have to be supportive when they are upset, insecure, and fragile. Non-monogamy tests all of us. Success is found in compassion.

Avoid invalidating a trigger

Before we move into a discussion of how to cope with triggers or somatic dysregulation, here's a final suggestion: please try not to invalidate triggers. We are all humans who make mistakes. At times, you'll be unaware that you've accidentally triggered your partner. Sometimes partners will express hurt regarding something you said or did when really they're telling you that they're becoming low-level triggered—and when that happens, invalidation can skyrocket a partner's low-level trigger to something much bigger. If a partner tells you that something upsets them, believe them.

How you can help a triggered partner

Imagine you're having an upsetting conversation with your partner and it's escalating. They've been softly crying, but now they are crying harder and their breathing has changed. Their face shows their pain. This is a good time to step in and attempt to get in front of what may be a triggered emotional state. At this point, you might verbally recognize the somatic changes by saying, "Love, your breathing has changed and your brow is furrowed. Is there anything that I can do to help you?" This wording may feel weird, awkward, and maybe even cheesy to you, but it's also purposeful and effective. I'll tell you why.

First off, when you simply verbalize your *perception* of your partner, such as noting "your breathing has changed," they can't (or shouldn't) argue with your perception of them. That's how you see them. However, if you say to your partner, "You look upset," or ask them, "Are you mad at me?" the response will often be a defensive "I'm not upset!" or "God, you always think I'm mad at you. I wasn't mad, but I am now." These are common and predictable responses when we make up a story or try to interpret our partner's tone, facial expressions, or body language—or, worse yet, make it about us. Typically, these assessments feel invasive to us and make us defensive. Operationally defining what we experience of our partner, such as, "Your voice just got louder," is less threatening than our interpretations of these changes, which may be inaccurate to begin with.

Second, when you ask, "Is there anything I can do to help you?" you're more likely to get a positive response, such as, "Yes, can you give me a hug?" or "Please spoon me," or "Can you just tell me that everything will be okay?" But if we instead verbalize our guess regarding what they need, they are more likely to respond negatively. For instance, you might guess that they need touch and ask, "Sweetie, can I give you a hug? You look like you need one." To this, "Sweetie" might reply, "Don't touch me. I'm furious at you right now. That's the last thing I want."

In summary, when we report observable evidence that our partner is beginning to get upset with an open offer to help, they are more likely to tell us exactly what they need to calm down their nervous system. And if this is something we can give them, we can often work through the uncomfortable conversation with both people staying in their Resilient Zone. And this, in turn, increases your likelihood of finding a productive and supportive resolution to the conversation.

Helping yourself when triggered

Let's imagine that despite your best efforts to watch your breath, engage in mindfulness, and practice somatic tracking, you still find yourself triggered. What can you do?

1. **Ask for what you need.** Let your partner know how they can help you. You need not wait for them to ask. Remember, they're not a mind reader. Do you need a hug? Do you need to hear them say that they love you? Do you need a break? You need to tell them.

2. **Don't power through the disagreement.** If you ignore that you are in the high zone—panicked, enraged, etc.—or in the low zone—checked out, numb, and so on—several things may happen. First, you may not remember the conversation the next day due to being so upset, thus rendering the whole thing a waste of time. Second, you may become so upset that you say something you regret. Third, you may become so checked out and overwhelmed that you agree to things you truly aren't okay with in an attempt to make the upsetting conversation end. None of this is good. Avoid powering through at all costs.

3. **Tell your partner what you're experiencing.** If you are having trouble focusing, let them know. If you are so overwhelmed that you are having trouble following their words, they need to know that as well. They may be able to help you get grounded again, or the two of you might decide to take a time-out. And since we are on the topic, let's talk about that.

4. **Take a proper time-out.** A proper time-out is a powerful tool. It can allow one or both partners to become grounded and centered again before they regroup to finish an uncomfortable conversation. (Now, I'm guessing you have some concept of what a "time-out" is. But I find that left to their own devices, people attempt a time-out in a very poor, if not horribly destructive, way. Part of what we're going to cover in this chapter and the next is how to take a much more constructive time-out.)

To share a typical scenario of how couples often take their time-outs, and show how you can do it better, let's look to Devin and Stephanie, a couple of seven years who've been dating a third person, Ava, for two years. They love her very much and consider her family. But the two have been fighting for the last hour about whether they should take Ava on their vacation to Hawaii. Devin feels that vacations are something special, something for just the two of them, and they should stay that way. But Stephanie is pushing for change.

Finally, in anger and frustration, Devin shouts, "Screw this! You just go to Hawaii with Ava without me. I'm out of here!" She stomps out, slamming the door behind her.

Stephanie collapses onto the bed in tears. She doesn't know if Devin has just broken up with her. She doesn't know when or if she is coming back. She feels abandoned and angry that Devin didn't work the issue through with her before leaving. She's pissed, hurt, and scared.

Now let's imagine a proper time-out.

Again, Devin and Stephanie. The two of them have been fighting for the last hour about whether they should take Ava on their vacation to Hawaii. Luckily, Devin has learned to mindfully watch her thoughts, feelings, and sensations. She can feel herself about to lose it. Her cheeks have gotten hot, and she can feel the adrenaline and tension in her body. She turns to Stephanie and says, "Look, I love you, but I'm really pissed at you right now. I need to take a time-out to calm down. I'll come back in an hour and we can finish this conversation then."

With that, Devin leaves and goes on a jog through the neighborhood. While she's away, Stephanie is left knowing three important things: first, that she is loved; second, that she is not being abandoned; and finally, that the conversation is not being abandoned either. Devin respects the importance of resolving their disagreement enough to take a time-out when she knows she is going into a destructive emotional place. Stephanie trusts Devin, and although they're both upset, she knows that they will work through this.

What, exactly, has left Stephanie in such a secure place? Let's break down what Devin said. First, "I love you." Her reaffirmation of her love for Stephanie, even when she's pissed and about to leave, eases Stephanie's fear that Devin is abandoning her, is fed up with her, or is breaking up with her—all core fears that can be triggered by a time-out. Second, she acknowledged, "I need to take a time-out to calm down." This sentence lets Stephanie know that Devin is not leaving in attempt to be passive-aggressive or punishing, but rather because she is exercising self-care. And finally, she said, "I'll come back in an hour and we can finish this conversation then." This lets Stephanie know that she is not being avoidant or trying to get out of an uncomfortable conversation.

Proper time-outs allow for good self-care. When the ego is running the show, that part of you that wants to "power through" a fight, no matter how emotionally compromised you are, may win. But with a proper time-out, you have a fighting chance to regain composure and have a productive conversation. You're keeping your higher self in charge, and you're prioritizing your relationship. Remember, a non-monogamous relationship in which the ego is primary and your partner is secondary never works in the end. So put your ego in your back pocket and take a time-out when needed, or allow your partner to take that time-out when requested. You'll both be glad you did.

The double trigger

Now let's discuss the dreaded double trigger moment that sometimes occurs within a fight. A "double trigger" is a term I coined to denote the moment both partners are triggered simultaneously. When we are triggered, it is almost impossible to stay in our Resilient Zone. And as I mentioned earlier, people rarely feel like they're grounded in their current chronological age when triggered. So in a double trigger moment, you basically have two overwhelmed children who may either be tantruming or crying in a heap, with no caretaker in sight to help improve the interaction. As you can imagine, this is when a couple is at their very, very worst and judgment is poor.

To illustrate, I'll give you an example: Leo and Ashley have been together for three years. Ashley is an entrepreneur and a badass businesswoman. Leo is a gentle artist. As a child, Ashley's father was a drug addict with anger management issues. From the time she was twelve, her mother taught her how to manage her father. She felt like her father's caregiver from a very young age. She found him vile and weak.

Leo's childhood was much different. His parents were kind but often clueless. He didn't feel he could go to them for help. He was bullied—emotionally and physically—at school throughout much of his childhood. As an adult, he still flinches at loud noises or aggressive body movements from others.

If Ashley perceives Leo as weak, she tends to lose her temper. If Leo perceives Ashley as aggressive, he tends to unconsciously cower. Both behaviors set the other off, leading to a negative spiral. Ashley has been known to lose it and shout, "You're so timid and weak! I despise you right now. How am I supposed to rely on you? You're a child." Leo, meanwhile, has been known to pull out of his cowered state long enough to shoot back, "Ashley, you're emotionally abusive. You're a bully, and I don't know why I stay with you."

The arguments that ensue can last for hours.

How can you deescalate such a compromised moment with no adults in the room? Well, first off, you need to have an established plan in advance—something that looks like this:

1. Take a time-out. Both partners need to take a break as soon as either is aware of the dysregulation, the sooner the better.
2. Ground yourself. Both partners need to use this time-out to ground themselves and get back into their Resilient Zone.

Remember deep breathing, resourcing, and staying mindful and present while tracking your body to regain calm.

3. Help each other stay grounded. Once you reengage, use grounding techniques within the discussion. Ask your partner what they need. Perhaps they need to hold your hand or hear that it's going to be okay. But remember to ask rather than assume.

4. Try to discover what triggered your partner. Ask them if they have any awareness of which old wounds, if any, got poked at by the discussion. But be careful. If you are too quick to assume that they've been triggered by old wounds, they may feel you're invalidating their very real present upset. So be clear that you are simply opening a discussion. If both of you are able to verbalize the history behind your upset, it will give you a chance to show compassion for one another's history. Operating from this grounded, conscious place, you will be ready for compassionate, connected communication.

5. Use mirroring, empathizing, and validating from Imago Dialogue. If your partner can verbalize what past trauma got triggered, mirror how your argument got linked to that past trauma. Empathize with feelings that link back to the trauma and validate why having this past trauma triggered is upsetting. (This is next-level stuff. If you are not able to do this for each other, please don't be hard on yourself.)

6. Seek out a therapist or mediator. If you can't work out the double trigger on your own, get help. Some trauma triggers run too deep to be dealt with alone, and a professional's help is needed.

Back to Ashley and Leo. By using the steps above, Ashley was able to see that she was projecting her old story about her father onto Leo, and Leo was able to see that his bullying history was getting triggered in their fights. This awareness of their trauma triggers did not mean that they didn't have real issues in the present: Ashley felt Leo had a tendency to sugarcoat and minimized issues in their non-monogamous relationship. She wanted him to "have more of a spine" and speak up. And Leo felt that Ashley was too much of a control freak regarding their relationship. He wanted her to quit micromanaging him and to back off a little. But as they discussed these two relationship concerns, Ashley made a point of using a soft voice and keeping her body language minimized so as not to trigger Leo's bullying history, and Leo practiced his grounding techniques and some newly learned assertiveness skills from a class he had taken. These new skills allowed him to confront Ashley in a stronger and more confident manner that was not as reminiscent of her father. Both of their efforts allowed them to stay in their Resilient Zone more often and effectively work through their relationship issues. Over time, their double trigger moments became much more manageable and rare.

Chapter Thirteen

EPIC CONNECTED COMMUNICATION

Earlier, I mentioned the three components of your internal compass: emotions, physical sensations, and thoughts. We've gone through exercises that ask you to look within and check in with all three of those parts to make the best decisions for yourself. This same system can be applied to communication with your partner as well. My communication approach, called EPIC, has four parts: 1) emotional connection, 2) physical connection, 3) intellectual (thought) connection, and 4) compassionate connection. All of these ways of connecting increase your chance of navigating even the most difficult conversations you might have as you travel the path of non-monogamy.

My clients are typically highly intelligent, which has served them well in their lives. They assume that this same strength will slay any relationship snafu; they operate as if cognitive reasoning is the end-all, be-all within relationship communication. They will use this tactic despite repeated failure, never achieving the deep, trusting, conscious, connected long-term relationship many of them desire until they learn a better way. I believe this pattern reflects how many people outside of my practice operate as well. This ineffective loop reminds me of that expression that doing the same thing repeatedly and expecting a different result is the truest indicator of insanity. Yep.

Perhaps you have resolved to stop being so defensive—promised yourself you'll fight the urge to lawyer up. Great. But do you know what you should be doing instead?

That's what this chapter addresses.

Whether you're going through the process of creating a non-monogamous relationship agreement, working through a disagreement after a play party, or attempting to love your partner better, the EPIC communication steps will guide you through.

Getting Prepared

First, utilizing the steps covered in the last chapter, make sure that you are both grounded. Don't even get started if you aren't grounded and in your Resilient Zone. If you are overwhelmed, either due to being in the low zone (dissociated, checked out, or numb) or being in the high zone (heart racing, angry, or highly anxious), your prefrontal cortex, the part of the brain responsible for negotiating between logic and emotions, will not be working so well. The result might be calling your partner a bitch or an asshole and then regretting it the next day. Nothing productive will occur.

So, are you in your Resilient Zone? Good. Now let's discuss a plan for better communication.

Determine Who Will Hold the Emotional Talking Stick

Figuring who is metaphorically going to "hold the talking stick" matters because it gives space for one person to express their thoughts, feelings, and sensations first. If you are holding the talking stick, your partner is there to hold space for you. In doing so, they are going to do everything to understand what you are going through, not just by listening but also by using the strategies we'll cover in this chapter. They will refrain from overpowering you or launching into a defense. They will stop themself from interrupting you, no matter how hard that might be for them. Instead, the two of you will follow each of these steps, with the knowledge that you will both get a turn. Approach it as an exercise in patience and compassion.

Talking Stick Holder: Assert Your Experience, Feelings, and Needs

Okay, talking stick holder. It's your turn. Using feeling words (happy, mad, sad, confused, etc.), express your experience. You can use the following example as a guide:

Donna and Mike, both in their forties, have been married for fifteen years. They have been in the swing lifestyle for years. They are pros, but pros screw up too. At a recent play party, Donna looked up from making out with her play partner, Chase, just in time to witness Mike knocking over and breaking her bear sculpture while he passionately made out with Veronica in their backyard. Afterward, he never apologized to her or made mention of it, despite knowing how important the sculpture was to her. She didn't sleep well that night and was still fuming the next morning. He went to work the next day, and upon arriving home, he *still* didn't mention it.

Donna finally said to Mike, "I need to talk to you. I'm upset with you. Can you hear me out?"

Mike checked in with himself to see if he was grounded. He'd had an extraordinarily stressful day. He was tired and was still spinning over something that had happened at work. So he said, "Sure. Of course. Just give me a few minutes." During that time, he went to the bathroom and made an effort to ground himself. He took several deep breaths, focused on getting present while letting go of the day's events, and talked to himself in the mirror, saying, "Let it go for now. Stay present with Donna." Once he felt he could hold his intent, he left the bathroom, sat down next to Donna, and said, "I'm ready."

Donna began, "Last night, while you were making out with Veronica, you knocked over and broke my bear sculpture. You know how special it is to me. It reminds me of our fifth anniversary vacation when you gave it to me. You made me feel so loved on that trip. I've always remembered our vacation to Big Bear especially fondly because of that. But you haven't said you're sorry. You haven't even brought it up. I waited until this morning. Nothing. I waited for a text while you were at work. Nothing. I feel so unloved by you. I'm just so freaking disappointed in you. You obviously don't give a shit about me."

Now, if Mike became defensive right now, he might lose his groundedness and presence. He and Donna could easily be off to the races, yelling at each other and heading toward a crash and burn. But couples therapy has helped Mike and Donna learn the steps of reflecting, validating, and empathizing during uncomfortable conversations like these. So he tries that now. He feels nervous and awkward about it, especially with Donna being so angry, but he persists anyway.

Let me pause the story here and tell you a bit about what Mike is about to attempt. Mirroring, empathizing, and validating are three core communication steps of what Harville Hendrix calls "Imago Dialogue" in *Getting the Love You Want.* The EPIC communication system is heavily influenced by the Imago Dialogue process. However, EPIC blends some of Harville's steps, has a less rigid structure, and has additional components of somatic psychotherapy, mindfulness, and research on compassion, thus creating a new approach.

Listener: Prepare Your Reflecting Approach

While utilizing the EPIC system, you will be reflecting your partner's story back to them both during Step 1: Emotional connection and Step 3: Intellectual connection (discussed below). Many of us are guilty of not truly listening when our partner is explaining their sadness, hurt, or anger. Instead, we formulate our reply as they speak, assuming we already know what they will say. To top it off, we often twist their intent to fit our own premanufactured view of their psyche. The combination of these two fallibilities often leads to our partner not feeling seen, thus adding an extra hurt to the pile.

Reflecting is designed to combat this. The act of reflecting is simply repeating back what you have heard. In doing so, we offer our partner the opportunity to correct us, add more, and know that they have been heard. In return, an upset partner might feel somewhat calmer. This technique, while it requires patience at first, will greatly reduce misunderstandings and increase a sense of being cared for. In the long run, it will save you time, increase your emotional connection, and reduce your argument recidivism. In other words, it's worth the effort!

So, let's set you up for success by making you aware of common mistakes. There are three missteps that can sabotage reflecting back to your partner: 1) reverting back to old patterns, 2) taking on more than you can handle, and 3) reflecting back when you are too upset.

Reverting back to old patterns

We often find ourselves reverting back to old, destructive patterns. If you cut your partner off left, right, and center as they speak in order to voice your defense, your new, improved communication will have died before it began. This sounds like common sense, but again, we humans tend to go back to old patterns. If you fall into this, have compassion for yourself and try again.

Taking on more than you can handle

The second common mistake is to repeat back more than what is humanly possible. Please don't bite off more than you can chew. It's tempting to let your partner completely finish explaining why they are hurt, even if they are going on at length. But people lose awareness of how long they have gone on when they are upset. Be cognizant of your memory limitations—and imagine what will happen when you can't summarize their lengthy monologue. Your partner might feel unheard and hurt, and decide that you don't care. So please, don't set yourself up for failure like that. Stop them at periodic intervals and create manageable sound bites so you are able to reflect back with success. That way, you will feel more confident and your partner will feel more seen.

Reflecting back when you are too upset

The third mistake is attempting to reflect back when you are too upset. Reflecting can become difficult if your partner's emotionality is dysregulating you or them. If you are not grounded, your upset might impair your focus so much so that you are unable to hear them, let alone reflect what they have said. You both have a responsibility not to yell, use a tone, or be emotionally abusive. Any of these three communication destroyers can dismantle a good start.

If you feel your partner has a tone or is yelling, try to stay away from saying, "You're yelling at me!" Say instead, "The volume and tone of your voice is upsetting me. Can you speak more softly and gently?" Now there is no argument. You haven't passed a negative judgment on the volume of their voice or the tone. You have simply expressed how their current volume and tone is emotionally impacting you. They can't or shouldn't say, "No, you're not upset," and there is little to be defensive about. You are simply stating how you are experiencing them. This communication is much more likely to get the response that you are hoping for.

When the sender pauses, or perhaps when you have asked them to pause, it's the receiver's task to repeat back what was said. Paraphrasing is okay, but analyzing, critiquing, modifying, or responding is not.

Reflecting language may start off with phrases such as, "If I got this right, I think you said . . ." or "So you're saying . . ." And then ask if there's more, perhaps by asking, "Is there more that you want me to know?" or by saying, "Tell me more."

Let's go back to Donna and Mike. Mike nervously attempts to reflect. He says to her, "Let me know if I have this right. Last night, when I broke your bear, I destroyed a precious memento that was symbolic of my love for you. The fact that I did not acknowledge that it happened or attempt to make amends added to your injury."

Donna replies, "Yes. That's right."

Mike reads her face. "Is there anything more that you want me to know?"

"No," she says. "That's about right." She sadly looks down.

Now that he's heard her confirmation, Mike can (gingerly) move into the next phase: emotional connection. (Note: Reflecting can be utilized through the lens of emotional connection, intellectual connection, or both. So now let's begin with the EPIC communication approach.)

Emotional Connection

Emotional connection is understanding another's emotional experience, or putting yourself in someone else's shoes. As with Imago Dialogue, empathizing is simply repeating back your partner's emotional language, such as sad, hurt, or angry. If the sender has not already expressed their emotions when they initially explained why they were upset, you can ask them for this information now.

Empathizing might be worded like, "I can imagine you might be feeling . . ." or "It sounds like you feel . . ."

Then you need to ask for confirmation: "Is that how you feel?" or "Is there more?"

Let's go back to Mike.

"It sounds like I really hurt you," he tells Donna. "You felt so loved on our anniversary in Big Bear. But when I broke your bear, you felt unloved. It sounds like it was crushing. I understand that you are sad and disappointed in me, especially since I didn't acknowledge the injury or try to make amends until you brought it up now. Is that correct? Is there anything more that you're feeling?"

"I just didn't know you had it in you to be so cruel and cold," Donna says. "It just hurts."

Mike struggles not to spiral into shame; he knows he has to stay present and with her. So, instead, he says, "I know. I must have seemed incredibly cruel and callous. I'm so sorry that I hurt you. Is there anything else that you're feeling?"

Donna sadly shakes her head no.

When the receiver attempts to emotionally connect with the sender, it is tempting and easy to slip into "thought language" such as: "It sounds like you feel as though I'm cruel and cold." But do you see how emotional language (disappointed, hurt, sad) is absent in this sentence? How that sentence expresses an idea, not an emotion? Emotional connection has to include emotional language in order to be heartfelt. And even if the thought is true, the sender may feel many various ways about that thought. So it's close, but no cigar.

The best way to distinguish the difference between a thought and a feeling is that a feeling can generally be described in one or two words, like happy, excited, frustrated, or scared. I have found in my practice that couples often go into expressing thoughts rather than feelings—probably because thoughts are easier and less scary to articulate. Staying in our head is an easy and common defense. It allows us to avoid facing our own vulnerability or our partner's feelings. However, such a heady place gets in the way of intimacy.

It is through the use of feeling words that your partner will feel seen by you.

Physical Connection

Physical connection can start with a somatic check-in. Are you still grounded in your body? If not, what would help?

Grounding can come from within or with your partner's help. If it's just you grounding yourself, you could do some deep breathing, put a weighted blanket on your lap, or hug a big pillow. If it's coming from your partner, you could ask for a hug or a hand on your knee, or to be the little spoon, while you talk through something hard. (Note: Physical check-ins and connection can happen before, during, or after your discussion. Any time you perceive that grounding is necessary for yourself or you partner, stop and move to this step.)

Going back to Donna and Mike:

They both take a second to check in with their bodies.

"How are you?" Mike asks. "Do you still feel grounded? Do you need anything in terms of touch?"

"No," she says. "I'm still too upset to be touched by you. Maybe later. But I am going to get some tea and a blanket and then we can continue to work through this."

"Okay," Mike says. "While you do that, I'm going to step outside for a couple of minutes."

While Donna boils water for her tea, Mike does some deep breathing on their front porch. Shortly, they reconvene in a more grounded space and move on to the next step.

Intellectual Connection

Connecting intellectually is validating or affirming that your partner's feelings or opinions are worthwhile and make sense. This one is powerful. For many of us, our childhood was filled with invalidations. For instance, a son says to his father, "I'm getting bullied at school. I don't know what to do. I'm really scared." Dad replies, "These are the moments that help you grow up, son. You just need to stand up to them. They'll back off. You'll be fine." Invalidation goes back to some of our most tender childhood wounds. Therefore, nothing creates a greater schism in an adult love relationship than invalidating our partner's feelings.

As damaging as invalidation is, validation is just as profoundly healing. It creates a sense of confidence and groundedness, and a deep knowing of being loved and seen. Therefore, validation from a loved one anchors the psyche. Again, think back to your childhood. Maybe you had a teacher, coach, or caregiver that got you, believed in you, and was able to nurture your gifts. Sometimes we only need one such person to change the course of our life. That's how powerful validation is.

In love relationships, validation can create a sense of calm within our body and connection to our partner while also conjuring feelings of love and gratitude. Meanwhile, invalidation creates sensations of dysregulation in the body, distance from our partner, and feelings of anger and loneliness. Our choice to validate or invalidate our loved ones becomes a massive contributor to whether we're cultivating a connected, conscious love that provides corrective experiences versus a toxic dynamic that retraumatizes childhood wounds.

Unfortunately, so often our first tendency when a romantic partner is upset with us is to invalidate. Within non-monogamy, this may occur if we fear that validating our partner may lead to us losing our freedom or losing an additional sexual or romantic relationship that we want to keep. When our partner's feelings scare us, we may unconsciously shut them down as quickly as possible—and in the short run, when they withdraw or fall silent, we may lie to ourselves, believing that we won the argument or set them straight. In reality, however, their silence is more likely indicative of a hopeless, helpless state, the precursor to emotional numbness, which is the antithesis of a connected, conscious love. Unfortunately, many of us are masters at invalidation, especially if we were invalidated as children. For many of us, this is a bad habit that has to be unlearned—a process that requires self-compassion and patience.

So, let's discuss how to intellectually connect and validate. Once the sender says there is "no more" to emote, the intellectual connection phase can begin. To start, the receiver simply lets the sender know that what they just expressed makes logical sense. (Keep in mind, you do not need to agree with everything that transpired or was said—you just need to confirm that it makes sense.)

Mike is not sentimental, so he probably wouldn't react the same way if Donna broke a gift given to him by a loved one. However, he understands that the bear meant a lot to Donna and he knows he screwed up by not addressing the issue immediately and making amends, so he can say from a truthful place, "It makes sense that you would be upset about my breaking the bear, since you saw him as a symbol of my love for you."

How to intellectually connect

Intellectual connection language may begin with, "What you're saying (or feeling) makes sense to me because . . ." or "That makes sense," or "I can understand where you are coming from because . . ."

I would encourage you to stick to what you can comfortably confirm. If you don't entirely understand where your partner is coming from, ask for more information. If you understand part of their experience, you might say, "This part makes sense to me, but help me understand, can you say more about [fill in the blank]?" This sentence structure is lovely because it does not put the sender on the defensive (in comparison to saying something like, "You make no sense to me," or "I have no clue what's going on with you").

Combining Emotional and Intellectual Connection

Now that we have looked at emotional and intellectual connection separately, let's go back to Donna and Mike's discussion and show what it looks like if Mike attempts to combine both while simultaneously reflecting back.

Mike thinks back to what he recently learned from their couples therapist about emotionally and intellectually connecting. "I get why you felt hurt, disappointed, and sad when I broke your bear, a memento from one of our best anniversaries, last night. It makes sense. It's a symbol of my love for you. I also understand that my lack of response or attempt to make amends just left you all the more hurt and sad. You didn't know that I had it in me to be so self-centered."

"Yes," Donna says. "That's true."

"Is there more?" Mike asks.

At this point, Donna might clarify her sadness, saying, "Honestly, I feel a little heartbroken. You're a better man than that. You've always been compassionate. You let me down."

At this, Mike will fight the urge to defend himself and simply reflect back with empathy, "I get it. I understand."

This is allowing her to understand that he sees her, which is the point of reflecting. She might respond by simply saying, "Yes," and then he can continue to reflect and empathize until she feels that he truly understands the story and her feelings. In doing so, she feels his love and begins to heal.

In the beginning, I would encourage you to break down the steps into three parts—emotional, physical, and intellectual connection—but eventually, these three stages may blend and simply become how you communicate with the world. This new, connected way of being may extend to your best friends, or even to your short chats with your grocery bagger. Everyone loves being empathized with, attended to, and validated. No one gets enough of that. When you reach this point, the three separate steps will evolve into something more fluid and organic.

Now back to Donna. She might reply by saying, "Yes, and the fact that *I* had to approach *you* almost twenty-four hours later made it worse. But hearing that you understand and care is appreciated, and it's a strong step toward me feeling better."

Attuning to our partner's emotional state is an art that can be forever improved upon. When we are truly present and mindful, we are better able to hear their words, pick up on their body language, and read their expressions, or even micro expressions, with more accuracy. We have the space within ourselves to allow another to exist without interrupting, shaming, or attempting to control them. The more emotionally healthy we are, the better able we will be to do this.

The stronger our inner core, the easier we're able to validate another person without losing touch with our own internal truth and sense of self. And the more we cultivate a secure attachment style, the more we will become an oak tree with deep roots. Validating another will become second nature. As this ability is cultivated, communicating with control, dominance, and manipulation tactics will fade and be replaced with validating and empathizing with our partner with ease.

Compassionate Connection

Once you move through emotional, physical, and intellectual connection, it's time to take action: it's time for a compassionate connection.

Once the sender has had their needs reflected and validated with empathy, the sender can then state what they need for repair. For instance, Donna expresses her need: "What I really need is an apology and a promise that you won't wait until the next day to address my feelings in the future if you know I'm hurt."

Now it's time to negotiate before Mike gets his turn holding the emotional talking stick. He might say, "I deeply apologize. I'm so sorry that I put you through this, Donna. I hate hurting you. And I'm so sorry for the delay. There are reasons, but for now I'll just say that there won't be such a delay going forward. I only have one ask. If we are in the midst of a party, I'll probably pull you into the bathroom to find out what is wrong, and if you say a full discussion can occur later, I'll want to hash it out in full after the party is over and our guests have left."

Donna might come back with, "Yes, that make sense. But please don't completely wait until the party is over. You know there are ways for us to briefly get away from guests to exchange a few words in private."

"Absolutely," Mike says. "Agreed."

They smile at each other.

"Can I give you a hug?" he asks.

In response, she extends her arms, and he, in turn, wraps his big, warm arms around her. Donna now feels seen, heard, and cared for, even though it will take a while before the upset completely fades. After a brief break, she is able to hand over the emotional talking stick to Mike.

Mike says, "I hesitate to discuss what was going on with me, because I know how upset you were. I have no excuse for breaking your bear in the first place. I should have been more aware. However, I do want to explain why it took me so long to address the issue. When I woke up this morning, you were sleeping and I didn't want to wake you. I intended to call once I got to work, but once I got there, we had an emergency staff meeting and I found out that our company is being sold and I might lose my job in the process. The whole office was in a panic. I got caught up in the chaos and completely forgot to call. I honestly was still completely panicked about that when I got home."

Donna is able to both emotionally and intellectually connect as she says, "Yes. You should have addressed it last night, but I can understand that the events at work had you panicked which made you forget to call me. It's not an excuse, but I get it." She follows with making sure she's hearing everything. "Did I hear you correctly? Is there anything else that you are feeling?" Here, she is reflecting, validating, and empathizing in one step, but also remembering to ask for more until she has heard everything.

"Yes," Mike says. "I knew that you were already upset with me for breaking your bear. I knew you were already disappointed in me. I was scared that the threat of losing my job would just make you more disappointed in me. We've already been struggling."

Donna reflects back with validation and empathy, "I can see how breaking my bear and the threat of losing your job became emotionally compounded in your mind. You must have been really fearful about how I might react." Her face softens as she feels his upset.

"Thank you," Mike says. "I believe that you get it."

They move to compassionate connection and negotiation.

"I'm still getting over my sadness," Donna says. "That will take time. But I'm calm enough to give you your turn. What do you need, Mike? Given my recent upset, please make your request reasonable."

Mike said, "Please just don't give up on me. I get that I need to earn your forgiveness and trust again. I'll make things right again, both at home and at work."

Donna replies, "I know you will. We will get through this together. We always have each other's back."

Now, things likely won't go so smoothly as this example portrays. However, I can promise you that those who refrain from invalidating their partner and who make a point to empathize will find themselves with calmer, more content loved ones.

And a word of advice: If you are new to these strategies or your relationship is struggling, don't combine the steps. If one or both of you is in the high zone (heightened uncomfortable emotion, such as anger or anxiety) or in the low zone (dissociating, checking out, withdrawing), then you need to stop and go back to the grounding strategies in Chapter 12. Then, once you're both grounded, break the steps down. And go slow! Being in the high or low zone is a sign of emotional dysregulation that requires a more slow, methodical, and boundaried structure to the discussion.

This recommendation holds true whether you own that you are out of your Resilient Zone or if only your partner perceives you this way. If your partner is perceiving you as upset, they may very well be dysregulated themselves and need grounding. Regardless, you aren't ready to combine steps. Combining the steps is for cool cucumbers who are present in their body and have been practicing the three steps for a while. Please be humble in this. Accept where you are and be patient. Patience will win out.

When you use the EPIC communication approach, you're more likely to stay grounded in your body and thus clearheaded while you connect with your loved one. This system is great for any relationship model, but let's face it, non-monogamy is more complex and challenging. We need all the tools we can get, and it takes time to learn how to practice them all well. But once we do, our chances of relationship success increase by leaps and bounds.

Chapter Fourteen

STEPPING OUT
OF DENIAL

When it comes to non-monogamy, even the most emotionally intelligent people can realize, in hindsight, that they have been in denial regarding certain aspects of their non-monogamous dynamic. We can go into a state of denial for many reasons, but often it occurs when reality becomes too emotionally overwhelming, or when it is in dissonance with our immediate desires. Here are six common denials that I see in my practice:

1. Love with Our Other Partners
Can Be Controlled

Many people believe that they can control love and, if need be, walk away from love. And maybe some folks can, but often such believers find out, the hard way, that they are dead wrong. Once love strikes, they can't walk away—or they simply don't want to.

Despite this truth, couples often include in their relationship agreement wording such as, "We will allow ourselves to date other people, but if one of us falls in love, that person will end the secondary relationship." Others truly believe it's not in their psychological makeup to love anyone else but their primary partner. Does this sound reasonable to you? To me it sounds like someone who's convinced themself that they're a robot.

If love with other partners happens, that doesn't mean that the primary or nesting partner relationship will inevitably be destroyed. It does mean that when the denial is ripped away and the reality of loving another sets in, one partner might be heartbroken or feel betrayed.

In juxtaposition, the reality-based couple that realizes they may end up falling in love with other partners if they date separately is in a much stronger position when it comes to weathering change and keeping their relationship healthy, because they can emotionally process and adjust in advance.

Let's take Madeleine and Frank. They had been swingers for five years. Over time, they grew frustrated because finding a couple they both liked seemed nearly impossible. So they decided to see other people. At first, they saw singles in the lifestyle. But over time, they decided they both wanted relationships with more depth. Soon, they were looking for partners outside of the lifestyle community. Once they both owned that they wanted deeper connections with others, Frank said, "But if one of us falls in love, we will end it, right?"—and Madeleine agreed.

After dating a few new people, they both found partners who had more substance, both intellectually and emotionally. Two years passed quickly. Frank started booking most of the month to see his girlfriend, Genevieve. Madeleine began to pull away and see Bruce more and more. Bruce was emotionally young, but he allowed Madeleine to take the reins in ways that Frank didn't and she loved him for that. She began to blossom and grow in unexpected ways. The two of them had endless fun adventures together. Meanwhile, Madeleine and Frank found that after ten years together, they had grown apart and had little to say to one another.

One night, it all came to a head.

"I can see what you're doing," Frank said. "You're pulling away from me. Break up with him. Let's just focus on each other."

Madeleine looked at him with a steely resolve that frightened Frank and simply said, "No."

Frank's face fell.

A year later, they were hiring a divorce mediator.

In contrast, let's look at Trinity and Ian, who navigated non-monogamy from a more reality-based lens. These two also began as swingers and had reached a similar point of wanting to play with other lovers separately and have deeper, connected relationships. At that point, they had a long talk.

"You know, if we do this, one or both of us might fall in love with our other partners," Ian said.

"I get that," Trinity said. "It's scary, isn't it?"

"Yes, and exciting," Ian said.

Trinity nodded.

What commenced after that was a discussion about how to keep their mental, emotional, and sexual connection so strong that it could withstand many loves, whether those loves materialized or not. They decided to read couple's communication skills books. They learned how to communicate with empathy and connection. They hired a sex-positive psychotherapist who also had a strong knowledge of attachment theory and EMDR training. She helped them clear old wounds that were creating barriers between them. They went to neo-tantra retreats and BDSM classes to learn new ways to connect more deeply and creatively with one another. They made sure that they maintained a vested interest in each other's intellectual and creative pursuits. They learned the importance of living in gratitude for one another. And through these action steps, they learned to love each other well. They grew to love each other so deeply that their other loves—and they did find other loves—simply added to their happiness.

That sounds like a lot of work, right? But why not reframe learning to love well as *fun*? Yes, at times it will feel like work. But the time you spend on it will be a fraction of the time you have spent at the gym or school, or cleaning your house. Isn't learning to love well as important as any of these things?

Loving well—and I'm talking about cultivating a conscious, connected love—does not happen organically. Unfortunately, Hollywood movies have misguided us. They send the message that love is easy if you choose the right person and portray intense connections between two people with unresolved psychic injuries as desirable. But the reality of a truly connected love is quite different. It has been consciously cultivated. It's more peaceful *and* it allows for a hot sexual dynamic.

2. Hierarchy Is Easily Maintained

Another area riddled with denial or naivete is the one surrounding the debate over hierarchical versus nonhierarchical non-monogamy. People get very opinionated about the concept of hierarchy. Some feel hierarchical non-monogamy is unsustainable and inherently unethical. But (not surprisingly) there is an opposing view too. Those who believe in a hierarchy might argue that treating a partner of two weeks as being on an even playing field with a spouse of ten years is unethical. I believe both camps have their valid points.

Let's discuss nonhierarchical versus hierarchical relationships a little bit more.

Nonhierarchical relationships come in various forms, but the commonality between them is the intention to treat every relationship as equal, powerful, and as important as the next. Hierarchical relationships, meanwhile, tend to assign levels of importance, priority, and power to each partner. Terms such as "primary," "secondary," and sometimes "tertiary" are often used to describe various levels of importance and commitment.

A hierarchy may be prescriptive or descriptive. A prescriptive hierarchy has an emotional component and implies that if a choice has to be made, the primary's needs will often come first over another partner's. If, however, the primary role is merely descriptive, the primary partner holds this status simply because it's practical. This partner has to be considered first due to commitments, such as parenting, marriage, and shared financial obligations, but not necessarily because they're more loved or emotionally valued than another partner.

Some have purposefully avoided these ranking terms, which may feel demeaning to other partners, by using terms like "nesting partner" or "anchor partner" to describe a higher level of entanglement. The nesting partner is often that person you foresee sharing a home with and potentially growing old with.

Most clients I see have some sort of hierarchy in their relationships. Of the individuals who see me, most go home to a primary or nesting relationship, triad, or V relationship. I get everything from swingers who always play together to poly folks who have many other lovers. Those other lovers may be important and deeply cared about, but they're usually not earmarked for major plans such as retirement and child-rearing, thereby making them relationships that one or both people are less emotionally invested in.

Now that we have covered these basic definitions, I want to talk about the ethical challenges inherent in these differing relationship models—but first, let's consider if you can truly pull off maintaining a prescriptive, primary relationship in the long term.

In order to consider this question, let's clarify the threats to maintaining the healthy integrity of an ethical hierarchy. Three of the biggest challenges are: 1) new relationship energy (NRE) or limerence, 2) typecasting, and 3) greater attunement with a new lover. Let's discuss all three.

Challenge #1: New relationship energy (NRE)

Because NRE with a new lover is so wonderfully blissful and powerful, it's a top challenger to maintaining a hierarchy within non-monogamy. Few things are as captivating and feel as good as intense NRE, which can be described as that natural drug high that occurs when you initially emotionally and/or sexually connect with a new lover.

When you feel attraction to someone, your body releases both dopamine and norepinephrine. Meanwhile, low levels of serotonin create obsessive thoughts of the new love interest. Other neurochemicals conspire with these influences to make you blissfully lose your judgment and ability to see the big picture . . . if you allow yourself to become lost in it. Together, these hormones make love or sexual attraction a pleasurable experience similar to the euphoria associated with use of cocaine or alcohol.

As you erotically ramp up for your next hot date by sexting, you may be experiencing NRE. You may be walking around with a smile on your face, sexually lit up, distracted, and excitedly awaiting the next nude or sexy message to arrive on your phone. You may say to yourself, *I haven't felt this good in years.*

But let's stop for a moment. Imagine how this can make a primary partner feel. Your body maybe physically there, but they are completely aware that you are emotionally gone. Even if you're seated right next to them, they know your thoughts are elsewhere. This loss can be heartbreaking for the partner watching this unfold.

Coping with NRE

If you are experiencing NRE, you know firsthand how it could be destructive to a primary or nesting partner relationship and thus the established hierarchy. Contending with it responsibly requires some effort. Frequent reality checks are needed because your mind will be prone to telling you lies under these conditions.

A mental reality check may sound something like this: *I am not going to leap to the conclusion that I have found my soul mate even though I'm experiencing a blissful natural high, a chemical cocktail coursing through every cell in my body. I may feel that I am head over heels in love, but I have to own that I don't really know my new partner yet. I only know the first onion layer of their personality.* This self-talk with help you hold yourself in check. This is a hard but often doable endeavor, especially if your primary relationship is strong, connected, and healthy.

Risk

There is, of course, a possibility that the NRE you're experiencing is a sign of a blossoming love. If love occurs, the hierarchy you've established may begin to break down, often in subtle ways. Perhaps the new lover is taken on a vacation when up until now only the primary couple went on vacation together. Maybe you find out the new partner has a pet name where before only you had one.

The risk of love developing with other partners can somewhat be reduced by having a more boundaried relationship, like swingers usually do. But if you are playing separately, please don't slip into denial regarding the doors you are opening. Love can happen. And if love happens, the chance that the hierarchy will begin to shift is a damn good bet.

Challenge #2: Typecasting

Many sex educators state that NRE is the biggest threat to the polyamorous primary relationship. However, in my practice, I've found that two phenomena might have NRE topped. The first is typecasting.

Just as it does with Hollywood actors, typecasting within non-monogamy occurs when one person is relegated to a certain archetype or role. What if you didn't sign up for that role?

This kind of situation usually plays out when couples hold delusions and assumptions about how things will unfold once they start to play separately. These assumptions are fed by lack of knowledge and denial. Many people honestly believe that they will remain primary in all major ways and continue to relate to each other as they always have once they introduce non-monogamy into the relationship. Instead, typecasting often occurs.

As we discussed in Chapter 6, what often unfolds in a non-monogamous relationship is that the primary gets cast in a Clark Kent role—the predictable one who shares responsibilities, such as child-rearing, cleaning the house, and other adulting. "Clark" is primary when it comes to nesting goals: family, home, and friendship. The new lover, meanwhile, gets cast as Superman—the sexy, romanticized one—and eventually becomes primary in areas like sex and carefree play.

Guess what? No one wants to be typecast to play the responsible, boring one. Nobody. Beyond Gary Chapman's five love languages is the love language of adventure, freedom, and carefree fun. Most people drawn to non-monogamy fall in love due to this shared love language. They pride themselves in being the adventure buddy. So how the hell did they get cast as the boring one? Unfortunately, this is a common problem when couples decide to play separately and typecasting causes a shift in roles.

If, however, a primary relationship has awareness of this phenomenon and takes action steps to shape it, they are more likely to be able to have some control in how this process manifests. For instance, as I mentioned before, couples who play together or swing are less likely to deal with typecasting because they are sharing sexual adventures together, thus maintaining a sexy, adventurous, carefree role in each other's life.

The farther down the poly train tracks one gets, the more hierarchy takes on a life of its own. Emotions aren't easily controlled—not authentically, anyway. The best way for a primary/nesting partner dynamic to stay healthy is for the couple to always stay mentally, emotionally, and physically connected. If any of these three connections slide, typecasting is almost certain to occur.

Let's look at two examples.

Paulina and Wes had been married for fifteen years. They had two beautiful kids they adore and successful careers. However, their sex life had waned. Troubled by this, they talked about bringing heat back into their bedroom by each taking on another lover. They agreed to set boundaries with any outside lovers while clearly stating that they, Paulina and Wes, were primaries and the outside lovers were secondary.

Soon, Paulina began to date Connor and Wes began to date Audrey. At first it was great. They enjoyed sharing their erotic adventure stories. The lovely by-product, as predicted, was that the two of them started fucking like rabbits again.

But then Paulina found out that Wes was multiply orgasmic with Audrey, and Wes began to be intimidated by Connor's physique (he was a personal trainer). Slowly, Paulina and Wes went back to having sex less. Concurrently, the heat with their outside lovers ramped up. Paulina discovered that she could have sex with Connor all night long—and by day they started taking CrossFit classes together. Meanwhile, Wes discovered BDSM with Audrey. He realized that he was kinky, and that this unmet need was one reason his sex life with Paulina had waned. Sex with Audrey was delicious for him.

It slowly became apparent that Connor was Paulina's sexual primary and Audrey was Wes's sexual primary. Paulina and Wes remained primary regarding raising their kids, sharing holidays together, visiting family, and planning for old age, but their sex life all but disappeared. This dynamic organically unfolded before they were even aware enough to steer this typecasting of themselves.

Meanwhile, let's go back to Trinity and Ian in the example from earlier in this chapter. They had NRE with their new loves, but the sexual chemistry remained strong between them. They made a point to carve out date nights, in which they both let go of their Mom/ Dad responsibility roles and morphed into their sexual archetypes. The process of getting ready for date night allowed that transition to happen. They tried not to watch each other transform for the date so the big reveal would be more of a surprise.

Some women are sex kittens. Trinity, once she discarded the mom sweatpants for a hot little black dress, was more of a sex goddess.

And Ian was more switchy, sometimes dominant, other times submissive. Trinity loved that about him. It allowed her to connect with him in many ways. The extra work they did to maintain connection (sexually, intellectually, and emotionally) stopped any sort of glaring typecasting from happening. Sure, each lover they took on offered different individual strengths, but since the two of them maintained a strong connection, they were able to enjoy their outside partners without sacrificing the happy, healthy relationship they had with each other.

These two couples illustrate how typecasting can unfold, and also how it can be managed or minimized. Regardless, only so much of this is within your control. All you can control is you. For instance, if you are in a ten-year relationship and your partner discovers that they are kinky, they are likely to go on a journey that leads them (happily) down a kinky rabbit hole. They may even discover a new, kinky family of friends. If that's not your thing, you may feel emotionally left. Meanwhile, your lover will likely feel more bonded to partners who can connect erotically to them in this way. This is beyond your control. What is in your control is finding another, equally compelling erotic connection with your partner—like neo-tantra, for example—that will allow you to maintain a unique and potent sexual bond with one another.

Challenge #3: Greater attunement with a new lover

The second monster challenge to hierarchy that tops NRE is when greater mental, emotional, and physical attunement is found with a new partner. This dynamic is even more intense than typecasting because it's all-encompassing. And it can easily occur.

Let's look at Clive and Amanda, who had been partners for ten years. When they first met, the connection was intense. They shared a ton of common interests. The sex was fantastic. Emotionally, they just got each other. The two of them were mentally, emotionally, and sexually connected. But that was a long time ago, and they've both changed.

When their therapist asked them to reassess the three areas of connection that had been so strong for them in the beginning, this is what Clive and Amanda discovered:

Mentally: They no longer shared the same interests. Clive was into action movies, role-playing games, and staying at home. Amanda was into social justice movements, parties, and travel.

Emotionally: Clive was sick of hearing Amanda complain about her mother and her boss. Amanda was sick of feeling emotionally unsupported by Clive.

Sexually: They were only having sex once a month at best. Built-up resentments and changes in sexual interests had created a wedge between them.

Now guess what happened when the sparkly new lovers, Mirabel and Jamal, arrived on the scene. Mirabel loved action movies and had been an active participant in a role-playing game every Tuesday for the last three years. She was bendy and an enthusiastic lover. She wanted to know everything about Clive, all his feelings. She was captivated.

Amanda met Jamal at a Black Lives Matter march. She dropped her protest sign amongst the crowd and Jamal quickly stepped in, held the crowd back, and helped her retrieve it. Upon rising back up, his eyes met hers and it was magic. Jamal is energetic. He loves a good party or travel adventure. Every cell in Amanda's body lit up upon their first kiss.

This phenomenon, way more worrisome for the original couple than the chemical cocktail of NRE, is a common dynamic. The primary couple has become disconnected, and they have each found a fierce mental, emotional, and sexual connection with their new lover.

When this dynamic is set into motion a chain reaction ensues that's hard to stop.

It's better to get in front of this dynamic with awareness and concerted effort. Prioritize staying mentally, emotionally, and sexually connected with your primary, and see if you can regard this effort as fun rather than work. If you maintain this firm foundation, the Jamal and Mirabel in your lives will simply add to your already wonderful existence. They will be a blessing, not a final straw.

3. The Couple's Feelings, Needs, and Desires Are All That Matter

"Couple privilege" is a term that gets many polyamorists up in arms—and for good reason. As we have discussed in a few other chapters, couple privilege can be defined as the advantage that an established couple has over additional partners. It can't be eliminated (not in a hierarchical relationship structure, anyway), but it can be managed. However, just like other types of identity that can afford privilege, such as race, socioeconomic status, or gender, those who have couple privilege often can't see it—a lack of awareness that can cause injuries to those who become its victims.

Couple privilege is most likely to rear its ugly head in prescriptive hierarchical relationships. In an effort to protect the primary relationship, the couple treats their other lovers in demeaning ways. Often, the primary couple is completely unaware of or in denial about the ways in which their lovers are being emotionally injured.

Privilege can manifest in many ways. I can't tell you how many times I've heard a swinger couple half-joke with trusted friends, "Oh, our other lovers are just human sex toys to us." Such an attitude leaks out in subtle ways and the other lovers sense it. It doesn't feel good. It's not hot and it's disrespectful. Now, if your lover's kink is to be objectified and they have consented to such a dynamic, that's one thing. But most of us aren't into being thought of as walking dildos or fleshlights.

It is true that misguided good intentions sometimes exist behind these unkindnesses. For instance, one partner may be a bit jealous of another lover, so their primary says, "Baby, they're just our sex toy. They aren't a threat to our love." Although this dehumanization can put the jealous partner at ease, what is the price of this comfort? There are better ways to work through a fear of abandonment or being less desired than to dehumanize other lovers.

Sometimes this inherent disrespect starts from the beginning. I'll give you an example. Ray is married to Julia. He sets off to look for a unicorn for them on popular dating sites. Since identifications such as non-monogamous, polyamorous, or pansexual may scare off a lot of women, he portrays himself as single rather than non-monogamous with an existing primary. Boom! He has already behaved in an unkind and misleading manner.

Why is what he did so bad? Imagine that Sue sees his profile and really digs it. She's non-monogamous but looking for a primary. She becomes emotionally invested and excited about him. It's not until their second date, where he can tell that she is "all in," that he tells her about Julia. Sue feels her heart sink and a deep sadness sweep over her. She pauses, then says, "I'm sorry. I'm looking for a primary. I'm not interested in this dynamic." He has been disrespectful to her time and to her feelings by hiding the truth.

Certainly, anyone who's been non-monogamous for long enough has been the victim of couple privilege. You know, that couple that courted you for weeks, but once you slept with them and they were satisfied, they stared at you silently until you sheepishly picked up your clothes and awkwardly backed out of their bedroom, feeling less than human? Or the couple that says, "You're part of the family! We love you. We want to share everything with you," and even introduces you to their children, but when the holidays roll around, no invitation is given to join the family and you're left spending the holidays alone? Such mixed messages are potentially heartbreaking and certainly not okay.

But just because a couple has a hierarchy doesn't mean that kind of cruelty is inevitable. It is possible to treat other partners with dignity, respect, and gratitude within a well-disclosed hierarchy with clarified boundaries. And of course, other partners can always walk away if the relationship no longer meets their needs at any point. They have their own agency. No one is trapped.

To bring in another example of how to do this well, let's look at Chloe and Anton, who've been dating for a couple of years. They started out playing separately, but as their relationship progressed, they decided they wanted to share lovers. They looked at their swinger friends. They looked at their poly friends. They decided they wanted to do a hybrid of the two extremes and decided to carve out time to look for lovers together. By sharing this discovery process, they felt they were more likely to find a lover they were equally excited about and attracted to.

Ultimately, they found two lovers, Amy and Angela, and they began to see each woman once a month—but they didn't limit the experience to simply sex. They took Amy to Six Flags. They took Angela to nice restaurants and parties. They built a true friendship with both of them. However, both women knew the limitations of the relationship. They knew, for example, that they wouldn't be asked to move in. They weren't going to be invited to celebrate Chloe and Anton's anniversary. But they also knew that Chloe and Anton honored them and showed appreciation and gratitude for them. The honesty, transparency, and integrity inherent in all interactions was consistent. Both Amy and Angela had other lovers and at times had primaries of their own.

This healthy dynamic is possible, and clear communication is the key. Boundaries and consent to relationship agreements can support this. Misleading or hiding facts from a new lover in order to lure them is not okay.

Hierarchies get unhealthy when a couple misleads other lovers or keeps them out of the loop regarding things that have a direct impact on them. This is common—and it's also a by-product of couple privilege. Primaries often don't tell other lovers about their fights, for instance. And while the intention may be good—perhaps they don't want to upset the other partner about things that don't directly concern them—the other partner will likely sense that something is wrong but have no idea what that something is, which can lead to anxiety and suffering. To be told, "No, everything is fine," when you know it's not is crazy-making. The partner is left wondering, *Are they mad at me? Are they going to break things off with me? Did I do something wrong?* The tension may have nothing to do with them, but they don't know that.

That is not to say that other partners need to know everything that goes on. If the negative energy is so palpable that it can't be hidden, an explanation should be given as a courtesy, even if it's simply to say, "It's not about you, and it's not anything that's going to cause any major shifts in our relationship or our relationship with you." Such a sentence will more than likely address some of the major fears the other partner is experiencing. And a follow-up sentence, such as, "Does that put your concerns to rest?" is even better. Again, compassion is key.

Remember, just as a fish can't see the water it swims in, you will not always have awareness of how couple privilege is affecting your other lovers. Therefore, it's crucial to check in with your partners. Let them know that you are aware of the concept of couple privilege and also that you may not always be aware of when it's impacting them. Do regular check-ins with them and let them know that the door is open if they feel a need to voice concerns at any juncture. Such open communication is a good start to combat this very real challenge.

Couples can also let other lovers know where they stand regarding their relationship model and boundaries. The bigger the commitment, the more the new lover needs to know. A hookup who we only intend to see once doesn't need to know every detail of a relationship agreement. But a lover who may be an ongoing partner needs to know about any relationship agreement that may impact them. Even a hookup should be treated with at least as much courtesy as you would give to a dinner guest. And no, this courtesy does not need to infringe upon hot, primal sex.

Let's look at some more examples of couples who have faced these issues and how they navigated them.

Lexi and Peter had been searching for a bull to fulfill Peter's cuckhold/hot wife fantasy. They found Damian, who advertised himself as a bull on a lifestyle dating site and had many positive reviews. They sent a few emails back and forth and he seemed like a good fit, so Lexi and Peter stated their desires to him:

We want a bull, probably for a one-time experience. We want him to come in and ravage Lexi while Peter sits in the corner on a chair. If anything is wrong, one of us will say, "red," at which point all sex should stop. We would like to know your safe word, hard nos, and anything else you would like to negotiate in advance as well. Lexi loves to have her hands held down. Oral and vaginal sex is on the table. Breath play, like choking, along with face slapping and anal, are hard nos.

Although some cuckholds love to be demeaned directly, Peter likes to be treated as invisible, unless he uses the safe word. Lexi might talk about Peter as if he's not in the room. Feel free to go with whatever she is saying. You can fuck her until she's exhausted. When she's spent or when you need to go, you can say your goodbyes and leave.

Other BDSM-related play, like restraining Lexi with rope, might be on the table, if we invite you back and you decide to play with us again. But this time, we want to keep it simple. Does that sound good to you?

Damian's response is:

Yes. I need to leave by 2:00 a.m. because I need to take my daughter to a birthday party by noon the next day. I'll bring

condoms. Please let me know if you have any other safe sex rules.
Does that sound cool to you two?

They all agree and plan a time to talk one last time right before their date to discuss any final feelings and safe sex practices.

Now, even this potential one-shot experience took a lot of communication. And it should be noted that scene negotiations can be much more lengthy and detailed. But Lexi and Peter were respectful to Damian by letting him know the extent of possible emotional and sexual connection. They aren't looking for a boyfriend but rather a one-night, hot fantasy. Damian is down for that. He also knows how he will be treated after sex. Peter probably won't say a word, and Lexi will simply say goodbye to him. Since he understands their dynamic, he won't be confused or insulted by Peter's silence. And, finally, he has a good sense of everyone's role, including his own, and has been asked if this scenario is hot to him. His desires have been considered and heard.

Now let's look at another scenario with this couple. After years of being swingers, Lexi and Peter decided they would like to date one special person. They reached out to Penelope, who they'd met at a lifestyle party months earlier and had maintained a friendship with ever since. They felt she would be a good fit because she was pansexual and kinky, and had been non-monogamous for several years. Also, she already had a lover whom she considered her top priority, which made it more likely she'd agree to the boundaries they intended to propose to her.

After texting back and forth with Penelope, they took her out to dinner and a show. They let her know that they weren't looking for love but rather a play partner and true friend they could see once a month. They let her know that they were aware of couple privilege and that while they did have boundaries, they would make an active attempt to be aware of that dynamic and attempt to avoid it.

This opened the door for Penelope to speak plainly. She told

Peter and Lexi a story of a past couple who shut her out and, eventually, abruptly dumped her without explanation when they hit hard times. She told them another story of a couple who courted her and developed a friendship with her, and then, once she had sex with them, never contacted her again, leaving her feeling used. She asked them if they were willing to hear what she would need from them.

Peter and Lexi assured her that they were all ears.

"I don't need to know about the hard times you are having at work or your sick grandma," Penelope said, "although please tell me if you would like to. But I *do* need to know if you two are having troubles that are due to me. I need to have room to express my feelings. And know that I intend to continue dating other people, because I would like a nesting partner of my own."

This all sounded just fine to Lexi and Peter.

Granted, this is just the beginning of these three expressing their wants and desires. And these wants and desires will change over time. But this is where they are now. And it's a fine start.

As you can see, reducing the effect of couple privilege is achievable if you're being considerate. So keep communication alive: hear all parties' needs, keeping all parties in the loop regarding emotions and events that may affect them, avoiding building false hopes; treat others with respect; and show them gratitude for what they bring to your life. In doing so, you'll make your lovers feel seen and appreciated.

4. Communication between Metamours Isn't Necessary

It's easy to dismiss the importance of having an established open door to communication with your partner's metamours. But this denial often has dire consequences down the road. As I've said before, being good at non-monogamy is akin to being good at chess. A good chess player is aware of the board as a whole. They know that their choices regarding one piece will have an impact on others. It follows, then, that a poor chess player may have tunnel vision—may focus exclusively on one piece and in the process leave all their other pieces unattended to. Similarly, a skilled non-monogamist considers everyone's needs, including their own, and is mindfully aware of each person's impact on the others, while the less skilled non-monogamist often emotionally melts into one lover at a time, fading out everyone else, and in doing so disrespects others' feelings, requests, and needs.

Paul, Ellie, and Sergio provide an example of this. Ellie has been seeing both Paul and Sergio for two and five years, respectively. For the health of such long-term poly relationships, it's necessary for metamours, in this case Paul and Sergio, to be civil with each other and feel safe to run requests, feelings, or thoughts by each other if need be. However, Paul and Sergio don't really care for each other and try to avoid talking or seeing each other as much as possible. Over time, tension has increased between them—mostly due to heightened misunderstandings and poor communication. Ellie is often asked to be the go-between. And as a result, both men are frequently pissed at Ellie.

Friday, March 25, is the anniversary of Ellie's first date with Sergio. They typically celebrate this date as any married couple might celebrate a wedding anniversary. Sometimes they go to a five-star restaurant. Sometimes they go on vacation. This year, however, March 25 is also the date of Paul's physics master's degree graduation ceremony and after-party. He is the first in his family to even get a college degree, let alone his master's. He is estranged from his family and moved to California to be close to Ellie.

Both men expect her to be with them on this day, and anything less will be seen as disrespectful. What's a girl to do?

Admittedly, this example is extreme, but you will find yourself in situations like this at times if you are full-on poly. The key is to insist that all parties communicate clearly from the beginning. Why? Because even if Sergio and Paul don't care for each other, if they have their communication cordial and open, both men will feel respected by each other—and from this place of three-way trust, difficult situations can be negotiated. In this case, for instance, both men will be more likely to negotiate time spent. Maybe Ellie can agree to go to the graduation ceremony and attend the after-party until 3:00 p.m., and then hop a plane to Vegas with Sergio at 8:00 p.m., leaving time for dancing at a Vegas nightclub by midnight. This is feasible, but only if the two men have some basic respect for each other and don't view the other as the enemy.

In other words, it's not enough for respect to exist between Paul and Ellie and Sergio and Ellie. Respect has to be maintained and nurtured between the metamours as well.

How does this translate to your form of non-monogamy? Well, if your partner takes on a new lover and they look like they'll be a keeper, perhaps you should meet them for coffee or at least have a short phone call. During that conversation, you can let them know that if they ever need clarity or need to express feelings, you're willing to listen. It doesn't have to be a grand effort. In the long run, even a small amount of communication can defuse a lot drama.

5. I Understand the Inherit Risks within Non-Monogamy

In the context of this book, risk involves the probability or degree to which one might lose something of value. Stating the obvious, you can't own a human—so what might you lose in a non-monogamous relationship? Let's make a list:

1) You or your partner might fall in love with someone else as a result of non-monogamous exploration, and you might fall out of love with your primary or nesting partner (or vice versa) in the process. This switcheroo may partially be due to attachment wiring; it's true, not everyone is wired

to be fully in love with more than one person simultaneously. For many, losing one's partner to another is the biggest fear of all.

2) You or your partner may realize that you aren't as much of a sexual match for each other as you thought. This realization sometimes happens as part of the discovery process that occurs once you become non-monogamous.

3) And here is the catch-all: You and your partner may grow apart in unforeseen ways as you explore non-monogamy.

From an attachment lens, these are the heavy-hitter fears. Despite the fact that you can't fully control whether any of these three fears will come to pass, setting relationship boundaries does have an impact. Relationship boundaries can be loose, such as, "Do whatever you want with whomever you want, but please inform me if any relationship gets serious." They can also be tight, such as, "We will only play together. We will only play with other couples. And we will end the night around 2:00 a.m." Neither loose nor tight boundaries are inherently healthier. Some partners who give each other a ton of rope are healthy and happy. In other partnerships, loose boundaries may lead to emotional chaos. In some partnerships, a lot of restrictions may feel safe. In others, such tight boundaries might set one or both partners up for failure. You simply have to find what's right for you and all parties involved. This discovery process will most likely include plenty of trial and error.

A loose non-monogamous relationship model requires something akin to a Buddhist-inspired non-attachment philosophy. To illustrate, consider this metaphor for life: Imagine you're looking into a stream. Some fish swim by, some floating leaves pass, and then a tin can bobs by. You are powerless to change any of that. All that is good and all that is bad is simply floating by. You cannot control, own, or keep any of what you see.

This mindset is a tall order for most people. As Buddhist monk

Thich Nhat Hahn once said, "You must love in such a way that the person you love feels free." This, my friend, is some next-level shit.

Freedom is a lovely goal, but please don't be in denial about your attachment injuries. If you have a lot of unhealed wounds, a loose relationship model might hurt your heart way too much—in fact, it could be downright traumatizing. So be honest with yourself regarding where you are right now.

Some of you may be reading these words and silently screaming, "But isn't it riskier to try to stifle, control, and trap someone in a rigid, soul-sucking relationship?"

Good point. Remember how I said that the degree of rigidity to fluidity within a relationship is not an indicator of emotional health? I meant that. But what *does* impact emotional health is authenticity. If you feel you can grow, explore, have fun, and be real within the boundaries of your relationship, that relationship has a good shot of being healthy for you.

Within a tight relationship model, if you feel you have to lie, hide your true nature, limit your growth, and numb your desires due to the strict boundaries in place, the restriction may be toxic for you. Similarly, within a loose relationship model, if you are experiencing anxiety, panic attacks, insomnia, dysregulation, a profound sense of abandonment, or fear of loss, those loose boundaries may be toxic for you.

More rigid boundaries tend to work best for most until self-confidence, along with confidence in one's partners, is gained. Those who have been non-monogamous successfully for years tend to kick off the training wheels and loosen their boundaries over time. This progression is healthy only if trust, love, communication, and compassion are maintained as boundaries are shed.

In my nineteen years and counting of being non-monogamous, I've experienced everything from being a swinger to poly to every hybrid in between. In my personal experience, swingers are like the accountants of non-monogamy. If you went to an accountant convention, you could pretty much bet that from one accountant to the next, they're all operating similarly due to shared laws and regulations. Swingers also tend to have similar, very boundaried, relationship agreements. The quintessential swinger practice is like a blue chip stock: less risk and more security.

A polyamorist might argue that with less risk comes less reward—that such rigid boundaries stifle authenticity and personal growth. But swingers' common counterargument is that risking your primary love is not worth it. Both stances are valid.

Hybrid relationships are those that fall somewhere in between the two extremes. These relationships are custom-made, and the designers are creating a relationship model that works best for them instead of buying an "off the rack" form of non-monogamy, such as the quintessential swinger package. Such hybrids may incorporate practices and norms that are swingerish and elements that move toward poly. An example might be a couple who plays together in threesomes, foursomes, and orgies here and there (swingerish behavior) but also has outside lovers (beginning to look like poly). They don't identify as swingers or as polyamorous but rather as, perhaps, a "modern couple."

Such couples may be taking on more risk than couples with swinger practices. However, the heightened attunement involved in creating a relationship model that is completely custom-made for them may set them up for greater success.

6. Our Relationship Model Won't Change Drastically

Many people I see in my practice say things like, "I will always be non-monogamous," or "I will always be a swinger. I can't imagine being polyamorous." No matter how open-minded a non-monogamous person is, they often can't foresee how much their relationship will shift over time. But then life happens. Things change.

A fluid relationship, by my definition, is one that shifts and adapts over time based on emotional needs and circumstances.

During anxiety-provoking times, one might be more drawn to a more conservative relationship model. In more committed relationships, this might play out if you get pregnant and you and your partner decide to be monogamous in practice for a while—during and directly after the pregnancy. Another life circumstance that may require a break from non-monogamous practices is the loss of a loved one. A break or a simplified relationship model may be necessary to allow you to grieve.

However, agreements will change over time as you and your partners have actual experiences, both social and/or sexual, that allow you to experientially discover what truly works. This fluidity is adaptive and healthy for the relationship.

Many factors can influence a major shift to a less boundaried relationship model. Perhaps a couple has been non-monogamous for years. Over time, trust and confidence has been built between them, and an ability to read each other during complicated non-monogamous dynamics has been cultivated. Or perhaps the couple has fewer stressors, such as young children or long work hours, in their life than they used to. A calmer, simpler life can allow more emotional room for the risks inherent in a less boundaried relationship model.

Many changes in life logistics will create the need to reevaluate your relationship agreements and your relationship model. The more you can accept that relationship fluidity is needed, the more likely it is that you will flourish within the world of non-monogamy.

Chapter Fifteen

CONSTRUCTING BOUNDARIES FOR HARM REDUCTION

Every so often, I find myself at a party with mostly monoga-mous-identified people. Many times, upon finding out that I specialize in non-monogamy, someone at the party will launch into describing a train wreck of a couple with horrible boundaries that was, of course, non-monogamous. Examples of the poor boundaries might be non-consensually and creepily hitting on monogamous-identified people in one moment and then having an embarrassing public fight the next, making a disconcerting scene.

When someone launches into one of these stories, I listen patiently and sip my wine as they ramble on, slinging around stereotypes and misguided assumptions, until they finish. Then I ask them, "Can I describe something to you?" If they say yes, I say, "Imagine walking into a party. As soon as you walk in the door, your five senses are overwhelmed. The smell of sex and sweat overwhelm you. Your eyes widen as you take in a massive orgy right before you that spills out into the side rooms. Out of nowhere, a naked person appears before you, grabs your hand, and pulls you toward the writhing, naked bodies without your consent. Is that what you picture when you think of a non-monogamous party?"

Often, their reply is an affirmative nod, accompanied by a sheepish laugh.

This little scene encompasses the boundary myths I often hear from those who have never dabbled in non-monogamy. This larger-than-life metaphor is designed to gently tease people with the ignorant view that non-monogamous people have no boundaries, no respect for social norms, and no interest in consent. (Side note: I follow up with telling them what it's actually like.)

We can always find someone who will validate any stereotype or prejudice—but successful, healthy non-monogamy is all about consensual interactions and boundaries that create a sense of emotional and physical safety. So what's right for you? Let's bat around ideas to help you formulate a relationship agreement.

First, Are You Sure You Want to Be Non-Monogamous?

If not, stop here and simply take time to read books about non-monogamy, join online support groups, listen to podcasts, and make friends with those in open relationships who can tell you more. Perhaps you need to stay in the information-gathering phase a bit longer.

If so, great! At this point, there is a series of considerations that applies regardless of what form of non-monogamy you lean toward. In this chapter, I'll delve into some main areas to formulate agreements around. The questions to ask yourself are endless, but I've included some ideas and samples to get you started.

What Safety and Privacy Practices Will You Put into Place?

What are your safe sex practices? Will you request STI lab results from potential partners? What sort of barriers will be used? Condoms? Dental dams?

If you have an online profile, do you want to show your face? If yes, who do you want to have access to your face? Many non-monogamous websites have security settings/privacy levels that may include: 1) allowing anyone to see your face, 2) only allowing website members to see your face, or 3) only allowing those you're interested in meeting to see your face.

Do you give out your real name online and/or at parties? Are there some people who know your real name and not others?

Will You Play with a Primary or Nesting Partner at Least Part of the Time?

If you want to have some sexy fun with your partner, here are some considerations specific to you.

Who are your other partners?

Will you only pursue lovers who identify as non-monogamous? Will you play only with couples, or also with singles? Is there anyone who is off-limits? Coworkers? Relatives? Dear friends?

Where will you meet your other partners?

Monogamous-oriented bars, non-monogamous parties, and non-monogamous dating sites are a few of your options here. The first is the most challenging for most. The last is often easiest.

If you're hoping for group play, I'd advise you to steer away from on-premise sex clubs, where you'll have little control over your environment. Instead, start with non-monogamous dating websites, where you will be better able to assert your boundaries. Once there, take some time and look around. At this point, if you haven't even had your first date or first party, there are already a million boundary decisions to consider, including:

How will you communicate?

Can either of you contact couples or singles on an alt sex website? Or will you always do this together?

If you intend to play together, once you're chatting with a couple or single, will it always be a group conversation, or might one of you "represent" both of you as a couple?

On your first date with a couple, do you want it to simply be a chemistry check date in which you assess whether there is a sexual connection? Or do you intend to jump right in and have sex spontaneously? (Newbies, I strongly recommend starting with a chemistry check date so you have at least a day to get in touch with your feelings.)

What will your party and group sex guidelines be?

How often will you check in with each other at the party while socializing? Every hour? Or is this not a concern?

What if one of you needs to let the other know that you are uncomfortable, but you don't want the other party attendees to know? What is your secret sentence, gesture, or course of action to easily transition to speaking privately? I've known some couples to simply say, "Sweetie, I left something in the car. Can you walk out with me?" or "Hon, I just got an urgent text. Can you step outside so I can talk to you about it?"

If in a group sex situation, will you, as partners, ever play in separate rooms? (I would encourage same-room play for those new at non-monogamy.)

And finally, how often will you have check-in conversations? (These should occur before and after any major event, like a play party or a date with another couple or single. They should also occur regularly, perhaps once a week, especially when you're new at all this. This is a good opportunity to discuss if any relationship agreements need to be modified.)

Will You Play Separately without Your Primary or Nesting Partner at Least Part of the Time?

Playing separately is a more complicated relationship model. And polyamory certainly is. If poly is your cup of tea, love is on board—or it's at least invited. This additional factor inherently creates a more emotionally delicate and challenging dynamic. So let's explore some possible question categories:

Where will you find partners?

Just as with swinging, poly folk can be found online, at parties, through common friends, or at bars. However, the process might be slower since deeper relationships are ideally wanted.

How much time will be spent with each lover?

If you play separately from your partner, how often will you see other partners in a given month? Once a week? Three times a week? Once a month? Will you spend any major holidays with your other lovers? Will your other lovers meet your friends and family?

What boundaries will you set around social media?

Will you talk about other partners on social media? Will you post pictures of them? Or do you plan to keep other loves hidden?

What will your disclosure agreements be?

How much do you want to know about your partner's relationships with other lovers? Do you want to know about their sexual practices? Is it hot and sexy or emotionally hard for you to hear about those things? If they get into something new—say, kink or tantric sex—that may shift their personality, do you want to know about it? If they have a date with a new lover, how much do you want to know? The new person's name? Where they're going? The address? When they're coming back?

I advise you not to choose a "don't ask, don't tell" relationship agreement. You can't emotionally adjust to what you don't know about. And when things do come out, as they inevitably will, finding out what has transpired all at once can often emotionally land as if your partner has been having an affair—even though you intellectually know that you have agreed to be kept in the dark.

When love comes on board, what do you want to know?

Do you want to know if your partner begins to have feelings for another partner? Or do you only want to know if they fall in love?

I would encourage the former. Information in bite-size pieces is way easier to digest. If we can process small bits of information over time, we are much more likely to remain emotionally resilient.

What is sacred?

Is there anything you want to keep sacred between you and your partner? Here is a list of a few things I've heard clients identify as sacred: a pet name, a kinky toy bag, a shared destination or vacation spot, anal sex, a favorite compliment.

It's important to communicate what is sacred to the best of your ability up front. Once your partner steps over that line, it can feel like a tiny, painful heartbreak—and it often can't be undone. So please, clearly define what is sacred to you.

Relationship Agreement Examples

As you flesh out your boundaries around where to find partners, communication with potential partners, play dynamics, etc., you're forming a relationship agreement document. One golden rule to remember is: if you haven't asked for something, it's unfair to punish your partner for not reading your mind and providing it. Assumptions will bite you in the ass within non-monogamy. A relationship agreement should be clearly stated or, better yet, put in writing. This doesn't mean it's set in concrete; it just means you have put a flexible, harm reduction model in place that can be operationally defined and changed as needed. For instance, instead of saying, "We will check in on each other every so often at the play party," the guideline might be, "We will check in with each other at the play party every forty-five minutes to an hour."

In the beginning, creating a relationship agreement that both people understand can be daunting. Oftentimes, someone thinks they were clear and their partner thinks they were as clear as mud. Some non-monogamous couples come to me cascading toward divorce, sobbing, and blaming each other for deep injuries. One partner might say, "He was fucking her for months and never told me." The other might say, "She said she wanted to be non-monogamous, but now that I have another lover, she's always crying and screaming at me!"

This need not be you and your partner. To help avoid that fate, let's look at some sample relationship agreements:

Quinn and Nate

She would like to find one deep love. He wants to have two or three other lovers who are friends, but he's not looking for a deep attachment. They both feel that they can emotionally handle what the other has requested. Here are a few of their agreements:

- Both have agreed that if Quinn intends to have sex with someone, Nate will meet that person or talk to them via Skype or FaceTime before she has sex with them. The same is true for a potential new lover for Nate. This agreement sets the stage for open communication.
- Both have agreed to attempt to date relatively stable, respectful, and kind people. They realize that the lovers they choose will impact their partner. (Note: Dating a disrespectful person is a great way to destabilize all your other relationships within non-monogamy. No relationship operates in a vacuum.)
- Quinn has asked to hear the sexual details of what happens after Nate has a sexy date because she thinks it's hot. She loves to fuck him right after he gets back while he whispers the details in her ear. Consequently, Nate has a policy of asking new lovers if they mind if the sexy details

are shared with his wife. Again, they try to be mindful of couple privilege and consent.

- Nate doesn't want to hear the details. It's a little hard for him. Quinn has agreed to respect that to the best of her ability. Again, boundaries are everything with non-monogamy.

- Regarding physical safety, both want to know the basic details of a date: day, time, person, and location address. They have defined their safe sex practices.

- Quinn has asked Nate to be home by 2:00 a.m. after dates. Knowing when he will return reduces her anxiety. (Note: I've noticed that for clients who suffer from anxiety, knowing when their partner will be home is often a game changer. It can be the difference between a tortured, sleepless night with a crying partner versus a partner who is happy to see you walk in the door. Again, they aren't trying to control you. They are trying to manage their anxiety, unresolved trauma, or attachment injuries.)

- Quinn and Nate have both set an ethical intention to try to break down couple privilege whenever possible. They listen to their other lovers' needs and create a line of open communication. Nate's lovers know and are encouraged to talk directly to Quinn if need be, and Quinn's lover knows he can reach out to Nate.

Obviously, a relationship agreement document can be much longer. Also, the above is simply a sample. Anything that you need for self-care may translate into a relationship agreement. You are limited only by your own ability to assert yourself and what the two of you are able to negotiate. Quinn and Nate's relationship agreements work well for them because their differences are honored. Quinn can have one deep love other than Nate, and Nate can have the variety he craves. In addition, an intention for open communication is set.

The impact of other lovers' emotional health on their relationship is acknowledged. Couple privilege is addressed. Some safety issues are covered, and both of their emotional needs are included. All in all, some solid bases are covered.

Josie and Phil

These two have decided to always play together and not take on any outside lovers. They identify as sexually non-monogamous and romantically monogamous (not looking to fall in love with anyone else). They are down for threesomes, foursomes, and group sex. They love dating other couples or seeing singles. They also love big parties, hotel takeovers, and lifestyle vacations. Here are some of their initial relationship agreements:

- Before they sleep with a single or couple, they will have a non-sexual chemistry check date to get a sense of the person(s) and have time to sleep on it. They realize that rushing things can lead to a yes that is not a true yes.
- They will communicate with such people in group texts or emails that they both have access to. Neither will communicate with potential lovers without their partner included. This agreement backs the intention to always play together.
- When they play, they will make a concerted effort to be sure that everyone feels attended to and no one feels left out.
- They will not give other partners pet names beyond generics like "honey." Anything more feels too intimate for them.
- Anal sex is off the table with other lovers. That's something they only do together.
- Lovers won't spend the night. Neither feels comfortable with that presently.

- They will not see any couple or single more than twice a month. This boundary is designed to mirror their intention that they are not looking for a connection any deeper than great friendship and fun sex.
- They have also decided upon their safe sex practices. (Note: I have purposely avoided specifics regarding safe sex practices in this chapter so as not to influence you. You must do your own risk assessment. What might be right for Josie and Phil may not be right for you. With that said, anyone practicing non-monogamy needs to make some conscious decisions on this topic.)

These agreements make sense for Josie and Phil since they are in keeping with their intention to remain romantically monogamous by setting intimacy boundaries around sex, flirting, and time spent with other lovers. By always including each other on text/email chains, they are reducing the chance of intimacy with others and upping the dynamic of shared adventure with each other. They are also being mindful of finding partners that are a good fit by having a chemistry check. And finally, the intention to not leave anyone out makes it less likely that they'll get caught up with new lovers and ignore each other. Simultaneously, couple privilege is loosely addressed, since this same intention implies that they will not sink into each other so much that their other partners might wonder why they came.

Chastity and Dean

These two have been lifestyle swingers for years and enjoy occasional threesomes. They have two kids. They always thought that they would never be down for love, but they fell in love with Lisbeth, one of their play partners. Lisbeth has a husband, Patrick, whom she loves dearly, and she and Patrick play separately. Patrick is happy that Lisbeth has found love with Chastity and Dean. Here are some of Chastity and Dean's relationship agreements:

- Either of them can play or go on dates with Lisbeth alone, but they have set the intention to attempt to keep that dynamic relatively even so that, ideally, they are both very connected to Lisbeth and no one ends up feeling left out or disrespected.

- They know that couple privilege is a concern despite the fact that Lisbeth has a primary, and have expressed this awareness to Lisbeth. They have invited Lisbeth to share any worry or upset she might have with them at any point. And in keeping with this sentiment, they have agreed to tell her if they have feelings/arguments that might impact her. They have expressed their intention to always be respectful of her and her needs.

- Although they aren't close with Lisbeth's husband, they have let him know that if he ever has any concerns, they are all ears.

- They will still go to play parties and share adventures together, just the two of them. This agreement backs their long-term intention to be adventure buddies. This is how they fell in love, and this is a main way their love is maintained.

- Safe sex practices have been established.

- At this point, Lisbeth will continue to celebrate holidays and take vacations with Patrick and their family rather than with Chastity and Dean. All three have agreed on this.

- They won't move Lisbeth, or any other lover, into their home. That feels like way too much to handle for them at this point. Lisbeth doesn't want that anyway. She is more than happy living with Patrick.

These relationship agreements work well for Chastity and Dean because they both honor their relationship and are respectful to

Lisbeth and Patrick. Couple privilege is addressed. And, finally, relationship agreements are set to maintain their love language of being adventure buddies.

Beatrice and Harvey

Beatrice and Harvey are in their fifties and have been together since their early thirties. They have practiced many forms of non-monogamy for over two decades, and at this point they are damn good at it. Consequently, they don't need many rules and boundaries. They have super high emotional intelligence regarding relationships. They realize these skills do not manifest organically, and therefore they have read books on how to love well and have taken couples bonding retreats together. They can read each other's faces and know what the other is thinking. They are both super empathetic to one another's needs and therefore have a lot of trust regarding each other's decisions around non-monogamy. They are also kinky. Harvey is Beatrice's submissive but he is switchy, meaning he enjoys being submissive but dominance is also in his wheelhouse.

Due to a large inheritance and sound investment decisions, these two are loaded. Three months ago, they purchased a small building that includes six condos. They live in one. The rest they rent out. In one condo are their lovers, Joseph and Kaitlyn. In another is Harvey's sub, Nick, and his partner, Rob. In a fourth is Rob's lover, Scott. They would like to create a fun, family-like atmosphere in the building. Here are some of their relationship agreements:

- The condo will only be rented out to lovers or close friends. The remaining condos will be used as Airbnbs for those in the kink community.
- They will spend two nights, at least, just with each other each week. One is a weeknight, one a weekend night, as a general rule, but exceptions can be made.
- Safe sex agreements have been made.

- They are free to see their shared lovers, Joseph and Kaitlyn, together or separately, but they always text or leave a note to let each other know where they are.
- When Harvey goes to play with his sub, Nick, he is to use a separate kinky toy bag. Harvey and Beatrice have a toy bag that is just for them. Harvey refers to Beatrice as his Mistress. No one but Beatrice owns him, and he is collared.
- Harvey and Beatrice don't play with anyone besides Joseph, Kaitlyn, and Nick.
- Once a month, they will have a condo potluck dinner or picnic. Everyone will be invited, including Nick's partner, Rob, and Rob's lover, Scott, thus creating a family-style vibe in the building.

These relationship agreements work for Beatrice and Harvey because they honor their need for autonomy, their love for each other, and their desire to build a sense of community within the building. Not many could pull off such a complex relational dynamic under one roof. However, because of all the work Beatrice and Harvey have put into their emotional intelligence and their understanding of psychology, they can—and they have earned it.

How Might Your Relationship Agreement Change Over Time?

An adaptable relationship agreement can prevent a lot of pain. As I've mentioned more than once, creating one does not mean you've agreed to a contract that's set in stone; rather, it means that you're engaging in a changeable harm-reduction process that takes into account the needs, desires, attachment injuries, and emotional readiness of all involved. It's a go-to if you find yourself in an argument. And it's a working document, open to revision, that can help partners think through different aspects of their relationship. To see how drastically a relationship agreement can grow and change, let's consider Hannah and Demetrius.

These two got married in their early twenties. Within a few years, they were in a polyfidelitous relationship with Bonnie. Their original relationship agreements included these points: there was no hierarchy, and Bonnie was invited to celebrate all major holidays with them; playing separately or together was okay; if there were any issues, the three would plan a time to talk together via video or in person. That went pretty well for two years—but then Bonnie moved to Boston for school, and following that Hannah and Demetrius grew apart from her. Her sexual interests changed, and she voiced a hope to find a primary of her own. So they all agreed to maintain a platonic friendship but end their romantic involvement.

After Bonnie left, Hannah and Demetrius decided that they'd like to make some major changes to how they operate. It was time to make some revisions to their relationship agreements.

First off, they decided to be adventure buddies for a while and experience different lovers together. Neither had had many sexual partners, so they decided that they wanted to play the field as a couple. Together, they got on a non-monogamous dating site. Their initial step was to make relationship agreements related to the dating site. They decided that they could both shop around on the site solo and mark as "favorites" the folks that they were interested in, but 1) before either of them decided to chat with someone, both had to feel some level of interest, 2) both of them had to agree to move forward before a date was scheduled, and 3) they wouldn't get into heavy sexual texting until they had met the couple or individual they were interested in.

Once they got familiar with the dating site, they found a cool event they were both excited to experience. They decided to go to a weekend swinger hotel takeover in Vegas. Their getaway would include parties on Friday and Saturday nights and pool parties on

Saturday and Sunday. This required another look at their relationship agreements. Here are some of their swing lifestyle party agreements:

- We will go to parties together. Our intention is to share an adventure.
- We will only play with a couple or single if we both are in clear agreement.
- We may consider participating in group sex at a party for the first time.
- If either of us starts to feel uncomfortable at all, we won't "take one for the team"; instead, we'll say a code sentence like, "I just realized I forgot something back in the room. Will you go with me?" or "I just got an urgent text. I need to make a call. Can you come with me?" and we'll both pack up to leave for a moment, or for the night, whatever is needed.
- We are both okay with full swap, but in the same room. For instance, if we are in a suite, it's not okay to go into the second room, out of each other's line of sight, to have sex.

As you can see, the relationship agreements that worked when Hannah and Demetrius were newly non-monogamous and poly-fidelitous with Bonnie are very different than the boundaries they needed during their expedition into the swing lifestyle world. The relationship agreements changed as they changed.

Some folks need to write their relationship agreements down rather than simply making verbal agreements. To determine if that's best for you, I invite you to ask yourself some questions: After a fight, do you have a vastly different memory of the fight than your partner? Do you or your partner have a poor memory? Do either of you tend to try to find loopholes in arguments if you're mad at the other?

If the answer to any of these questions is yes, you would be wise to write down your relationship agreements so you can reference them as needed. You can make addendums with dates or simply rewrite the agreements when necessary. These adjustments might be made as frequently as once a week or as infrequently as once a year, but such a written document can serve as an anchor when misunderstandings and/or chaos crops up within your relationship.

As I have mentioned previously, we all like to think that we're mature, that we don't have the same needs as little children—but in many ways, we really do. Even as adults, we need boundaries in order to function as our best selves. The boundaries actually make us feel safer and more relaxed, because we know where the wall is.

Only you and your partner(s) know if you need rigid versus flexible boundaries, or few versus many. And maybe you don't know. You may have to learn the hard way, through trial and error. But if you listen to your gut while educating yourself with non-monogamous resources, you will have enough of the basics down to put a pretty good harm-reduction model in place.

Chapter Sixteen

INFIDELITY AND AGREEMENT VIOLATIONS WITHIN NON-MONOGAMY

Folks often ask me, "If someone is non-monogamous, how can they cheat?" Well, easy. An infidelity is committed when a relationship agreement is broken. And since almost all non-monogamous relationships have relationship agreements, it is quite possible to commit an infidelity.

Let's back up and define fidelity. Fidelity is demonstrated by loyalty, respect, honesty, and support of another. So it follows that an *in*fidelity violates these intentions—and our partner(s).

With these anchor points defined, I invite you to realize that not all infidelities are created equally. There is a continuum—from a small boo-boo to behaviors that cause lasting pain. Recognizing the continuum encourages active mindfulness regarding how we are treating partners and how we are being treated.

Perhaps you are still questioning, "But isn't non-monogamy all about freedom? Do we really need all these relationship agreements?" Yes, it's about freedom, but it's also about being compassionate to our partners' needs. The trick is to find the balance between what makes the individual feel authentic and what makes the relationship most connected, healthy, and strong.

There is an upside and a downside to relationship agreements. They prevent harm—when both partners observe them faithfully. But once a relationship agreement is made, it can be violated, and even the most lenient relationship agreement can be broken.

There's a deeper question worth exploring here too, which is, "Why do some partners seemingly sabotage their non-monogamous relationship with broken agreements?" As we discussed in Chapter 4, the difference between a partner who forgets or simply misunderstands the rules versus a partner who has deep psychological issues is an important consideration. The former can usually correct their behavior after a few discussions. The latter, less so—and such a person often causes lasting and repeated injury within the relationship. Let's look at examples of both kinds of partners.

The Partner Who Makes Learning Curve Mistakes

If you have a partner who's proven themselves to be a thoughtful, kind person and they make a mistake within non-monogamy that feels outside of their usual character, their poor judgment may simply be a learning curve mistake. This theory is even more likely to be true if they are new to non-monogamy, or if the two of you recently made some changes to your relationship agreement. Such a partner usually will feel regret and make amends, and is likely to learn from the error of their ways.

Here's an example of a couple in which one partner makes a learning curve mistake. A couple new to non-monogamy goes to their first sex party with an agreement to check in with each other after a certain amount of time. One partner gets caught up and forgets to check in. The quiet spark of upset ignites here.

Now, a periodic check-in seems like an easy request, but at a really amazing non-monogamous party, it's easy to lose track of time. I've seen this cause huge fights between couples. But such a grievance can be worked through, especially if the one in error is not defensive, can validate and empathize with their partner's feelings, and learns from their mistakes. It's also an opportunity to see if the check-in rule you've made is reasonable. Perhaps checking in every thirty minutes is unrealistic, since the time goes by fast, and should be adjusted to once an hour. Mistakes are also an opportunity to learn.

The Partner with Deep-Seated Issues

A sign that you might have the second type of infidelitous partner is a lack of a clear learning curve. They rarely change after hurting you and are likely to break the same relationship agreements again and again.

You may not be able to recognize this type at first. They may seem very nurturing, as long as your upset doesn't interfere with their desires. But everything changes when your needs directly threaten what they want.

Such people have a pattern of repeated deception, and in a relationship they will break agreements time and again. They may even have a completely secret life with lovers you don't know about. This behavior runs way deeper than any relationship model can fix. This personality profile will find a way to betray trust regardless of how open-minded their partner is or how much freedom they have within the relationship. They may enjoy group sex with their partner or separate play allowed by their relationship agreement, but regardless, this personality profile will *still* want "something just for myself" that is secret and betrays their partner and their relationship agreements.

For some people, their need for a secret life is deeply psychological. Some are self-reported pleasers who lack assertiveness skills. They justify their deception by convincing themselves that they're protecting their partner from pain. Others have narcissistic tendencies and feel entitled to be unencumbered by another's needs and asks.

It doesn't matter if the deceiver has a partner who gives abundantly—emotionally, sexually, and financially. This isn't about how generous and kind their partner is. This psyche was built before the relationship ever began.

The source of this kind of behavior is often an incredibly controlling parent in childhood that hampered the child's ability to build a true sense of self. As adults, they project the over-controlling parent archetype onto their partner. This projection allows them to believe that their deception is justified because they believe their partner will never listen to their needs anyway (just like Mom or Dad). Thus, the story of their childhood is reconfirmed. Consequently, they lose their sense of self in the relationship (as they did in childhood) and project their anger about this (which is really anger at the controlling parent) onto their partner, thus rationalizing their deception. They're recreating a play that ends with the sentence, "You are always trying to control me." If you're a partner to a person who demonstrates these kinds of behaviors, please remember one thing: you need not put up with anything that feels psychologically damaging to you.

So, if non-monogamy doesn't fix this type's behavior patterns, what will? Probably an incredibly skilled, not easily duped therapist who will help them work through childhood issues while cultivating assertiveness, honesty, and a sense of self. I have known people who have worked through such issues and felt better about themselves on the other side. If you are dating such a person and discover the truth, you may need to lick your wounds and be reminded that asserting self-care needs is healthy, not controlling or selfish. If this archetype is willing to travel the long, hard road to health, the lies, deceit, and a secret life will no longer be necessary. But if they're not—it might be time to move on.

Is It Ever a Good Choice to Deceive
If You Break a Relationship Agreement?

For many of us, there may be times that we are tempted to hide our feelings, thoughts, or behaviors from our partner. Certainly, if your partner says, "Do I look ugly in this dress/suit?" we might decide to tell a white lie so as not to hurt their feelings. Also, if we make a huge mistake, like sleep with an unsanctioned person, we might lie if we know we will never do it again and we know our partner would be devastated by the truth.

However, there is another factor to consider before we choose to lie. We may believe that we are sparing our partner pain by hiding certain things, but because our partners can often read us better than anyone, they may sense that something is off—and then guess incorrectly about the source, asking questions like, "Are you mad at me?"; "Do you love someone more than me?"; or "Are you thinking of leaving me?"

Their specific guess may be wildly wrong, but what's correct is that something is not in order. So if you respond with something like, "Of course not! Why do you always think there is something wrong?"— you may cause your partner to lose faith in their own judgment, their instincts, which is one of the most damaging things a person can do to another human. So it's usually better to be honest, say what is authentic, and be compassionate as your partner hears you.

Healing from Violations
to Your Relationship Agreement

After a relationship agreement violation, you may feel disrespected and hurt. The existence of your partner's other lovers may be salt in the wound, exacerbating your pain. How can you stay grounded at such a time? How can the relationship heal? First, we need to discuss the responsibilities of both parties, the injurer and the injured.

Let's focus on the one in the wrong first. They have a responsibility to own their misdeed and actively attempt to make amends. These steps go way beyond "I'm sorry." These steps need to be coupled with an ongoing practice of empathizing and validating with their partner while actively attempting to make a repair.

Now to the injured party. What is your responsibility in this? First, let's start with self-compassion. You are human. You may go through a phase of yelling and crying. You may blame yourself if you feel you were gullible or forgave one time too many. But eventually, you need to get grounded and ask yourself a couple of questions—namely, "Do I want to stay and work this out?" and "Is my partner capable of making amends and improving?" What you're really asking here is, "Is my partner truly relationship ready?"

Someone who is "relationship ready" has the basic skills to love their partner *well*. Simply loving you is not enough. They may love you deeply, but that doesn't mean they're capable of loving you well. Many people have years of work to do before they're capable of getting a passing grade at loving someone well. And within non-monogamy, a heightened level of emotional intelligence is required. If your partner does not have the basic skills to love you well, you will most likely be hurt again. This knowledge should be figured into your decision regarding whether to stay or call it.

That said, if your partner has a track record of learning from mistakes and being considerate of your feelings and you decide to stay, at some point you'll have to process through the pain associated with the broken relationship agreement. This process may take hours or years, depending on the severity of the injury. But at some point, if you want the relationship to survive, you'll need to tame your inner rage monster who sends the message to your partner that they're a bad person. From a grounded place, you are more likely to realize that your partner is not a bad human but rather a perfectly good human whose behavior was bad. This is the difference between shame and guilt. If you can't make this transition, you may eventually find that a shift has occurred in your relationship and *you* have become the injurious partner. Shaming can feel emotionally abusive to the receiver, and often leads to hopelessness and helplessness. However, guilt often inspires our partner to improve and learn to love us better.

From this lens, trust can begin to be earned back, but that may require a break from non-monogamy. It will definitely take time and patience. I've noticed that the person who breaks the relationship agreement often thinks that their partner should be bright-eyed and bushy-tailed a week after the transgression, whereas the injured partner may still be healing a year later.

Beyond showing, through word and deed, that relationship agreements will be respected going forward, patience, love, compassion, and attraction heal a lot of relationship injuries. If the injured partner feels their partner lacks empathy, is impatient, and is pressuring them to get on with their sex life, they will stay stuck in their pain. However, if the injured partner feels their partner's empathy, validation, patience, love, attraction, and connection, they will often heal more quickly.

Don't Ask, Don't Tell Policies

Maybe while considering the secret-life guy scenario I posed above, you wondered, *But what if the secret life is sanctioned? What if my partner agrees to a "don't ask, don't tell" agreement? Isn't that a perfect solution? Then all of this discussion and potential pain can simply be avoided. Right?*

I'll be honest with you, I'm not a fan of this sort of arrangement. I know it can work for a while, but it rarely ends well.

Let's consider Uri and Constance. Long ago, they had dinner together at a lovely restaurant in Santa Barbara. On that fateful night, as they discussed sex and fantasies, Uri said to Constance, "I just want you to be happy, but I don't need to know everything you do."

Constance tilted her head to the side. "Really? Are you sure?"

"Yes," he said. "I'm sure. I trust you. I know you love me."

They stared into each other's eyes with love. In that moment, life was perfect.

Such trust sounds lovely, yes? But let's hit the pause button here and really think about the stage that has been set. In my experience, the one in Uri's position has something in his head like, *Maybe once a year she'll make out with one of her girlfriends,* or *Maybe she'll go to Vegas and make out with a male stripper after she tips him really well.* The one proposing the "don't ask, don't tell" relationship often tells themselves a story about what their partner will do—one they feel they would be able to handle well if the truth were to come to light.

Ten years after that night at the restaurant, Constance and Uri's relationship had been good and relatively peaceful. Uri had hooked up with other people here and there while on business trips, but he hadn't cultivated anything ongoing and his sexcapades were infrequent. As agreed on that fateful night, he'd never told Constance about his experiences and had never asked her what she was up to either. But one day Constance approached him and said, "I have to tell you something."

Uri's stomach tightened a little.

"I need you to sit down," she continued.

Worried now, he took a seat and waited.

"I know we agreed to a don't ask, don't tell relationship," Constance said slowly, "but it's reached a point that I have to tell you. I can't hide it anymore. I've been seeing someone for two years now. His name is Ben, and we are in love."

Uri had a small, quiet explosion in his brain. He dumbly repeated, "You're in love? You've been seeing him for two years?"

Constance was confused by his reaction. *Why is he acting this way?* she thought.

Do you see how Uri reacted like a partner who'd just found out about an affair? Well, that's what it felt like to him, because he had forfeited the natural emotional adjustment process inherent in communicative non-monogamy. He was getting ten years' worth of news in just a few sentences.

By contrast, consensual non-monogamy that includes open communication would have created a situation in which Uri would have slowly (by comparison) adjusted to shifts in relationship dynamics. These small adjustments over time are much more manageable for the psyche. It's sort of like easing yourself into the kiddie pool versus being abruptly picked up and dumped into the big pool.

If, for instance, Uri had been privy to Constance having one-night stands every so often while on business travel during the first five years of their relationship, he would have had the chance to adjust to that and perhaps request boundaries around her activities. However, due to the "don't ask, don't tell" agreement, this process never had the chance to unfold.

At five years, Constance might have told Uri that she wanted a deeper attachment. If they reached common ground on this desire, she might have begun to see a guy in their town once a month. This might have gone on for another three years. Uri would have had an adjustment process associated with this leg of the journey as well.

By year eight, when Constance met Ben, Uri would have learned a lot of coping skills regarding non-monogamy and would be much better equipped for this new chapter. Then Uri wouldn't have a mini bomb go off in his mind when Constance told him about Ben. He'd be equipped and able to deal.

Communication Styles

As you can see, there is no skirting the heavy work of communication within a non-monogamous relationship. The chickens always come home to roost eventually. It's much better to address needs, wants, and desires as they come up. In my humble opinion, neither infidelity nor "don't ask, don't tell" relationships allow one to escape the hard work—at least not without a lot of damage.

If you're the sort of person who gives up the first time you get some emotional pushback from your partner, non-monogamy may not be for you. Why? Because giving up often leads to feeling resentment toward your partner. Not good. Or cheating. Worse still. Sometimes, getting your voice heard takes making repeated attempts to clearly let your partner know your needs.

In 2003, when my partner at the time first brought up an interest in non-monogamy, I responded with massive pushback, but he didn't give up on the discussion. He addressed my fears and let me know that he had my back and always would. He stood up for his needs while listening to mine. It would have been sad indeed if he had lost his voice on his first request and simply decided to cheat instead. A whole, amazing journey would have been lost.

This leads to how honesty shows up in our communication styles. Let's talk about three types: blunt talkers, sugarcoaters, and finessers. Each of the three has a different psychological makeup.

When you are in love with a blunt talker, it can sometimes feel like being tied to the tail of a bull that's navigating a china shop. The forceful style can be painful, but the bull finds its way through, for better or worse. Although the blunt talker could learn some kindness and diplomacy from those who finesse, at least this person isn't blowing smoke up your ass. You know where you stand. This type tends to be honest but lacks the empathy that fuels a gentler approach. If you can tolerate their style, clear relationship agreements can be reached that reduce the chance of relationship agreement violations due to lack of understanding. But you have to have a thick skin.

Sugarcoaters, on the other hand, soften their request so much that the reality of the request or situation is frequently lost. Often, the receiving partner doesn't even realize what they've agreed to. Sugarcoaters and their partners will inevitably get into big fights in which the partner feels the sugarcoater has deceived them and acted without their consent. Meanwhile, the sugarcoater believes they've been transparent and is in denial about the deception inherent in their approach. They almost always justify their behavior as an attempt to maintain harmony—which is ironic, since sugarcoaters tend to have a ton of drama in their non-monogamous relationships.

Finally, the finesser is someone who has cultivated emotional intelligence, empathy, and an ability to read people. This type knows how to honestly convey their needs in an authentic way that their partner can easily hear. *How* one makes a request within non-monogamy matters. Timing matters. Getting a read on your partner's "emotional gas tank" level matters. Any request has the potential to poke attachment injuries. Finessers navigate these difficult waters like expert surfers.

The most successful non-monogamous partners are those who can have authentic communication, who can assert their needs without crushing the needs of their partners. I hope you have partners who love you well—with kindness, honesty, and compassion. However, if relationship agreements between you and your partner have been broken, there is almost certainly hope. Couples can heal and even have a better relationship on the other side of a relationship injury. It takes emotional fortitude and a willingness to do the work. But, in relationships, it's worth it. We don't get to cut corners, not if we want to get close to our true, ideal vision of love.

Chapter Seventeen

STAYING CONNECTED

Have you ever felt alone even though your partner is sitting right next to you, because they're engrossed in their phone and ignoring you? Or perhaps you are lying on the bed with four hotties right after group sex, and you feel totally disconnected from your partner. It happens. Even couples that are good at non-monogamy will hit this disconnection hurdle at one point or another. But it doesn't have to continue. Let's look at some common occurrences of disconnection and address how to take action steps to reconnect.

Technology's Impact on Connection

Technology is a beautiful thing. It helps us connect to the world. However, we can become lost in it and forget good boundaries—which can cause us to lose our connection to the person(s) we should be prioritizing. This makes our partners feel taken for granted and resentful. And when technology and non-monogamy become co-conspirators in disconnection, some escalated hurt feelings can happen real quick.

Consider Kendra and Diego, who've been dating for two years. They have a date at LACMA, their favorite art museum. Kendra has been working hard all week and has been looking forward to time with Diego on this much-needed day off. Art is something they both love, and it's always been a bonding experience for them. In the entrance line, however, Diego is lost in his phone, constantly texting.

Kendra isn't sure, but she feels in her gut that Diego's texting with Sonya, his new lover. She likes Sonya, but isn't this *their* time? She fears being accused of being jealous and controlling if she says something. She feels a deep sadness and turns away from him, alternately looking at the queue of people before her and staring at her feet. He is too captivated by his phone to notice this tiny heartbreak happening right next to him.

Now observe Sandra and Joe. They've been married for ten years. After a long workday, they climb into bed together at 10:00 p.m. Joe's looking forward to spooning as they fall asleep. Sometimes he's the big spoon and sometimes he's the little spoon, despite his six-four frame. He loves that Sandra cuddles him too.

As Joe turns off the table lamp, the light of Sandra's laptop fills the room. This has become the new norm over the last two weeks. He shrugs to himself and wonders why he allowed himself to hope that tonight would be different. He rolls over. He can tell she's swiping through dating profiles by how the light in the room shifts. *Swipe. Swipe. Swipe. Sigh.* He feels so lonely and is second-guessing whether they made the right decision to open up their relationship.

Both of these situations are sad, and they may sound familiar. But technology need not be an ongoing issue that blocks connection, love, and sex. With many of the couples I see in therapy, a few conversations around healthy boundaries often solve the issue quickly.

Let's go back to Kendra and Diego.

In therapy, Kendra confronts Diego. "You know, it really hurt me that you were texting the whole time that we were at LACMA," she says. "That was supposed to be our time."

"It wasn't the whole time," Diego replies defensively. "It was just when we were in line. God, you're so jealous! How is this ever going to work?"

Kendra briefly looks at me before her posture collapses and she quietly, but tearfully, focuses on the floor.

I prompt Diego to pose a question.

"What were you feeling while we were at LACMA?" he asks.

Kendra, still quite and tearful, says, "I just felt so left and sad. I thought that day was going to be our day. It didn't feel like that at all. I felt so lonely."

"What would have felt better?" Diego asks.

"I don't mind you texting with Sonya," Kendra says, "but there are times that are special, like when we are on a date or when we are watching our favorite show together. I'd like those times to be *our* time, without screens distracting us."

Diego's face softens. "Of course, we can do that. I'm sorry that you felt lonely. I know how much you love to share art with me. We're both new at this. We'll figure it out. We always do. It's going to be okay."

Kendra leans over and puts her head on his shoulder. He pets her head while they reach out to hold hands.

With a few empathizing, validating, and grounding words from Diego, Kendra was able to ask for the boundaries that would alleviate the technology-induced disconnect between them. Communication that could have led to a massive fight instead resolved quickly and led to a greater sense of connection.

The technology issue is often just that easy to resolve, even if it's been causing pain for quite some time. Couples simply need to carve out quality time for the two of them. Once those boundaries are set, things get much easier.

As for Joe and Sandra—the next day, Joe comes home from work to find Sandra sitting on the sofa, deeply focused on her laptop. She barely looks up at him when he walks in.

He puts down his briefcase and goes to the bathroom. When he comes out, Sandra says, without looking up, "Do you want to order Thai?"

Joe stops and looks at her.

She finally looks up. "What?!"

At this, Joe's feelings—still simmering from the previous night—boil over. "You're always on that thing!" he explodes. "It's like you're addicted. Can you even put it down?"

This conflict is common. Shopping for a new lover can light us up—specifically, when we find a hot person who excites us, our midbrain dopamine system lights up, giving us that happy and reinforcing neurochemical release. It can be as habit-forming as pulling the slot machine lever in Vegas. And if our life circumstances (job, kids, etc.) are stressful, searching for a new partner can feel like a stress relief, or even an escape. But behaviors that offer stress release can inadvertently hurt your partner.

For most, setting limits is easily done. But for Sandra, it's not so easy. In therapy, she says, "I'm just so stressed from work that I feel I need it. I know my swiping is getting out of control. I know it's hurting Joe. But it's hard to stop."

We discuss other ways to manage stress. Exercise? Hanging out with friends? Self-care of some other sort? As a last resort, we discuss her perhaps seeing a psychiatrist, if compulsivity has been a struggle in her life, something that might be best managed with meds.

By the end of our session, the two of them have set some boundaries around screen time. Sandra feels she can get a handle on this issue without the help of a psychiatrist—compulsivity has not been a struggle until now—so she agrees to try some of the other self-care approaches I suggested.

Balance is key. Having good boundaries will make your partner feel safe.

Reconnecting After Your Partner Goes on a Date

The keys rattle and the doorknob turns. Your partner has just arrived home after a hot night of sex and adventure with their other lover.

How do you feel? Turned on? Full of anxiety? Emotions vary wildly, and so do needs and desires. What you need may be incredibly different from what your partner needs when it's their turn to hear the knob turn. Some may want to be fucked while stories of the night are whispered in their ear. But for those who are filled with anxiety, that scenario may be their worst nightmare. They may simply want their partner to go take a shower, come to bed, gently spoon them, and whisper, "I missed you," and "I love you" before they fall back to sleep.

As we discussed in Chapter 6, creating an after-date ritual will do wonders for the strength and health of your relationship. Reconnecting after your partner has gone off on a date is a key practice to help keep your connection loving, secure, and sexually solid.

Phil and Natalia have been dating for a year. They'd both been non-monogamous for years before ever meeting. Their relationship is new, passionate, and exciting.

Phil is a very, very naughty man. He can't wait to fuck Natalia as soon as she gets back from her threesome with a new couple in her life, Jack and Tyler. The knob turns. He rushes up to greet her. He swings the door open with a big smile. She can't help but burst into a giggle. He scoops her up and carries her back to the bedroom. There is nothing that turns him on more than throwing her down on the bed when her body is still lit up from hours of sexual attendance. And she loves him for it.

Now let's look at another couple, Sunny and Rose. Sunny is still having a hard time with Rose's new lover. She lies in bed, waiting for Rose to come home from her date. Finally, she hears the front door open and then the shower turn on (Rose is adhering to Sunny's request to wash off the scent of her other lover before crawling into bed). Rose gets in bed, pets Sunny's head, cuddles up to her, and whispers in her ear, "I love you so much. You're my bright light."

Sunny's anxiety softens. "I love you too," she says, and they fall asleep in each other's arms.

Phil and Sunny's emotional reactions and consequent needs couldn't be more different. And both are completely valid. In these examples, Natalia and Rose beautifully attuned with their partners' individual needs with ease, which is what intimacy-building and connection are all about.

However, it won't always be this easy. What if you can't give your partner what they need or it's counter to what you need? Let's go back to these same couples and imagine it all going down differently.

Natalia walks up to her front door. She's exhausted and annoyed. She's never had a MMF threesome, and this was her big night with Jack and Tyler. It was a huge disappointment. Jack was selfish and ego driven in his approach, and although Tyler was great, he could only do so much to counteract Jack's bad energy.

Natalia puts her key in the door. Before she can turn it, Phil swings the door open with a massive grin, all lit up like a happy puppy. Upon seeing her face, however, his face falls. He can read her moods like no one else.

"I know how much you were looking forward to this," she says, "but I just need to sleep. We'll have sex as soon as this bad mojo leaves my body. I'll probably be fine in the morning."

Notice that although she says no to what he originally wanted, she offers what she *can* do instead of dismissing him altogether. When we offer what we can do, even if it's given a bit later or it's something different from what was originally anticipated, our partner still feels our effort to care for their needs.

Let's go back to Rose. When she comes home from her date, she feels sad. She turns the key, enters her apartment, and heads straight for the bathroom to shower, per Sunny's request, but she does so begrudgingly. She feels slut-shamed, and it's not hot for her at all. She wishes Sunny could have compersion for her.

After showering, she quietly crawls into bed. They exchange cuddles and I love yous, then fall asleep. But at breakfast the next morning, she sighs and quickly launches in.

"I know you get triggered when you can smell another lover on me, but having to take a shower after a date makes me feel shamed by you. It makes me feel like you perceive me as dirty. I want you to share my happiness with me."

Sunny pauses to think, then connects with Rose's eyes. "It's not that I think you're dirty. It's more that I need you to do a little ritual that lets me know that you have transitioned from your date to being present with me." After further consideration, she says, "How about I get up and take a shower with you when you get back? I'll be a little sleepy, but it could be a quick little erotic ritual that makes me part of your erotic night instead of separate from it."

Rose smiles, relieved. "That sounds way better. Let's try that."

Reconnecting After a Shared Adventure

You might wonder why a couple would need to reconnect after a shared adventure like a sex party or a chemistry check date; they were both present, after all. But the fact is, because they are both individuals who don't have a shared hive mind, they will not have had the exact same experience or emotional response to whatever events transpired, although both were there. Perhaps one or both were left feeling adrift by something that occurred. Therefore, a post-adventure discussion may be in order.

There are different ways to do this. You and your partner can share evening highlights, letdowns, and things you'd like to do again or perhaps do differently. Or maybe what you need is entirely non-verbal. Maybe you need cuddles, sex, or a massage to reestablish the bond you share together, just the two of you. Whatever your post-adventure ritual is, it should be designed to move you through the bad feelings while increasing empathy, validation, love, and sexual connection.

Kelly and Tom, a couple of six years, have an informal ritual of discussing the pros and cons of a chemistry check date during the car ride home. They explore how they felt about the other couple and whether they would like to see them again. They often giggle as they share their experiences.

Todd and Terrell have a morning-after pattern following a sex party the night before. Upon waking, they cuddle in bed, and then they get up, cook breakfast together, and return to the bedroom for breakfast in bed. While eating, they discuss the night before over waffles and orange juice.

Maintaining a conscious practice of reconnecting and staying connected during your non-monogamous journey is important. Technology, our own fears, and other factors might get in the way, but they can be surmounted. Remember your healthy habits, and you will be rewarded with a much happier, connected partnership.

The Power of Gratitude

For some, non-monogamy is like walking into a land of limitless temptations and delights. With all this potential amazingness, it's easy to take what you already have for granted. For that reason, I invite you to, from this point forward, develop an active practice of gratitude for your partner.

When you think of your partner with gratitude, notice what memories come up. When you connect with everything that is wonderful about them, what shifts in your thoughts? What feelings and sensations arise in your body? Let the images fill your mind's eye and notice how your life is better because of their presence in it.

A practice of relationship gratitude is one of the most powerful ways to increase happiness within a partnership. As Stan Tatkin writes in *Wired for Love*, we are more wired for war and survival than for love. Scanning for danger keeps a wild animal safe. But this same programming breaks down our love relationships. So a practice of gratitude is literally a method to rewire your brain for love and connection. Your practice of gratitude throughout your day may initially feel forced, but it will eventually become the way your brain naturally processes the world around you.

Gratitude can be expressed in so many ways. Ask your partner what best conveys your gratitude and love to them. Some people adore prolonged, loving eye contact, expressed words of appreciation, or gifts. Others love acts of service, compliments, or passionate sex, to name a few. Allow yourself to go beyond the five basic love languages. If your partner's love language is carefree adventure and freedom, then they feel loved when sharing an adventure with you, whether it's travel, skydiving, or sex. If you express love for your partner in their love language, they will feel your gratitude much more deeply. This is an incredible way to build connection and a strong bond in your relationship.

Reconnecting and maintaining connection within a non-monogamous relationship is crucial to its success. Building healthy practices (like reconnection rituals and gratitude practices) while simultaneously maintaining awareness of potential hurdles (like compulsive screen use or a critical mind) will allow a couple to maintain a happy, loving connection within non-monogamy. Keep an eye on the big picture of your relationship; even watch it as if you and your partner(s) are characters in your own movie. Are you practicing gratitude and connection? Your mindful awareness will aid you in achieving the conscious, connected relationships of your dreams.

Chapter Eighteen

THE PILLARS OF STABILITY IN A NON-MONOGAMOUS RELATIONSHIP

Mental, emotional, and sexual connection are the three power cores that create stability in a long-term non-monogamous relationship. If these three areas are fortified pillars, non-monogamy is much more likely to add to your relationship rather than tear it down. Why is this so important?

Imagine Will and Linda, who fell in love when they were twenty and twenty-three, respectively. They felt as connected as two people could feel—mentally, emotionally, and sexually. Their three pillars were strong and sturdy. In the beginning, they had sex like wild beasties, sometimes several times a day. Both were fascinated by each other's interests: Linda was proud to be with a human rights activist and photojournalist. Will admired Linda's artistic spirit and drive.

However, fifteen years into their relationship, they let go of some of the freedom and adventure they'd previously enjoyed in order to have children. Their two young children made having sex, even quicky sex, incredibly challenging, and their sex life got stale.

Early in their relationship, these two had shared many common interests. But over time, their interests had diverged. Will had quit his photojournalism job for a more reliable job as an accountant so he could support their family. Linda had stopped acting to be a stay-at-home mom and taken on a part-time job as an office manager. Neither felt fulfilled.

Emotionally, Linda needed to vent about her boss and Will needed to talk about his controlling mother. Secretly, Will was fed up and wished Linda would finally get a new job. Linda, meanwhile, was frustrated. She wished Will would finally stand up to his mom rather than continuing to enable her. Both caught themselves daydreaming while the other spoke. They felt unhappy, trapped, and bored.

One night, over drinks, they began to discuss opening up their relationship. They thought that taking on separate lovers might spice things up. One of them could stay home and watch the kids while the other went on a date. It seemed like a great plan to give both of them a break from responsibility.

They moved forward and soon both had separate lovers. And things worked. Free time shifted from daydreaming while the other spoke to sharing thoughts and feelings about this new sexual journey. The rest of their spare time was spent bent over their phone or laptop, captivated by their new lovers. Both felt invigorated again. Both smiled more. Their plan to recreate spice in their lives worked—but their ultimate intention of increased closeness was lost in the fervor. And they certainly didn't anticipate what would happen next.

Soon, Linda fell for Rico. He loved the gym, just like she did, and they became fitness partners. Linda discovered that they shared similar spiritual interests as well. He practiced yoga and meditation, and had even studied tantric sex. Will was often too tired for such things due to working long hours at his job. She found herself feeling more and more distant from Will and texting Rico more frequently.

Meanwhile, Will fell for Sophie. She too had a love for photography and social justice issues. They became lost in this common bond and would go to marches together, sharing their passion for a valiant cause while capturing it through film. Their sexual chemistry was through the roof.

So what happened to Will and Linda's connection? Back in their early twenties, their three pillars were as strong as could be. They felt incredibly connected on every level—mentally, emotionally, and sexually—but over the years they had grown divergently. Accumulatively, these changes had brought them out of alignment. Meanwhile, Rico and Sophie connected to the identities they had now, at ages thirty-five and thirty-eight, which cast a harsh light on just how disconnected they had become. Linda and Will's connection could not hold a candle to their connection with their new lovers. Instead of non-monogamy adding spice to the marriage, it simply shined a spotlight on how much they had grown apart.

Will and Linda came into therapy truly wondering if their marriage would survive. They were shell-shocked, because so much of the literature on non-monogamy that they had read made this path seem like the answer for everything.

Sometimes couples like Will and Linda find a way to reconnect. Other times it's too late to reconnect or reconfigure their non-monogamous connections. Despite loving each other, they may no longer be "in love" with each other—and may be finding deep love with the new partner. This dual progression of falling out of love as primaries and in love with new lovers may lead to their deciding to simply be friends or to end their connection entirely.

Okay! Now you have this tale of warning. With it, my hope is that you will be more able to combat this dynamic head-on. Now let's discuss each of the three core pillars separately.

Pillar One: Intellectual Connection

We all have a natural inclination for self-expansion and are happiest in relationships that encourage us to grow. The more our lover causes us to expand intellectually, the more connected and attracted to them we will be.

Ideally, when you are intellectually connected to your partner, they inspire your exploration of your intellection passion—whether it's art, science, travel, comic conventions, festival culture, you name it. This dynamic creates shared meaning. Renowned couples therapist John Gottman puts "shared meaning" at the very top of his "Sound Relationship House," a model for a strong, happy relationship. He suggests that couples create shared meaning through the use of rituals, roles, goals, and symbols. So let's discuss how to do that.

Creating intellectual connection practices

What shared practices, traditions, experiences, or goals can you and your partner put in place and nurture to make sure your intellectual connection stays alive and passionate in your relationship? Is your shared intellectual passion travel? If so, plan vacations together often. Do you share a love of literature? If so, read to each other before bedtime or listen and discuss books on road trips. Do you both love inspirational or spiritual thought? Then send texts sharing articles that inspire you throughout your day. These rituals keep your intellectual connection to your partner healthy, just like going to the gym keeps your body fit. Maintain your intellectual connection as a daily practice and you will be rewarded with a happier life. Furthermore, this will mean that any new and intellectually captivating lovers or partners will more likely enhance rather than threaten your already established partnership(s).

Pillar Two: Emotional Connection

As couples therapist Susan Johnson states in *Hold Me Tight*, most of us want our partner to meet our emotional needs in three ways:

1. Accessibility: Can I get your attention when I need it? Can you listen to what I am saying? Am I a top priority to you?

2. Responsiveness: Will you make an effort to comfort me when I am anxious, sad, lonely, or afraid? Are you effective at comforting me?
3. Engagement: Do you care about my well-being even when we are not together? Do you care about my joys, hurts, and fears? Will you care about me consistently and reliably?

A consistent pattern of accessibility, responsiveness, and engagement will create a resilient, unflappable, and secure partnership. This stability is a great starting point for a non-monogamous journey.

During the happy times, such couples will be better able to fully embrace the fun of their experience, whether it's a simple chemistry check date or full-on group sex. In addition, if you know your partner has your back, uncomfortable feelings like jealousy and insecurity will be lessened. Within disagreements, such partners are better able to problem-solve, less likely to catastrophize, more able to forgive, and better able to cope with power struggles or disappointments.

Increasing your emotional connection

- First off, utilize the communication skills we discussed in Chapter 13, especially when processing hard feelings. Please don't over-rely on logic to tackle your emotional difficulties. Difficult feelings have to be worked through, not around.
- Second, remember to create carefree time for increased bonding. As mentioned, most of my clients have a love language beyond the famous five: freedom, carefree fun, and adventure. Emotional connection wanes when freedom and adventure is forgotten and responsibility takes center stage. Can you relate? If so, remember to cultivate adventure together regularly. If you can't help but talk about responsibilities (kids and work) during a lovely dinner, then find an activity that makes such conversations

more difficult. Learn to scuba dive together. Go rock climbing. Go play putt-putt golf. Anything that won't allow you to slip into responsibility-laden patterns.

- Third, continue treating your partner as you would on a hot first date. Such an intention will send the message to your partner that you have active gratitude for them. Right now, as a little exercise, think about your words and behavior within your relationship in the last week. Would any of the actions you've taken or words you've uttered to your partner cause a hot new date to walk out on you? If so, cut it out! You shouldn't be treating your partner that way. Time for an attitude adjustment. Cherish your partner. They deserve such care way more than a hot stranger does.

If you maintain accessibility, responsiveness, and engagement along with great communication skills, adventurous bonding, and respectful treatment, you and your partner will be much more likely to stay emotionally connected.

Pillar Three: Sexual Connection

My clients, who almost always identify as either kinky, non-monogamous, or both, are bright people who usually describe themselves as highly sexual. As couples, at least initially, they had epic, connected sex. And when their sex life dies, they often assume that it's due to reasons directly related to sex, like their partner doesn't like their body anymore or doesn't think their sexual skill level is advanced enough.

In my experience, it is never that simple. When a couple's sex life dies, it's often because of a long history of disrespect, misattunements, boundary violations, and small or large heartbreaks in and out of the bedroom. I'm still a bit dumbfounded when a client says something like, "Well, maybe my partner wasn't ever kinky and non-monogamous to begin with. Perhaps it was all a lie to get me to invest in the relationship." Such a client usually will not or cannot process the long history of injuries that have gotten them to their current, sexless state.

A lack of sex is almost never a consequence of something so straightforward as sexual misattunements alone. I believe this is especially true for my clients who *love* sex, most of whom chose their partner partially due to their stellar sexual chemistry in the beginning.

Of the three core pillars, staying sexually connected can be the most challenging. The next chapter will be devoted to ways to stay sexually connected within non-monogamy—but for now, let's discuss what blocks our sexual flow.

In a long-term relationship, everything inside and out of the bedroom can impact whether you want to have sex with your partner. In *Come as You Are,* a book about women's sexuality, Emily Nagoski provides the brilliant analogy for women's desire: as a car with two brake pedals and one gas pedal. The gas pedal, Nagoski says, is a woman's erotic pathway—in other words, the stuff that turns her on. Some women like candlelight, soft music, and flowers. Others like being tied up and given a good spanking. The two brakes, meanwhile, are stand-ins for external and internal factors. For instance, maybe the bedroom door's lock has been busted for years and your five-year-old now has a tendency to walk right in whenever she has a nightmare or needs water. That would be an external, logistical factor inhibiting sexual desire. Perhaps you fear that your lover isn't truly attracted to you. That would be an internal, psychological factor that's getting in the way. A lover can have all the candles lit, the soft music playing, and the gas pedal floored, Nagoski says, but if even one of the brake pedals is on, the car will not move.

Although *Come as You Are* focuses on female sexuality, I feel all genders can relate to this analogy. For the purposes of this book, I'm going to assume that you are smart enough to get that lock on the bedroom door, along with all related logistical sexual blocks, fixed.

Therefore, we'll focus here on the psychological factors that can destroy sexual arousal and impact the health of a non-monogamous relationship. And just to clarify, both intimate play with your partner or group play with your partner can be negatively impacted by these following bad behaviors.

Psychological factors that put the brakes on sexual connection

First, I should note that psychological factors that put the brakes on sexual arousal can be external (coming from your partner's psyche) or internal (coming from your psyche). And although these psychological factors may impact our intellectual or emotional connection outside of the bedroom first, all things lead back to the bedroom in the end. Let's explore.

Laziness, disrespect, and self-entitlement

Most of us want a true partner. When we feel our partner is lazy, disrespectful, or entitled, all three of our pillars are compromised. We feel our partner doesn't understand us (intellectual pillar). We feel our partner doesn't care about us (emotional pillar). And we feel our partner doesn't care about being sexy for us (sexual pillar). This behavioral triple threat puts on the external brakes hard, leading to a sexually flatlined partner.

Disrespect and laziness often show up in seemingly trivial ways. For example, I often hear stories of one partner going off on another for loading the dishwasher incorrectly for the fifth time. The argument is never truly about loading the dishwasher. It's about respect, or lack thereof. The partner who loads the dishwasher incorrectly, or who doesn't do their share of household duties, is sending a message to their partner (who values a tidy household) that their needs are unimportant.

No one wants to have sex with someone who repeatedly disrespects them. Such an inconsiderate person often seems childlike to their partner. And it should go without saying that there is no better way to become desexualized than to come off like a helpless child. It often doesn't occur to the slacking partner that they aren't getting laid because they aren't loading the dishwasher correctly, but such accumulative patterns of behavior often lead to just that. Whether you see these behaviors in your partner or are being accused of them yourself, please don't ignore these issues. They will eventually leak into your bedroom.

Taking your partner for granted

Taking a partner for granted may hit your relationship's emotional pillar first, but the sexual pillar will soon follow. In contrast, when we listen to what makes our partner feel loved and invest in them by fulfilling these needs, they know they are cherished. And when we feel cherished, we are more open to connection and adventure of all kinds.

In contrast, if you slack in this regard, how do you think your partner will respond when you have an ask related to non-monogamy? They might think, *Oh, you want a threesome? When was the last time you did something for me?* A partner who feels taken for granted is not an authentically generous partner. If you and your partner know what makes each other feel cared for and strive to fulfill these needs, your relationship—and sex life—will thrive.

Appearing bored by your partner

Appearing bored by your partner may hit the intellectual pillar initially, but the sexual pillar soon follows suit. Whether you appear bored because your partner is complaining about their boss for the hundredth time or because you are choosing your phone over them, they notice. Within non-monogamy, this can be incredibly detrimental. Because guess what? Your partner is probably going on dates with someone who is captivated by everything they are, say, and do. If you're ignoring them, it's not shocking that they will want to be with that new lover who makes them feel so wonderful about themself.

Fading into being the bored partner is a type of relationship laziness. Unless we are on the way out and intending to break up with our partner, it's our responsibility to stay engaged, whether it's through flirting, sharing an article, or going on a new adventure together.

A lack of effort to flirt or invite flirtation

Let's talk about flirting, a core component of your sexual pillar. Maintaining a flirtation is arguably more important within a non-monogamous relationship than it is within a monogamous partnership. Why? Well, because you will naturally flirt with new lovers, and your partner will see that—and if the contrast between how you relate to your partner and your new lover is noticeable, it will likely be hurtful to them, leaving them feeling like the boring partner that you do adulting with.

You may be thinking to yourself, *Well, I don't plan to rub their face in it*. Right. Well, simply hiding your flirtations is not a sustainable solution. Even if your partner isn't aware of it, *you'll* know. And when you relabel your partner as "the responsible one," that's the beginning of going down a very bad road, especially if your love language is freedom, carefree fun, and adventure.

Your partner witnesses your sexual vitality and inspiration with other lovers when they believe you are uninspired with them

Similar to flirting, but perhaps even more painful to a long-term partner, is being sexually lit up with a new lover but erotically lackluster with your long-standing partner. This can be heartbreaking to witness and a hard hit to our emotional pillar. New relationship energy is natural, so it's unreasonable to ask you to numb your attraction to your new lover, but it's important to make sure your partner clearly knows, feels, and sees your fire for them as well, unless you have a consensually companionate relationship. So please make efforts both during one-on-one play and group play to let your partner know how desirable they are to you. This effort will contribute to the integrity of both your emotional and sexual relational pillars.

Disrespecting boundaries

A boundary is not something to push through; rather, it's a limit that should be remembered and respected. Most of us know this. But it's easy to become a sugar-lusting, out-of-control kid in a candy store on your non-monogamous journey and forget the boundaries that your partner has asked of you.

Here are a few common boundaries I've heard couples verbalize regarding group play:

- We will always be in the same room while playing with other lovers.
- In a foursome between one MF couple and another MF couple (straight guys/pansexual gals), it has been decided that the women can play together, but other than that, all play will be side by side, with no swapping of partners.
- At a play party, we will stay in the common social area and at most just watch the sexual play in the back room.
- No anal play with other partners.
- During group sex, you can play with whomever you like except for [insert name], because they were disrespectful to me recently and it would hurt me to see you with them.

Regardless of whether you think that the above boundaries are fair, if a boundary has been agreed to, that agreement needs to be upheld. Pressuring your partner in the middle of the party when they are liquored up, feel put on the spot, or feel pressured to please you is not considerate, loving, or respectful. It is not consensual play, and even if you get your way and feel giddy about it, I promise you that it will all backfire eventually, when your partner no longer trusts you.

Failing to attune with your partner emotionally or sexually in the bedroom

For some people, sexual attuning comes easily. They can read micro facial expressions and body language moment to moment (a heightened ability to read people that likely began when they were a baby in the arms of a caregiver who mirrored facial expressions) and adjust accordingly. Consequently, they're able to play their lover like a gifted musician.

Not all of us have this cultivated skill, however. If you're unable to read lovers well, developing an erotic communication style will help. This skill may take time—but eventually, seduction will replace awkwardly poking around and asking nervously, "How does that feel?" A sexual tone of voice, a confident demeanor, and fluid movements can be coupled with inquiry to culminate as an informative dirty talk dynamic that is hot as all fuck even as it includes attaining consent and affirmation.

If we're aware of these sexual roadblocks that exist both in and out of the bedroom, we can better maintain a healthy sexual connection with our partner. The flavor of this connection may vary; what matters is that you have a strong enough bond that an outside lover is not seen as a threat but rather as a contributor who expands your partner's happiness.

We are all human and non-monogamy is challenging, but the more you remember and avoid these sexual connection roadblocks that occur in and out of the bedroom, the more likely it is that you will stay sexually connected to your partner and thus maintain a happy and sexually vital relationship with them.

Chapter Nineteen

INTIMACY THROUGH BDSM AND NEO-TANTRIC PRACTICES

Regardless of your relationship model, you may reach a point in which sexual revitalization is needed. Yes, you heard me right: long-term non-monogamous relationships struggle with sexual heat waning too.

Don't get me wrong. Being open can help the sizzle last longer. Amazing threesomes and shared sexual adventures can maintain the heat between you for quite some time. But you can't have a threesome every day, now can you?

So, what can a primary or nesting couple do to keep things sustainably hot and connected? Neo-tantric practices and BDSM are two options.

"BDSM" stands for bondage and discipline, dominance and submission, and, finally, sadism and masochism. Regardless of your previous conceptions of BDSM, for now, I invite you to think of it as heavily psychological sensation play. Similarly, you may have confusion regarding neo-tantra or tantric sex, which is the modern, westernized variation of classical tantra from India. But for the purpose of this chapter, think of both simply as practices that heighten consciousness and union with your partner.

Why BDSM and neo-tantra? Because both effectively work in tandem with the neurochemicals of NRE (new relationship energy)—also called limerence—*and* the main neurochemical of long-term couples, oxytocin (the cuddle hormone), which makes them powerful ways to keep a relationship hot over time.

Before we get started exploring these two options, let me share some thoughts. As a couples therapist, I noticed early on that once NRE fades, the sex begins to dwindle as well. Long-term non-monogamous couples may find that they aren't fucking like bunnies as they used to; instead, they're only having sex when they go to a sex party, see other lovers, or play separately.

As I witnessed this pattern, I found myself scratching my head. I refused to believe that we were all doomed to simply cuddle in front of the television and forgo sex after a certain point in a relationship. So what was supposed to replace NRE? After much dedication to this question, I discovered the answer: intimacy.

Unfortunately, many of us suck at intimacy. If you don't believe me, take a neo-tantra class. You will experience firsthand how even the most basic tantric intimacy exercise results in a giggly, squirming group of adults in less than a minute. This is because intimacy and true connection terrifies us. But if you are brave, both neo-tantra and BDSM are great pathways to build a capacity for intimacy and maintain it.

Often, I see long-term couples struggle to recapture the NRE they had at the beginning of their relationship—but this is not a sustainable approach. Trying to reignite NRE can feel like swimming upstream. Why fight to recreate a chemical cocktail that has faded when you can work with what exists now—the oxytocin?

I am not suggesting abandoning the new and exciting, but let's face it, activities like skydiving or a threesome take considerable planning and organizing. Incorporating a practice of kink and neo-tantra within a long-term non-monogamous relationship, in contrast, 1) only requires planning between the two of you, 2) creates daily bonding erotic rituals, and 3) can work regardless of your present neurochemistry, as long as you both feel positively about each other. From that deep root, epic sex and love can be cultivated and maintained, so it's worth the effort.

The Integration of Neo-tantra and Mindfulness into Non-Monogamy

I find that many people are resistant to neo-tantra. They'll see one video in which two people are simply staring into each other's eyes at length, and they get nervous. She has her hand on his heart, he has his hand on her heart, and the viewer thinks, *Oh, hell no.* Or they write it off as "hippie shit." Or perhaps they're queer, Black, or brown, and they notice that the neo-tantra community looks very white and heteronormative. Regardless, I encourage you to question or push through your mental resistance. Even a sex life that gives a light homage to neo-tantra will be better off for it. There are easy ways to incorporate what we might call "tantra light."

When we have tantric sex, we are present, aware of our body, aware of our partner's body, and tracking this experience moment by moment. For some people, mindfulness (being present and aware) during sex comes naturally. But, alas, it's also natural for our minds to wander. Anxiety may eat away at the edges of our awareness (and enjoyment). There is ample opportunity to zone out. We may play pornographic films in our brains, evaluate our own sexual performance, worry about the kids, or wonder what our butt looks like. All of this monkey mind activity takes us away from deep connection and great sex. Neo-tantra brings us back. The following neo-tantra-inspired five steps are a great way to start.

Step One: Clear negative energy and be present

Make sure both of you have freed yourself from negative emotional energy and can be present for one another before you ramp up toward eroticism. I've had so many couples come into my office with a tale of spontaneous sex gone awry due to one of them initiating sex without first checking in on their partner's emotional state. Simply asking your partner, "How are you?" can be a game changer. Let's consider the following scenarios.

Hailey is at the stove cooking dinner. While cooking, she is thinking about her asshole boss who keeps criticizing her, her mom who keeps pressuring her, and her daughter who keeps waking her in the middle of the night because she's wet the bed.

Remy comes home from work. He's had a great day. He's happy, horny, and can't wait to fuck his gorgeous wife. He comes up behind cranky Hailey, who is brooding in silence. He loves those short shorts she's wearing. He scoops up her breasts and lightly tweaks her nipples while softly kissing her neck. Hailey almost elbows him as she struggles to free herself from his embrace. Remy feels completely rejected and hurt. He storms off, muttering, "What the fuck?" under his breath. Hailey bursts into tears while her burgers burn.

What went wrong here?

Because Hailey was stewing in anger and anxiety, she was easily kicked into her autonomic nervous system's threat response (fight, flight, or freeze) when Remy touched her. She wasn't in a receptive place. When unexpected sexual touch is paired with angry or anxious thoughts, it can trigger body memories of any non-consensual sexual attention we have experienced across our life. Hailey was already in her sympathetic nervous system (fight or flight) before Remy walked in the door. Remy unknowingly paired his sensual touch with all of her distress.

Now let's imagine their night going down a better way.

Remy texts Hailey before he leaves work and asks, "How was your day?" She tells him how terrible it was, so his approach upon entering their place is much different. It's slower. He takes time to connect with her emotionally. Later, after dinner, he suggests drawing her a bath and washing her hair. She says yes, and he proceeds by lighting some candles and putting on some sensual music. This sensual care allows her to switch from her sympathetic nervous system to her parasympathetic nervous system, a place of calm. Once calm, she may be able to find her sensual self again. As her nervous system shifts into her parasympathetic, her thoughts and feelings also switch over to a more positive and present place. She is much more capable of connecting with Remy—rather than brooding over the past or worrying about the future, she can be in the here and now. From this centered, grounded, present place, she is more capable of connecting and then ramping up into passion. She's also better able to 1) track her own body, 2) have enhanced intuition regarding his body, and 3) cultivate deeper intimacy between them.

Keep in mind, after such a hard day, Hailey might just need to be tucked into bed after this bath. Some men make the mistake of only nurturing their partner if they intend to ramp up to sex, which leads to accumulative resentment in their partner over time. Part of neo-tantra is honoring your partner. If Remy lovingly meets Hailey's needs without pressure for sex, she will be more willing and eager the next time around.

What rituals can you create to clear negativity from the day and switch over to a present place with your partner? First, attempt to connect to a place of calm as you let go of your Mommy/Daddy or professional archetype. These are non-sexual headspaces. Allow a transformation into your inner sex kitten or sexual god or goddess. From this headspace of presence, connection—and maybe even epic sex—will be possible.

Step Two: Focus on eye contact and breath

Maintaining eye contact when possible is also an important way to connect in the here and now. Rock salt lamps in the bedroom create a perfect, soft glow that make eye contact more visible while enhancing the beauty and sensuality of your lover's body.

Breathing slow and deep with your partner can enhance your connection to one another while enhancing awareness of your body and theirs.

A basic neo-tantric exercise is to sit cross-legged in front of your partner, their hand on your heart, your hand on their heart, and simply breathe together while looking into each other's eyes. This can be incredibly intense, even after a minute. But why is that? Well, because most of us haven't built a tolerance for the deep connection that we crave. Most of us don't know what baby steps to take to attempt to build it. This basic tantric exercise is a meditation, but a meditation that you are doing together. It's always connecting, and it's often erotic and love-enhancing.

Step Three: Slow down . . . at least part of the time

Fast, spontaneous fucking can be amazing. There is no argument there. It has its place. But I'd also invite you to carve out a place for slowness. It's in the slowness that one can deeply connect and notice the details. Shifts in your body, your partner's body, and how they move together enter your awareness more easily when you slow down. If you meet each of these subtle changes with an attuned response, you're likely to be a better lover to your partner. This practice will increase your connection the next time you fuck fast and hard, because these memories and knowledge will stay with you.

Step Four: Track your body

As you connect erotically with your partner, I invite you to track your body. If you have a trauma history, this may be hard. Such people are often disconnected from their body. But as you build a practice of tracking your body sensations in and out of the bedroom, you will notice more detailed and intricate sensations. And simply noticing those sensations within your body tends to make them more intense.

As you get better at tracking your body, you may find that you can actually experience the sensation of moving energy in your body. This energy movement is a key step toward achieving a tantric orgasm. Noticing negative body sensations is also key. Awareness of this information can enable you to better guide your lover away from uncomfortable touch, thus setting them up for success in optimizing your pleasure.

You can further this experience by noticing what your body needs to do to release energy. The more we move and create sound that mirrors our feelings and body sensations, the more powerful our release—whether that's an orgasm, body tremors, tears, or laughter. I encourage you to let all of this out. The body is healthier and happier when we allow it to release its energy.

Step Five: Track your partner's body

Part of neo-tantra is also tracking your partner's body. This can be done simply by watching or mirroring their breath, noticing changes in smell, noticing how their body reacts to touch. This can also be achieved by asking them what they sense within their body or asking them to verbalize shifts in the energy flow within their body. If they are highly aroused, they may reach a point where it is difficult to speak, but if they are able and willing, this is another way to connect.

What does all this have to do with being non-monogamous? I believe it has everything to do with it. One of the challenges of non-monogamy is that we can easily emotionally disconnect from our main partners for many reasons. We may shut down emotionally as a way to protect ourselves from getting hurt. We may disconnect due to being overwhelmed by power battles related to relationship agreements. Or we may numb out to avoid feeling left while witnessing a partner's NRE for a new lover. These are just a few examples. Neo-tantra is a powerful tool that can melt through much of that, allowing us to reconnect on a deep soul and body level and keep our relationships strong.

The Integration of BDSM and Non-monogamy

And now on to another deeply psychological and connecting practice: BDSM. The erotic bond cultivated through Dom/sub play can be a delicious way for a couple to stay connected within a non-monogamous relationship. (Note: It is beyond the scope of this book to discuss all the knowledge, skill, and emotional intelligence required to become involved in safe, sane, consensual BDSM. But if BDSM interests you, by all means, explore. It is up to you to embark upon your own educational journey, until you feel confident that your exploration of BDSM will be safe for yourself and your partner's mind, body, and spirit. If practiced safely, sanely, and consensually, with an intention of deeper attunement to your lover, it's a great way to reconnect.)

Let's consider the Dom role first.

Dominants

To be a great Dom, one must be very present and read their partner's body incredibly well. The by-product of this attunement is a deeper emotional connection. Now, there are a ton of folks who believe they are a great Dom because they are skilled. For instance, they know Shibari rope-tying or are a kick-ass flogger—but the best Doms also have a deep emotional intelligence. They are far from narcissistic or self-absorbed, and they want the best for their submissives. They maintain great boundaries and have stellar judgment and instincts. Their hyper-attunement and care can lead to deep and meaningful connections with their sub(s).

If you decide to explore kink, please do it wisely. Take some classes at your local sex toy store or dungeon and read some books. To participate in safe, sane, consensual BDSM, knowledge is necessary. Instinct is not enough—not even close.

Submissives

Submitting healthily within a BDSM relationship also requires great boundaries, stellar judgment, and great instincts. In addition, it requires an ability to assert yourself. The submissive needs to have confidence in their own ability to convey needed boundaries at any point. This communication may occur by negotiating a scene or creating a contract beforehand, or by asserting boundaries during a scene by using safe words or non-verbal safe gestures. Why might all these safety precautions be needed? Well, let's think about it.

Let's say you find yourself restrained, facedown, ass up, with a ball gag in your mouth. These restraints have made two of your defensive responses, fight and flight, impossible. This is a big deal, especially if you are alone with your partner. Having a safe word and a safe non-verbal cue allows you to have the ability to stop the action at any point. If this trust and vulnerability is honored by your Dom through thoughtfulness, care, skill, knowledge, and attunement, a deeper connection will unfold. Honored vulnerability is bonding.

We tend to eroticize what scares us. This is tender material. It explains why rape fantasies are one of the top fantasies for women and being a cuckhold is a common fantasy for kinky men. Does anyone want to be raped in real life? No. On the contrary, it's often a worst-imaginable fear. But within a scene that has been correctly and carefully negotiated with a trusted partner, one can experience something that is not only hot but also healing—a corrective experience. To do something so scary and have it play out well in a safe and erotic way can be very bonding.

Within D/s play, sometimes the sub will drop into a dreamy, blissful psychological and sensory experience called "subspace." Subspace can be broken down into two types: physiological and psychological. Physiological subspace is induced through sustained sensation play, especially from impact toys (e.g., a bare hand, flogger, paddle, cane, etc.). It is caused when endorphins, adrenaline, and other neurochemicals are released into the body, creating a natural drug high most likened to morphine. The actual sensation varies among individuals, but is often described as a warm, floaty, spacey, serene feeling. Some even liken it to a spiritual experience.

Psychological subspace is induced by psychological dynamics crafted by the Dom, or simply cultivated by the Dom's demeanor or energy. The sensation is very much an altered state where the submissive becomes relaxed, blissful, suggestible, floaty, and warm.

Subspace is a delicious place to be in. To have one's partner hold and protect you in such a state of complete abandon and bliss is very bonding. The Dom/sub dynamic can be incredibly powerful and at its best can manifest some shared mind-blowing, life-altering experiences.

These are a few reasons why BDSM can be a great way for a primary or long-term couple to stay deeply connected when there is love and trust.

Both BDSM and neo-tantric practices can help a non-monogamous couple stay connected or reconnect after seeing other lovers or having experiences that leave them feeling adrift from each other. Both sexual modalities have the power to melt away our sense of separateness and reestablish intimacy.

Chapter Twenty

COMING OUT

A book on non-monogamy would not be complete without discussing coming out. You may associate coming out as a struggle relegated to the LGBTQ population, but in my private practice, kinky folks, sex workers, and non-monogamous people struggle as well. Coming out . . . what a daunting proposition.

These days, I'm almost completely out. But I remember crying while talking to a gay male therapist at a San Diego couples therapy conference back around 2011 about my coming-out process as non-monogamous. He comforted me and let me know that any coming-out process, whether you are coming out as kinky, non-monogamous, or gay, can be emotionally difficult—and those feelings are valid.

Not everyone who is non-monogamous will choose to come out. But for some, feeling deeply connected with their partner is inherently linked to having their relationship recognized and validated by those around them. If this resonates, this chapter is for you.

As a sex-positive psychotherapist, I realize that being as out as I am is a luxury. It's a privilege and a rare thing indeed. Most people can't come out to family and friends because of fear (whether real or imagined) of negative consequences. But it should be noted that coming out is not like a door that is either wide open or locked shut—it's on a continuum. No need to be completely out if it doesn't serve you.

For me, it was a slow process. At first, only swing lifestyle friends knew that I was non-monogamous. My ex-husband and I started out playing with couples in 2003 and then slowly became part of the swing lifestyle community.

My first coming-out step was telling my therapist. After telling her, I remember saying, "I feel like a grapefruit-size weight has been removed from my core." She smiled and was kind and supportive.

It wasn't until many years later that I told two of my coworkers. I thought they might judge me—but instead, a huge sea change occurred in our friendship that took our connection to a deeper level.

Today, I would say that I'm 99 percent out, and by the time you're reading this book, I'll be 100 percent out. I have found that coming out has tremendously improved my happiness. Why? Mainly because I believe authenticity is one of the grand keys to happiness, along with a practice of gratitude, living mindfully, and finding meaning in life. You are giving yourself the gift of congruency: the person you are on the outside is the same as the person you are on the inside.

In our culture of sexual shame, however, coming out puts many people at risk for damaging their family relationships, careers, or emotional stability. If you are in this category, coming out may not be worth it. It takes a lot of emotional energy to come out, and if your emotional gas tank doesn't have enough fuel in it, then perhaps the timing isn't right.

The Benefits of Coming Out

So let's talk about some key reasons to come out. First, there are many perks that come with authenticity. There are strong drawbacks as well, but right now let's focus on the positives.

When you are out, you can speak freely about your life. Non-monogamy may very well extend past the confines of your sex life, and may include friends, community, activities, and loved ones. With all of that considered, you may discover that non-monogamy accounts for at least 30 percent of your life. If you are out, you can freely talk about your relationships, your weekend plans—hell, your life plans. Over time, you may become more comfortable in your own skin. You may find that non-monogamy is not merely a practice for you but also your orientation and your identity. Hiding something that is so integral to your nature may begin to feel unhealthy for you.

Normalizing non-monogamy

There are also social implications to coming out. When you come out, you give permission to others to move through their fears and come out as well. These days, with social media, this permission may be simply to those in your close circle, or it could be to your worldwide followers.

In living our big, bold truth, we model that we need not live in fear or shame. And helping others move through their shame and toward their truth is one of the greatest gifts one can give. A society crippled in shame is a society that can be controlled. A society living in authenticity is optimizing its populace toward its collective human potential.

Furthermore, when we come out, it makes others in less privileged positions feel that they too can explore non-monogamy and perhaps begin their process of considering how out they want to be. This is why it's so great to see non-monogamy gaining steam via progressive TV shows like *Insecure* and through sex-positive educators of all ethnicities and genders on social media.

We are still in a time when monogamous folks tend to know only about the most incapable non-monogamous practitioners. As more healthy non-monogamous couples come out, the masses will be able to see that non-monogamy is a viable relationship model.

Honoring all your partners

Another key reason to come out, in the case of polyamory, is to be sure that all your loves feel recognized and honored. Being a hidden partner can be emotionally difficult. For some, their sadness may only hit them when they aren't invited to a major family gathering or holiday event. For others, it may be a more pervasive sadness. Logically, they may understand the necessity of being closeted, but that doesn't mean their heart won't crave being recognized. They may want confirmation that you're proud to be with them, that your relationship is real and recognized by loved ones. Being in the shadows can be difficult.

Should You Come Out?

If you are weighing the pros and cons of coming out, Dr. Elisabeth Sheff suggests asking this question: "Is it relevant (appropriate), necessary, and safe to come out to this person or in this situation?" So let's consider each part of this question.

Is it appropriate?

It's important to consider how our disclosure will impact the lives of the newly informed. For instance, you may have a fragile, elderly mother with anxiety and physical health issues who is isolated in a small town. You may hold off telling her for the sake of her health unless someone outs you or your orientation can no longer be hidden. This choice is not being cowardly; it's compassionate. There is a delicate balance between our need for having an authentic sense of self and the welfare of our loved ones. Sometimes it's hard to balance self-care/self-love and love for others. We can only do the best we can.

Is it necessary?

What meaning you attach to coming out will determine what course is best for you. For instance, I've known plenty of folks who simply don't see a need to come out, such as swingers who aren't hiding other loved ones. They feel their sex life is their business alone. Furthermore, many have told me that they enjoy having a little secret.

They find it fun that they have a "naughty little secret" with their partner, and that's part of what keeps their connection hot.

In contrast, if you have two partners and are deeply in love with both of them, you may want to bring them both to your family's holiday party—in which case it may be necessary for you to come out.

Is it safe?

I believe people need to earn our vulnerability. Instead of coming out all at once in a big Facebook announcement, pick a chosen few places to start. Picture a dartboard. This is your inner circle diagram.

Included in your inner circle—closer to the bull's eye—are those who have earned your trust regarding non-monogamy and other vulnerable truths about you. As your trust in a person's open-mindedness and kindness decreases, the farther out that person should be on your dartboard. Perhaps they are in the second, third, or fourth circle out. Some may be pushed off the board completely.

An easy way to test family and friends is to ask them questions about pop culture or the news related to non-monogamy. For instance: "Hey, Carrie, did you see that show on non-monogamy on HBO? What did you think?"

If Carrie's reply is, "I think they're crazy and dysfunctional and risking everything they love," you may decide that she's not a safe person to tell and it's not necessary to tell her. Now, if your emotional gas tank is full, you may decide to disclose to her, but if not, you may decide that she hasn't earned your disclosure yet and possibly never will. The more a friend or family member has responded to you in a toxic way, the further out they should be pushed from your inner circle.

You may decide to take on a family member who has behaved in a toxic or bigoted way despite knowing the risks. I get it. Sometimes we need to for our own self-validation. Or it may be necessary in the case of a polyamorous relationship. I only suggest that you wait until you truly have the emotional energy to do so.

Also, please be honest with yourself about the risks of coming out. You can only control you. It's important to have a voice, but other people's responses are beyond your control. It's okay to hope for the best as long as you are prepared for something less than ideal. It's human to fantasize about a warm, loving, and embracing response from Mom and Dad, but they may not be able to give that to you.

Besides choosing who we come out to carefully, timing is key. It's not wise to come out when you're pissed at your right-wing uncle Marvin who's spouting off about the latest thing he heard on Fox News. It's not good timing to come out to the coworker you have a crush on while you're drunk at the company Christmas party. Choose a time that feels calm and good to you with little distractions or stress.

Another consideration, beyond who and when, is *where* we come out. Choose an atmosphere that will not have disruptive interruptions. This choice will vary depending on your sensitivities. A quiet restaurant, a hike, or a walk on the beach are good settings for such an important conversation.

When choosing how far to come out, consider the community that you reside in and perhaps the religious community you are affiliated with. If you live in a big city like Los Angeles or New York, both of which have massive non-monogamous populations, your worries will largely be diminished. However, if you live in a small, conservative town in which gossip and bigotry run rampant, coming out may not be emotionally or physically safe for you. Even legal concerns, such as parental custody, may be greater in such a situation.

Also, can you trust the person you are telling to keep a secret? There are some lovely, caring people out there who can't keep a secret to save their life. If you come out to open-minded Aunt Beverly only to have her tell gossipy Aunt Beatrice, who tells the rest of your conservative family, you might find yourself in an emotional crisis and your gas tank on empty.

Finally, please don't feel guilty if you decide that you aren't ready or don't want to come out. Self-care is paramount here.

Emotional Care for Coming Out

Once you have chosen the who, when, and where, it's time to ground and emotionally prepare yourself. Your looming coming-out conversations may have you feeling a bit nervous. If so, know that even though you can't control other people's reaction, you do have the power to set the tone that increases your chances for a positive outcome. First and foremost, that means keeping calm before and during the conversation.

Practice runs

One of the best ways to be calm and collected for this conversation is to do several practice runs in advance. This can be done either by writing a back-and-forth discussion in your journal or practicing in the mirror. Run through possible objections, questions, and reactions in your head and write out or verbalize your response. If unsure about some of your responses, run them by a trusted friend or partner. Although there's no way to predict every possible response, you'll feel much more confident if you've desensitized and prepared yourself a bit this way.

And again, setting boundaries is key here. If you don't want to answer some of the questions you're asked or don't feel answering them will be constructive, let the person asking know that you aren't comfortable answering. Here are some common questions from family or friends that look through a monogamous lens:

Are you being manipulated, pressured into this, or exploited by your partner? OR Are you pressuring your partner into this?

This question is based in fear and steeped in ignorance regarding non-monogamous relationships. One of the best ways to knock down such fears is to humanize your partner and to educate the people you're talking to via easy-to-digest articles or books on what healthy, respectful non-monogamy looks like.

How can you participate in such immoral, sexually deviant behavior?

First, you may need to unpack what, exactly, the person you're speaking to believes is immoral. They may be assuming that this is a form of cheating, or that non-monogamy is the equivalent of not having emotional or sexual boundaries. In other words, they may be assuming that you will have sex with just about anyone. People make up all sorts of stories about non-monogamy. If you unpack their assumptions around non-monogamy, and then clarify and address them, you may be able to reduce some of their fears.

But again, remember your boundaries. How much does family really need to know about the goings-on within your bedroom? That's your call.

What about your children?

This is a good time to throw out some Elisabeth Sheff quotes from *The Polyamorists Next Door* about the higher rate of emotional well-being and well adjustment amongst children with polyamorous parents as compared to children with monogamous parents.

Do we have to meet your other partners?

If you want to share holidays or get married to your other partners, the answer is probably yes.

Is this just a phase?

Often, this question stems from the hope that this threatening news will simply go away and thus there will be no need to process any grief or loss regarding their attachments to your future.

It may be helpful to point out to whomever you're coming out to that their effort to dismiss your reality may be easier for them but feels incredibly invalidating to you. This reality check may help them realize that they need to work through their feelings.

How will I explain this to other family members?

Often what is underlying such a question is a fear of being judged, so perhaps a conversation about the feelings hidden underneath this question is appropriate here. But please remember, your relationships are something to celebrate, not something to apologize for. And at the end of the day, it's not your job to help Aunt Martha figure out how to deal with Uncle Bob.

Explaining non-monogamy to family is often more of an ongoing dialogue than a one-time conversation. It takes patience, compassion, and constantly reasserting the boundaries you need and deserve.

Grounding techniques

Don't forget to utilize the grounding techniques learned earlier in this book. You can use them before, during, and after your coming-out discussion. Find ways to stay in your Resilient Zone. Even if the recipient of your news goes down this road and gets upset, you need not go with them. If you remain calm, they will be more likely to return to a state of calm as well.

Self-care after disclosing

So the conversation has run its course; now is a time for self-care. I usually felt better than ever once I came out to someone, but not always.

If the conversation you've just had has depleted your emotional gas tank, it's time to replenish. Perhaps you need a hug, a massage, or head pets from a partner. If a partner is not accessible, going to a place with a high level of negative ions, like the beach, can be incredibly grounding. Finally, a mindful yoga session, jogging, or walking are all great ways to ground and release anxiety from the body.

Coming Out to Kids

Coming out to children is a very different emotional process with different considerations than coming out to the adults in your life.

Elisabeth Sheff's *The Polyamorists Next Door* is a great reference for non-monogamous parents. First off, it's important to note that, according to Sheff, the kids are all right. Looking at the results of her fifteen-year ethnographic study of polyamorous families with children, she says, "These children seemed remarkably articulate, intelligent, self-confident, and well-adjusted. . . . The children in these families appeared to be thriving with the plentiful resources and adult attention their families provided."

Children who are born into a polyamorous relationship will need little explanation of it. They grew up with it, so they understand it—in fact, it's normal to them. However, children whose parent(s) become polyamorous after the children are born will need more support and explanation. It's important to present your relationship in a way that leaves your children secure and understanding that your family will not be hurt by the changes you are making.

Some children will need more reassurance than others due to their specific circumstances. For instance, if a child's friend's parents just divorced due to an infidelity, they may view other partners as a potential threat. Such children need to know that their world is still secure—that their parents' many partners are not indicative of impending divorce.

One thing that remains the same with children from both monogamous and non-monogamous families is that they want to hear as little about their parents' and/or caregivers' sex life as possible. And it's not necessary for them to know such details anyhow.

Children need to know that your door is always open if they have issues they want to discuss. For instance, they may need help deciding what to tell a questioning peer. (My advice: Due to stepfamilies, having multiple parents is normal, so kids can simply explain to another kid at school, "That's my other dad," and most kids will make their own assumptions without questioning it. Poly families don't usually stand out as much as you might think, and their children face fewer questions because of this fact. They often blend.)

Children tend to understand multiple loves more easily than adults. They know their parents love them and all their siblings, so it's easy for them to imagine their parents loving more than one partner. As Sheff writes, "What mattered to the children was that they had five loving and attentive adults caring for them, taking them places, picking them up from school, and putting them to bed at night."

There are many benefits to raising children in a poly household, including modeling authenticity despite typical societal views. And if polyamory is not involved, as is the case with swinging, then many parents choose not to address their sexual lifestyle to their children at all. The kids only need know that Mom and Dad are going to a party or out with friends. It's rare, in fact, that swingers come out to their children. Again, kids don't want or need to know about your sex life.

Legal considerations are also important. Please educate yourself on the laws in your state regarding polyamory and how they may impact your family, especially regarding custody and housing. Again, Elisabeth Sheff has many articles on this topic.

As extended families who live together become increasingly rare, polyamorous families are one way that some people are counteracting the isolation of the nuclear family and finding ways to increase caretaking options for children. In a poly household, it's common for other partners to visit regularly, stay overnight, and sometimes move in. In situations like this, lovers may take on roles similar to those of aunts and uncles, or sometimes even coparents—a safety net of love that, at its best, can actually be wonderful for a child.

My Final Wish

I close with my best wishes for your future. Non-monogamy inherently pokes at our old attachment injuries; that's unavoidable. But it need not create mounting scar tissue. My intention throughout this book has been to create a template for increased intimacy, trust, and deep connection in your open relationship. When we are able to put ego in our back pocket and lead with love and compassion, we have a good shot at having much happiness within non-monogamy. We can even heal old attachment injuries from this loving place.

You deserve compassion, patience, and understanding. You deserve to be truly seen and heard. Your partners deserve this as well. Good luck to you, and remember: connected, conscious love can only be found by those willing to open deeply.

WORKS CITED

Anapol, Deborah. *The New Love without Limits*. Intinet Resource Center. March 1, 1997.

Bergland, Christopher. "The Neuroscience of Empathy." *Psychology Today*, October 13, 2013. https://www.psychologytoday.com/us/blog/the-athletes-way/201310/the-neuroscience-empathy.

Bockarova, Mariana, PhD. "The Forgotten Attachment Style: Disorganized Attachment." *Psychology Today*, September 23, 2019. https://www.psychologytoday.com/us/blog/romantically-attached/201909/the-forgotten-attachment-style-disorganized-attachment.

Brogaard, Berit, DMSci, PhD. "Attachment Styles Can't Change, Can They?" *Psychology Today*, February 12, 2015. https://www.psychologytoday.com/us/blog/the-mysteries-love/201502/attachment-styles-cant-change-can-they.

Brogaard, Berit, DMSci, PhD. "The True Nature of Jealousy: Evolution, Fear, and Anger All Play a Part." *Psychology Today*, September 29, 2016. https://www.psychologytoday.com/us/blog/the-mysteries-love/201609/the-true-nature-jealousy.

Burleigh, Tyler, Serge Desmarais, Robin Milhausen, and Jessica Wood. "Reasons for Sex and Relational Outcomes in Consensually Nonmonogamous and Monogamous Relationships: A Self-Determination Theory Approach." *Journal of Social and Personal Relationships* 35, no. 4 (March 23, 2018): 632–654.

Buss, David M. *The Dangerous Passion: Why Jealousy is as Necessary as Love and Sex.* New York: Free Press, 2011.

Chodron, Pema. *When Things Fall Apart.* Boulder: Shambhala Publications, 2016.

Claire, Kimberly, and Robert McGinley. "Changes in the Swinging Lifestyle: a US National and Historical Comparison." *Culture, Health, and Sexuality* 21, no. 10 (May 2018): 1–14.

The Dalai Lama. "Only Genuine Compassion Will Do." *Lion's Roar,* November 5, 2020. https://www.lionsroar.com/only-genuine-compassion-will-do.

Dodgson, Lindsay. "Ashley Madison Now has 60 Million Users. Two Men Told Us Why They Use It." *Insider,* April 22, 2019. https://www.insider.com/why-men-use-ashley-madison-online-dating-2019-4.

Easton, Dossie, and Janet Hardy. *The Ethical Slut.* Celestial Arts. 2009.

Eckel, Sara. "Listening to Jealousy." *Psychology Today,* November 1, 2016. https://www.psychologytoday.com/us/articles/201611/listening-jealousy.

Edwards, Scott. "Love and the Brain." *Harvard Medical School,* Spring 2015. https://hms.harvard.edu/news-events/publications-archive/brain/love-brain.

Gaba, Sherry, LCSW. "Understanding Fight, Flight, Freeze and the Fawn Response." *Psychology Today,* August 22, 2020. https://www.psychologytoday.com/us/blog/addiction-and-recovery/202008/understanding-fight-flight-freeze-and-the-fawn-response.

Gelfand, Michele, PhD. "The Secret Life of Social Norms." Ted: Ideas Worth Spreading, October 28, 2018. https://www.ted.com/talks/michele_gelfand_phd_the_secret_life_of_social_norms.

Gottman, John, and Nan Silver. *What Makes Love Last?: How to Build Trust and Avoid Betrayal.* New York: Simon & Schuster, 2013.

Greenberg, Elinor, PhD. "What Three Factors Predict if a Child will Become a Narcissist?" *Psychology Today,* January 1, 2020. https://www

.psychologytoday.com/us/blog/understanding-narcissism/202001
/what-three-factors-predict-if-child-will-become-narcissist.

Hahn, Thich Nhat. *True Love: A Practice for Awakening the Heart.* Boulder: Shambhala Publications, 2006.

Hendriix, Harville, PhD. *Getting the Love You Want.* New York: St. Martin's Griffin, 2008.

Heller, Diane P. "The Four Attachment Styles and Not Taking Things Personally." Smart Couple 204, July 12, 2018. https://www.youtube.com/watch?v=ifymItcTOl0.

Heller, Diane P. "What's Your Attachment Style." https://dianepooleheller.com/attachment-styles.

Henderson, Shelby. "Three Toxic Parenting Styles that Turn Kids into Narcissists." *Your Tango,* July 28, 2020. https://www.yourtango.com/2017303382/3-toxic-parenting-styles-cause-narcissism-childhood.

Johnson, Sue, EdD. *Hold Me Tight.* New York: Little, Brown Spark, 2008.

Kimberly, Claire, and Robert McGinley. "Changes in the Swinging Lifestyle: a US National and Historical Comparison." *Culture, Health & Sexuality* 21, no.2 (2019) 219–232.

Kohn, Isabelle. "Why Do We Think Polyamory is Only for the Rich, White and Privileged?" *Mel,* 2020. https://melmagazine.com/en-us/story/why-do-we-think-polyamory-is-only-for-the-rich-white-and-privileged.

Levin, Amir, and Rachel S.F. Heller. *Attached.* New York: Penguin, 2011.

Levine, EC, et al. "Open Relationships, Nonconsensual Nonmonogamy, and Monogamy Among U.S. Adults: Findings from the 2012 National Survey of Sexual Health and Behavior." *Archive of Sexual Behavior* 47, no.5 (July 2018): 1439–1450.

Mariposa, Mel. "Polynormativity and the New Poly Paradigm." Polysingleish.com, February 1, 2013. https://polysingleish.com/2013/02/01/polynormativity-and-the-new-poly-paradigm.

The Mask You Live In. Written, directed, and produced by Jennifer Siebel Newsom. The Representation Project. January 25, 2015.

Miler-Karas, Elaine. Trauma Resilience Model®: Healing One Step at a Time. Trauma Resource Institute. Revised edition. January 2019.

Mogilski, JK, et al. "Jealousy, Consent, and Compersion within Monogamous and Consensually Non-Monogamous Romantic Relationships." *Archives of Sexual Behavior* 48 (2019): 1811–1828.

Moore, Peter. "Young Americans are Less Wedded to Monogamy than their Elders." Today.yougov.com, October 3, 2016. https://today.yougov.com/topics/lifestyle/articles-reports/2016/10/03/young-americans-less-wedded-monogamy.

Nagoski, Emily. *Come as You Are.* New York: Simon & Schuster, 2015.

National Institute of Mental Health. "Any Mood Disorder." November 2017. https://www.nimh.nih.gov/health/statistics/any-mood-disorder.shtml.

Perel, Esther. *Mating in Captivity: Unlocking Erotic Intelligence.* New York: HarperCollins Publishers, 2006.

Powell-Twagirumukiza, Neesha. "These People are Queering Ethical Non-monogamy." *The Body*, August 22, 2019. https://www.thebody.com/article/these-people-are-queering-ethical-non-monogamy.

Reisterer, Benjamin. "The Three Equations for Insight and Transformation." *Individual Counseling*, October 14, 2015. https://www.mindfulcounselinggr.com/blog/2016/1/25/the-3-equations-for-insight-and-transformation.

Rickert, Eve, and Franklin Veaux. *More Than Two.* Portland: Thorntree Press, 2015.

Ryan, Christopher. *Sex at Dawn.* New York: HarperCollins Publishers, 2010.

Savage, Dan. "The Problem with Polynormativity." *The Stranger*, January 30, 2013. https://www.thestranger.com/slog/archives/2013/01/30/the-problem-with-polynormativity.

Schairer, Sara. "What's the Difference Between Empathy, Sympathy, and Compassion?" *The Chopra Center*. July 31, 2017. https://chopra .com/articles/whats-the-difference-between-empathy-sympathy -and-compassion

Sharma, Roma. "Understanding Our Ego States." Medium, November 9, 2017. https://medium.com/romasharma/understanding-our-ego -states-77893182c269.

Sheff, Elisabeth. *The Polyamorist Next Door*. Washington, DC: Rowman & Littlefield, 2014.

Sheff, Elisabeth A., PhD. "Updated Estimate of Number of Non-Monogamous People in the U.S." *Psychology Today*, May 27, 2019.

Taormino, Tristan. *Opening Up*. Minneapolis: Cleis Press, 2008.

Tatkin, Stan. *Wired for Love: How Understanding Your Partner's Brain and Attachment Style Can Help You Defuse Conflict and Build a Secure Relationship*. Brattleboro: Echo Point Books & Media, LLC, 2012.

Van Der Kolk, Bessel. *The Body Keeps the Score*. New York: Penguin Books, 2015.

Well, Tara, PhD, "Compassion is Better than Empathy: Neuroscience Explains Why." March 4, 2017. https://www.psychologytoday. com/us/blog/the-clarity/201703/compassion-is-better-empathy.

Wilber, Matika, and Adrienne Keene, "Decolonizing Sex." *All My Relations* podcast. Season 1, episode 5. March 19, 2019. Buzzsprout. https://www.buzzsprout.com/262196/1001592.

The World of Work Project, "The Johari Window: A Helpful Interpersonal Awareness Tool." 2019. https://worldofwork.io/2019/07 /the-johari-window.

Zane, Zachary, "Who Really Practices Polyamory." *Rolling Stone*. November 12, 2018. https://www.rollingstone.com/culture/culture-features /polyamory-bisexual-study-pansexual-754696.

ACKNOWLEDGMENTS

I must express my reverence for a few of the pioneers in this field, Tristan Taormino, Janet Hardy, and Dossie Easton, whose contributions laid the groundwork for my work to flourish. You allowed me to go forth with confidence. I'm so grateful to you.

Limitless gratitude to my mother for being a "happy pregnant lady" whose consistent love built a deep resiliency in me that has helped me to stay grounded during even the most trying of times. To my beloved Grandma Loree, your modeling of being a bold, joyous light gave me permission to transcend fear and unapologetically shine bright.

Sending big love and thanks to my wonderful friends, Hudsy Brooke Hawn and Pierre Theodore, who were ever present when I had early-stage cancer during part of the development of this book. Your unconditional love and help allowed me to stay on course.

My deepest regard goes to my dear friend, Jennifer Burton-Flier, LMFT, for being a key catalyst in my development in the areas of attachment theory, mental health, EMDR, and somatic psychotherapy that are so interwoven in this book. Thank you, my inspiring friend.

Thank you to Richard Marz for being a key male muse and creative visionary who could see who I would become even before I did and helped me get there.

Thank you to my loveable, creative, highly intelligent clients, both past and present. I learn so much from you every day and you are a blessing. You inspire me to be a better therapist. You make my profession a joy.

Unlimited thanks to Brooke Warner, president of Warner Coaching, Inc. and publisher of She Writes Press, for being the best "Book Domme" a gal could ask for. You helped me polish my rough diamond into something I could be proud of. And thank you to Jamye Waxman for referring me to Brooke.

Huge love and gratitude to my dear friends who took the time to read and give me feedback on my book and/or emotionally supported me during the writing of the book, including, Hudsy Brooke Hawn, Heather Goldberg, Pierre Theodore, Andrea Mikonowicz, LMFT, Julia Greco LCSW, Jennifer Burton-Flier, LMFT, Babatunde Akinboboye, Lenora Claire, and Demetrius Asekomeh. I'm a much better human due to your influence in my life.

Big thank you to hypnotherapist Jordan Wolan, who got me over my writer's block after one session despite years of spinning my wheels. And much appreciation to music composer Tim "Spartacus" Despic for modeling the intense writer's work ethic that motivated me to hire Jordan.

A profound gratitude to Debra Linesch, PhD, LMFT, ATR-BC and Paige Asawa, PhD, LMFT, ATR-BC of Loyola Marymount's Marital and Family Art Therapy program, as well as my former therapist, Narda Smith, LMFT, who were powerful surrogate LA mother figures that shifted me. Narda, you were the first person that I came out to as non-monogamous outside of the non-monogamous community. Your shame-free response allowed me to go forth toward my true path unencumbered.

Finally, I want to thank everyone at She Writes Press who contributed to my book's completion, such as project manager Samantha Strom, copy editor Krissa Lagos, and again, Brooke Warner.

GLOSSARY

ambivalent attachment style. Ambivalently attached people have had caregivers who were inconsistent or unreliable. Because of the lack of consistency, they doubted as children whether their needs would be met and coped by clinging to their caregivers. These patterns are projected into their adult relationships. This style is not fixed and the adult can become more secure if they are committed to healing.

asexual. The lack of sexual attraction to others, or a low interest in sexual activity. Some consider asexuality to be a sexual orientation. Others describe it as an absence of sexual orientation. Asexuals may have an interest in romantic relationships.

attachment injury. An emotional wound, such as a betrayal of trust, abuse, neglect, or abandonment at a crucial time of need within an intimate or interdependent relationship.

avoidant attachment style. In the avoidant attachment style, caregivers' emotionally unavailable, insensitive, and even hostile responses to a child's need for connection formed a coping strategy of disconnection in the child. In adulthood, that person may completely avoid relationships, sabotage relationships, or keep people at a distance. They tend to view themselves as independent or a lone wolf. This style is not fixed and the adult can become more secure if they are committed to healing.

BDSM. A composite acronym for Bondage and Discipline (B&D), Dominance and Submission (D&S), Sadism and Masochism (S&M). BDSM refers to any activities or lifestyles between consenting adults which include some or all of these aspects.

borderline personality disorder (BPD). A mental illness marked by an ongoing pattern of varying moods, self-image, and behavior. These symptoms often result in impulsive actions and problems in relationships. People with borderline personality disorder may experience intense episodes of anger, depression, and anxiety that can last from a few hours to days. With the proper treatment, the severity of symptoms related to BPD can often decrease.

cisgender. Someone who identifies as the gender they were assigned at birth.

closed relationship. Any romantic relationship, such as a monogamous relationship or a polyfidelitous relationship, that specifically excludes the possibility of sexual or romantic connections outside of the partners involved.

compersion. A feeling of joy from other's pleasure—specifically, a positive emotional reaction to a lover's other relationships. Coined by the Kerista Commune.

consensual non-monogamy (CNM). An umbrella term for relationships, such as polyamory and the swing lifestyle, in which all partners involved are aware and give clear consent to engage in romantic and/or sexual relationships are not monogamous.

couple privilege. The advantage that an established couple has over a single. In non-monogamy, this is especially pronounced when a new person is added to a relationship, whether the new person is dating one or both of the individuals that comprise the couple.

dominant. A person who takes on a leadership role while consensually and erotically controlling a submissive participant. This type of partnership is often referred to in the BDSM community as a D/s partnership.

dialectical behavior therapy (DBT). A modified type of cognitive behavioral therapy that combines approaches such as mindfulness, acceptance, and emotion regulation. Its main goals are to teach people how to live in the present, develop coping skills, regulate emotions, and improve relationships with others.

disorganized attachment style. Usually seen in people who have been physically, verbally, or sexually abused in their childhood. A disorganized attachment style develops when the child's caregivers are also a source of fear. In adulthood, people with this attachment style are extremely inconsistent in their behavior, have little trust, and are caught in an internal conflict of wanting but fearing intimacy and love. This style is not fixed. The adult can become more secure if they are willing to seek out the required help, such as a psychotherapist, to heal.

don't ask, don't tell. A relationship agreement in which one or both people in a relationship are allowed to have other sexual or romantic relationships as long as no information about the other partners or activities is disclosed to the other partner.

double trigger. The moment between two people in a relationship in which both are emotionally triggered simultaneously by one another, rendering both people compromised and therefore unable to soothe their partner or themselves effectively. This is a term I coined after repeatedly witnessing this psychological dynamic in my private practice with couples. Once a couple is aware of the psychodynamics that set off their double trigger, it's possible to do the work to disarm or reduce it. This healing may require individual and couples therapy.

dyad. Something that consists of two elements, parts, or people.

EMDR. Eye movement desensitization and reprocessing (EMDR) is a psychotherapy modality that was originally designed by Francine Shapiro to alleviate the distress associated with traumatic memories. EMDR therapy facilitates the accessing and processing of traumatic or dysregulating memories in order to bring them to an adaptive resolution.

ethical non-monogamy. Any relationship that is not sexually and/or emotionally exclusive with the consensual agreement and full knowledge of all the partners involved.

fawn response. In childhood, the fawn response is an attempt to please an abusive perpetrator in order to escape or reduce mistreatment. In adulthood, the person may continue to attempt to please people in order to avoid any conflict.

fight, flight, freeze response. The body's natural and automatic reaction to danger, driven by the autonomic nervous system.

fluid bond. When partners make an intentional decision to have unprotected, barrier-free sex and exchange bodily fluids.

genderqueer. Denoting or relating to a person who does not subscribe to conventional binary gender distinctions and identifies with neither, both, or a combination of male and female genders.

grounding techniques. Coping strategies to help calm and reconnect the mind and body to the present that can help bring a person out of a panic attack, a PTSD flashback, an unwanted memory, a distressing emotion, or a dissociation.

hierarchy. An established ranking of partners where certain partners have priority or primary status over others.

high zone. A physiological state of hyperarousal or activation of the brain and nervous system. Associated feelings may include being nervous, anxious, angry, panicked, terrified, etc.

Imago Dialogue. A communication strategy in which both parties agree to a basic ground rule: to talk one person at a time. The person speaking is "sending." The person listening is "receiving." The receiver is responsible for moving through each of the three main steps of Imago: mirroring, empathizing, and validating.

jealousy. A complex emotion that typically refers to a combination of negative thoughts and feelings, including: insecurity, fear, anxiety, anger, resentment, inadequacy, helplessness, and/or disgust over an anticipated loss of something or someone of great personal value, particularly in reference to a human connection.

kink. An umbrella term that refers to erotic activity that falls outside of societal norms and often refers to BDSM and fetishes.

LGBTQIA+. An inclusive acronym for lesbian, gay, bisexual, transgender, queer/ questioning, intersex, agender/asexual, plus other gender and sexual labels, identifiers and experiences.

limerence. the state of being infatuated or obsessed with another person, typically experienced involuntarily and characterized by a strong desire for reciprocation of one's feelings but not primarily for a sexual relationship.

low zone. Hypo-arousal of the brain and nervous system. Associated feelings and sensations may include: tiredness, sadness, exhaustion, disconnection, dissociation, a sense of paralysis, not wanting to move, low energy, numbness, flat affect, etc.

metamour. A romantic and/or sexual partner of one's partner with whom one does not share a direct sexual or loving relationship.

monogamish. A relationship that is mostly monogamous, but exceptions are made to bend the conventional rules of monogamy with the consent of both partners. The term was coined by Dan Savage.

mono/poly relationship: One partner is monogamous while their partner has other sexual and or romantic partners.

narcissistic personality disorder (NPD). A mental condition in which people have an inflated sense of their own importance, a deep need for excessive attention and admiration, troubled relationships, and a lack of empathy for others. NPD is usually treatment resistant because their behavior is egosyntonic (their behaviors are acceptable to them).

neo-tantra. The modern, Western variation of tantra, this is a sexuality-driven spiritual path rooted in philosophies that emphasize the importance of being present and the power of touch. It's unlike classical tantra, which does not focus on sex.

nesting or anchor partner: A non-monogamous partner who shares a home or finances with another partner without implying hierarchy or priority over other relationships.

new relationship energy (NRE). A state of heightened positive emotions, sexual thoughts, and excitement that's driven by the body's neurochemicals and experienced at the beginning of sexual and romantic relationships.

nonhierarchical polyamorous relationship. Each partner forms agreements according to the needs and preferences of all, without the expectation that any one particular relationship will take precedence over another.

open marriage. Any marriage in which partners have consensually agreed to allow outside sexual relationships, outside romantic relationships, or both.

open relationship. A consensual, non-monogamous relationship in which both partners are allowed to have sexual and/or romantic attachments with others.

parasympathetic nervous system. The part of the involuntary autonomic nervous system that serves to slow the heart rate, increase intestinal and glandular activity, and relax the sphincter muscles.

polyamory. The practice of engaging in multiple romantic relationships; this may or may not include sex with the consent of all the people involved.

polyandry. A form of polygamy in which a woman has two or more husbands.

polycule. A connected network of non-monogamous relationships.

poly family. A polyamorous group whose members consider each other to be family, regardless of whether or not they share a residence.

polyfidelitous. A romantic relationship, sexual or not, that involves more than two people but does not allow the partners within that relationship to seek additional partners outside the relationship unless there is consent from all the existing members. The term polyfidelity was coined by the Kerista Commune.

polygamy. The state or practice of having multiple wedded spouses at the same time, regardless of the sex of those spouses.

polygyny. The state or practice of having multiple wedded wives at the same time.

polynormativity. Social norms perpetuated by the media that limit people's perception of what non-monogamy is and can be related to relationship models, relationship agreements, physical presentation, age, sexual orientation, gender, and ethnicity.

polysaturated. The state of not being open to new polyamorous relationships due to feeling that there is not enough emotional bandwidth for additional partners or due to time constraints that might make new relationships difficult.

positive affect tolerance. The ability to tolerate and integrate positive emotions and events into a shared positive experience of self.

primary partner. The person deemed the priority amongst partners in a non-monogamous hierarchy.

quad. A polyamorous relationship structure that involves four people who are romantically and/or sexually connected.

relationship anarchy. A form of polyamory that distinguishes itself by stating that there need not be a formal distinction between different types of sexual, romantic, or platonic relationships. Relationship anarchists look at each relationship (romantic or otherwise) individually and refrain from categorizing by societal norms such as "just friends," "in a relationship," etc.

resilient zone. The resilient zone refers to a state of mind and body well-being. In our resilient zone we can handle stress and react with our best self. Stress can shift us out of the resilient zone into our high or low zone.

secondary partner. In a hierarchical relationship, the person who, either by intent or by circumstance, is given less in terms of time, energy, and priority than their partner's primary partner.

secure attachment style. The capacity to emotionally connect well and securely in relationships with others while also having the ability to act autonomously as appropriate. In childhood, caregivers were a secure base from which the child could explore the world and become more independent. This style is deeply rooted in psychological health and is less likely to shift.

solo poly. An individual who identifies as polyamorous but has an independent or single lifestyle.

Somatically. Of, related to, or affecting the body. Somatic psychology can be defined as the study of the mind/body interface or the interaction of our body structures with our mind and actions.

submissive. An erotic participant who willingly and consensually gives up some or all of their control to a dominant partner. This type of partnership is often referred to in the BDSM community as a dominant/submissive (D/s) relationship.

swinging. The practice of having multiple sexual partners outside of an existing romantic relationship, most often with the understanding that the focus of those relationships is primarily sexual rather than romantic. Emotional bonds of friendship are commonly allowed and embraced.

switch. Within BDSM, a person can shift between the dominant role and the submissive role.

sympathetic nervous system. Part of the autonomic nervous system that directs the body's rapid, involuntary response to dangerous or stressful situations, such as fight and flight.

tertiary partner. A partner in a hierarchical non-monogamous relationship that is third in priority after the primary and secondary partners. The relationship with this partner is usually quite casual, with little expectations related to emotional or practical support, time, or energy.

transgender. An umbrella term for those whose gender differs from that which they were assigned at birth.

triad. A polyamorous relationship composed of three people who are romantically and/or sexually involved with each other.

trigger. A stimulus, such as a smell, sound, or sight, that sparks feelings of trauma or an intense emotional reaction, regardless of your current mood.

unicorn. A bisexual, non-monogamous person (usually a woman) who may be open to having sex or becoming romantically involved with both men and women but most often a male/female non-monogamous couple.

vee. A relationship made up of three people in which person A is romantically and/or sexually involved with person B and C, but B and C are not involved with each other. The term is derived from the letter "V," in which one person acts as the "hinge" of the V, seeing two partners who are not romantically and/or sexually involved with each other.

veto power. A relationship agreement that gives one person the power to end or disallow another person's additional relationships or specific activities. Most common in prescriptive primary/secondary relationships.

w. A non-monogamous relationship formation in which the center peak of the W represents a person who is linked to two partners (the W's two bottom points), who in turn have their own outside partners (the W's outside top peaks).

ABOUT THE AUTHOR

Kate Loree, LMFT, is a sex-positive licensed marriage and family therapist with a specialty in non-monogamous, kink, LGBTQ, and sex worker communities. In addition to her master's in marriage and family therapy, she also has an MBA and is a registered art therapist (ATR). She is an EDSE certified sex educator and an EMDR certified therapist with additional training in the Trauma Resiliency Model (TRM) for the treatment of trauma. She has been practicing psychotherapy since 2003. She cohosts her own sex-positive podcast, *Open Deeply*, with Sunny Megatron, has been featured in Buzzfeed videos, and has been a guest on Playboy Radio and many podcasts, including *American Sex*, *Sluts and Scholars*, and *Sex Nerd Sandra*. She has written for Good Vibrations and *Hollywood Magazine* and is a frequent public speaker. Her private practice resides in Encino, CA.

For more information, including webinars, speaking engagements, or to sign up for Kate's newsletter, go to KateLoree.com.

SELECTED TITLES FROM SHE WRITES PRESS

She Writes Press is an independent publishing company
founded to serve women writers everywhere.
Visit us at www.shewritespress.com.

Big Wild Love: The Unstoppable Power of Letting Go by Jill Sherer Murray. $16.95, 978-1-63152-852-1. After staying in a dead-end relationship for twelve years, Jill Sherer Murray finally let go—and ultimately attracted the love she wanted. Here, she shares how, along with a process to help readers get unstuck and find their own big, wild love.

Erotic Integrity: How to be True to Yourself Sexually by Claudia Six, PhD. $16.95, 978-1-63152-079-2. Dr. Claudia Six, a respected clinical sexologist and relationship coach, presents her unique method to uncovering your true sexual desires and attaining a more authentic and satisfying sexuality.

Fetish Girl: A Memoir of Sex, Domination, and Motherhood by Bella LaVey. $16.95, 978-1-63152-435-6. A kinky roller coaster ride through addiction, violence, motherhood, sex, and the creation of Evil Kitty, Bella LaVey's larger-than-life dominatrix persona, this singular memoir is the story of a woman attracted to extremes who is willing to go to great lengths to uncover and make peace with her true nature.

In Search of Pure Lust: A Memoir by Lise Weil. $16.95, 978-1-63152-385-4. Through the lens of her personal experiences as a lesbian coming of age in the '70s and '80s, Lise Weil documents an important chapter in lesbian history, her own long and difficult relationship history, and how her eventual dive into Zen practice became a turning point in her quest for love.

Daring to Date Again: A Memoir by Ann Anderson Evans. $16.95, 978-1-63152-909-2. A hilarious, no-holds-barred memoir about a legal secretary turned professor who dives back into the dating pool headfirst after twelve years of celibacy.

First Date Stories: Women's Romantic to Ridiculous Midlife Adventures by Jodi Klein. $16.95, 978-1-64742-185-4. A collection of hopeful, hilarious, and horrific tales—plus dating tips and inspirational quotes—designed to remind women in their mid-thirties and beyond that not all first dates are created equal, and sometimes they can be the beginning of something wonderful.

9 781647 423353